C0-AJX-095

A Comparison of Small and Medium Sized Enterprises in Europe and in the USA

Developed from a study commissioned by the European Capital Markets Institute, this book examines the impact of private equity and capital markets on the development of small and medium sized enterprises (SMEs) in the United States and the European Union. It also seeks to understand the nature of institutional policy towards SMEs, and the extent to which it can aid development.

Using data from a variety of sources, the authors provide an overview of SMEs followed by detailed analyses of:

- private equity and venture capital
- markets for SME publicly quoted stocks
- SME developments and constraints
- capital markets

This volume also offers a strong introduction and glossary, as well as international case studies, all to aid the reader's understanding. It should have broad appeal to markets in the spheres of finance, economics and business.

Solomon M. Karmel is a tenured Lecturer at the London School of Economics, UK. **Justin Bryon** is a Director at Nmás1, Spain.

Routledge Studies in Business Organisations and Networks

1 Democracy and Efficiency in the Economic Enterprise
Edited by Ugo Pagano and Robert Rowthorn

2 Towards a Competence Theory of the Firm
Edited by Nicolai J. Foss and Christian Knudsen

3 Uncertainty and Economic Evolution
Essays in honour of Armen A. Alchian
Edited by John R. Lott Jr

4 The End of the Professions?
The restructuring of professional work
Edited by Jane Broadbent, Michael Dietrich and Jennifer Roberts

5 Shopfloor Matters
Labor-management relations in twentieth-century American manufacturing
David Fairris

6 The Organisation of the Firm
International business perspectives
Edited by Ram Mudambi and Martin Ricketts

7 Organizing Industrial Activities Across Firm Boundaries
Anna Dubois

8 Economic Organisation, Capabilities and Coordination
Edited by Nicolai Foss and Brian J. Loasby

9 The Changing Boundaries of the Firm
Explaining evolving inter-firm relations
Edited by Massimo G. Colombo

10 Authority and Control in Modern Industry
Theoretical and empirical perspectives
Edited by Paul L. Robertson

11 Interfirm Networks
Organization and industrial competitiveness
Edited by Anna Grandori

12 Privatization and Supply Chain Management
Andrew Cox, Lisa Harris and David Parker

13 The Governance of Large Technical Systems
Edited by Olivier Coutard

14 Stability and Change in High-Tech Enterprises
Organisational practices and routines
Neil Costello

15 The New Mutualism in Public Policy
Johnston Birchall

16 An Econometric Analysis of the Real Estate Market and Investment
Peijie Wang

17 Managing Buyer–Supplier Relations
The winning edge through specification management
Rajesh Nellore

18 Supply Chains, Markets and Power
Mapping buyer and supplier power regimes
Andrew Cox, Paul Ireland, Chris Lonsdale, Joe Sanderson and Glyn Watson

19 Managing Professional Identities
Knowledge, performativity, and the 'new' professional
Edited by Mike Dent and Stephen Whitehead

20 A Comparison of Small and Medium Sized Enterprises in Europe and in the USA
Solomon M. Karmel and Justin Bryon

A Comparison of Small and Medium Sized Enterprises in Europe and in the USA

Solomon M. Karmel and Justin Bryon

London and New York

First published 2002 by Routledge
11 New Fetter Lane, London EC4P 4EE

Simultaneously published in the USA and Canada
by Routledge
29 West 35th Street, New York, NY 10001

Routledge is an imprint of the Taylor & Francis Group

Typeset in Times by Wearset Ltd, Boldon, Tyne and Wear
Printed and bound in Great Britain by St Edmundsbury Press,
Bury St Edmunds, Suffolk

British Library Cataloguing in Publication Data
A catalogue record for this book is available from the British Library

Library of Congress Cataloging in Publication Data
Bryon, Justin
A comparison of small and medium sized enterprises in Europe and in the USA : European capital markets institute / [Justin Bryon, Solomon Karmel].
p. cm. – (Routledge studies in business organization and networks; 20)
Includes bibliographical references and index.
1. Small business–Europe. 2. Entrepreneurship–Europe.
3. Small business–United States. 4. Entrepreneurship–United States. I. Karmel, Solomon M. (Solomon Mark), 1965– II. Title. III. Series.

HD2346.E85 B79 2002
338.6'42'094–dc21

2001048328

ISBN 0-415-26780-3

Contents

Figures

Tables

Contributors

Dun & Bradstreet

D&B is the leading provider of business information for credit, marketing, purchasing, and receivables management decisions worldwide. Over 100,000 companies regularly use their information. D&B maintains a global database of more than 62 million companies – updating it over one million times per day. It gathers business information in 209 countries around the world, covering 186 currencies.

IESE: International Graduate School of Management of the University of Navarra in Barcelona, Spain

IESE is the graduate business school of the University of Navarra. It offers MBA, Executive MBA and Ph.D. in Management degrees, as well as a wide range of open enrolment and customised programmes for corporate clients and continuing education programmes for alumni. Its programmes are designed to meet the needs of management professionals at every stage of their careers.

The London School of Economics

The London School of Economics and Political Science (LSE) concentrates on teaching and research across the full range of the social, political and economic sciences. Founded in 1895 by Beatrice and Sidney Webb, the LSE is one of the largest colleges within the University of London and has an outstanding reputation for academic excellence nationally and internationally. The school is a world centre for advanced research in the social, political and economic sciences.

Morgan Stanley Dean Witter

Morgan Stanley is a global financial services firm and a market leader in securities, asset management and credit services. With more than 600 offices in 28 countries, Morgan Stanley connects people, ideas and capital to help clients achieve their financial aspirations.

Nmás1

Nmás1 is a spin-off of the corporate finance and private equity arms of Morgan Stanley in Spain, following the acquisition of AB Asesores by the latter in 1998. It has a 16-year track record of advising small and mid sized companies both in Spain and abroad. As well as traditional corporate finance activities, Nmás1 manages Dinamia – Spain's only quoted venture capital fund. It also provides specialist advice in the areas of structured finance, TMT and wealth management. In emerging markets, it advises multilateral institutions and public administrations on privatisations and concessions as well as corporate and project finance for small and mid sized companies looking to invest in emerging markets.

Sponsors

Euronext

Euronext is the first cross-border European exchange organisation, created in September 2000 by the merger of the exchanges in Paris, Amsterdam and Brussels. Euronext manages both regulated and unregulated markets and offers a complete and varied range of services encompassing all exchange activity, including listing of financial instruments, trading in securities and derivatives (including futures and options on stocks and a variety of interest rate and commodity derivatives), clearing, settlement and custody of securities.

As of December 2000, Euronext was Europe's largest exchange organisation in terms of cash trading volumes through the central order book, and the second largest in terms of number and total market capitalisation of listed companies.

European Capital Markets Institute

The European Capital Markets Institute (ECMI) was founded in 1993 as an independent non-profit organisation aiming to serve as a central forum for practitioners and academics. The principal objective of the Institute is to initiate projects, programmes and conferences related to the functioning and growth of the European capital markets and to the development of cross-border trading and investment. ECMI has published several research projects as well as studies in its Short Paper series.

ECMI's membership displays some 140–member institutions of the highest standard in the fields of banking, broking, fund management as well as leading universities and stock exchanges from more than twenty-five countries.

The Spanish stock exchanges of Barcelona, Bilbao, Madrid and Valencia

Stock exchanges in Spain (Barcelona, Bilbao, Madrid and Valencia), interconnected in a single trading platform since 1989, are the official secondary markets, which trade shares, fixed-income securities, warrants and convertible bonds. The four exchanges represented, for the year 2000, a stock market capitalisation of €537 billion while its turnover exceeded €1.6 trillion.

The governing bodies of the four exchanges, along with other financial institutions, signed in June 2000 a protocol aiming to build a holding company of all Spanish markets. The new company, called Bolsas y Mercados Españoles, has figures of which, for the year 2000, will be able to post near €150 million in terms of gross profits. The company will be responsible for the unity of action, decision-making and strategic co-ordination of the Spanish markets.

Preface

This study, commissioned by the European Capital Markets Institute (ECMI), contains research and analysis conducted by Morgan Stanley Dean Witter in collaboration with Nmás1 and the London School of Economics, with data provided by Dun & Bradstreet, and additional research provided by IESE – the International Graduate School of Management of the University of Navarra in Barcelona, Spain.

The study discusses the nature and characteristics of small and medium sized enterprises (SMEs) private equity and capital markets in Europe and the United States. It analyses the link between SMEs and capital markets on both sides of the Atlantic, and provides answers to the central question posed: 'Despite the relative success of SMEs in Europe, why do SMEs in the USA appear to have closer, more profitable ties to private equity and capital markets?'

The introduction lays out the themes and definitions. The first section provides a comparative statistical analysis of developments on both sides of the Atlantic. The next section homes in on differences within the European Union, to gain a better sense of the relationship between SMEs and private equity, capital markets and policy, country by country. Overall, as factors that explain different intensities of risk equity and capital market activity on both sides of the Atlantic, we focus on tax and savings policies; the degree to which markets are legally unified and regionally clustered; and the impact of cyclical economic factors. 'Cultures of entrepreneurial dynamism' are also considered.

Acknowledgements

Solomon M. Karmel and Justin Bryon wish to thank the European Capital Markets Institute for commissioning Morgan Stanley Dean Witter in collaboration with Nmás1 and the London School of Economics to write this work.

In particular, they wish to thank the President of ECMI, Antonio Zoido, the Vice President John Langton as well as all the members of the ECMI Board of Directors and Advisory Board for their assistance and support during the process.

Furthermore they wish to extend their thanks to the other sponsors of the project. Euronext on the one hand and the Spanish stock exchanges of Barcelona, Bilbao, Madrid and Valencia on the other.

In addition to their gratitude to ECMI and the other sponsors, the authors also wish to thank several people for their contribution to this report. Juan Miranda and Guillermo Arboli of Nmás1 provided essential editorial suggestions and detailed written commentary for several sections. Iñigo Laspiur, also of Nmás1, for general research, particularly on Italy and Damian Barrera for research on Spain. Beatriz Zavala and Angélica Maldonado of Morgan Stanley Dean Witter for research into capital markets and private equity. Wolf Stein at the London School of Economics contributed to our knowledge base and research on Germany; Adam Steinhouse, also at the LSE, provided research on France; Juan Roure Alomar and Juan Luis Segurado at IESE contributed to our understanding of VC players in Europe; and Miles Nicholls, Glenn Porter, Paul Pitts and Graham Walker of Dun & Bradstreet provided essential proprietary data on SMEs in Europe and the US.

Above all, we are deeply grateful to Ramon Adarraga, Secretary General of ECMI, Santiago Ximénez, his Deputy, for their careful critiques and generous support of our research. The authors of this report are honoured to have been given the opportunity to research and analyse SMEs and capital markets in Europe and the US for the European Capital Markets Institute.

Introduction

This study focuses on the relationship between small and medium sized enterprises (SMEs), private equity and capital markets on both sides of the Atlantic. Specifically, it examines the impact of private equity and capital markets on SME development in the United States and the European Union. It looks at the financial enabling environment for SMEs and provides conclusions and recommendations for change. The European Capital Markets Institute (ECMI) apriori sees SMEs as an important engine of growth and employment. Its objective in initiating the study is primarily to understand the relevance of private equity, particularly venture capital, and capital markets on SME development. A further objective is to understand the nature of institutional policy towards SMEs, gather to what extent it aids development, and what lessons can be learnt.

Focus of inquiry

The central focus of inquiry can be summarised as follows: US and European SMEs have roughly similar turnover, are at a similar stage of economic development and operate within economic blocs of roughly the same size.[1] Nonetheless, SMEs in Europe are more numerous than in the US, and they account for a larger share of GDP. Indeed, the substantial growth of European SMEs in the post-Second World War period helps to explain why Europe experienced higher growth rates than the US (the 1990s excepted).[2]

> *Central question*: 'Despite the relative success of SMEs in Europe, why do SMEs in the USA appear to have closer, more profitable ties to private equity and capital markets?'

Subordinate questions to the one above include: If capital markets are indeed less central to European SMEs and less dynamic, is it economically important to change this state of affairs? What strategies would be required if this is a desired policy objective?

Other subordinate questions and hypotheses

To find answers to our central line of inquiry, we tested the following questions, some of which are popular themes in the policy-making community at the highest levels, as well as in academia and among the broader investment community.

- **Cyclical factors** *Are differences in SME capital markets primarily the result of cyclical trends?* With the US growing faster than Europe during the 1990s – the first decade since the war[3] that it has done so – perhaps the development of US private equity and capital markets simply correlates with comparatively explosive US growth rates and comparatively laggard European ones.
- **Entrepreneurial culture** *With an envious eye cast towards the dynamism of Silicon Valley in the 1990s, it is increasingly popular to discuss a culture of entrepreneurial activity that allegedly has a hand in 'making it all happen'.* Especially with respect to the type of high-growth firms that attract the attention of capital markets, 'entrepreneurial culture' appears to matter. Does it? A second hypothesis, that culture provides the answer, appears in contradiction with the first. Cyclical trends are potentially quite fleeting whereas culture might be portrayed as far more ingrained or 'structural'.
- **Single market** The US has been a unified market, with no internal tariffs and one currency, for most of its history since 1787,[4] and Europe had only created a mostly unified market, with a mostly unified currency, by the late 1990s. *Do Europe's less unified, nationally dispersed markets for labour, goods and services provide the answer to the 'missing capital market momentum?'* If so, this might imply that Europe is likely to catch up as soon as the fetters currently blocking market union are removed.
- **Synergistic clustering** *Is a kind of market failure at work in Europe due to tight 'clustering' of financial activity, with the early market leadership of US small-cap financial markets creating a semi-monopolistic momentum?* Just as one street may become known within a town as the place to buy shoes and cluster shoe stores, perhaps following NASDAQ, downtown Manhattan is the place to go public, with NASDAQ as the only exchange with the momentum and brand status to attract the attention of the most successful entrepreneurs and their companies and the liquidity to absorb sectoral changes without significantly affecting the whole market?
- **Regulatory framework** Is the issue more tied to policy, with tax regimes and savings or restrictive regulatory regimes in Europe hindering growth of capital markets for SMEs and thus also private equity?

Central findings

Several hypotheses on the link between SMEs and capital markets in Europe and the US lead to logical and valid arguments, but some appear more important than others do. We critique the hypotheses listed above in order of apparent validity and importance, and then provide additional, key findings from the study.

Fiscal framework

European tax and savings policies are comparatively prejudicial towards public and especially private equity markets, and hence, SME participation in equity markets. The same is also true for private equity. This is the most serious problem facing SMEs in their search for funding from dynamic private equity/capital markets. Taxes are higher on firm profits, on Venture Capital (VC) activity, and on individual private gains than in America. But far more important than this, pension schemes and other institutional investments are not as diverse, not as privatised, and more strictly regulated in a way that punishes the activities of the most important link between 'true SMEs'[5] and risk capital: institutional funds and VCs.

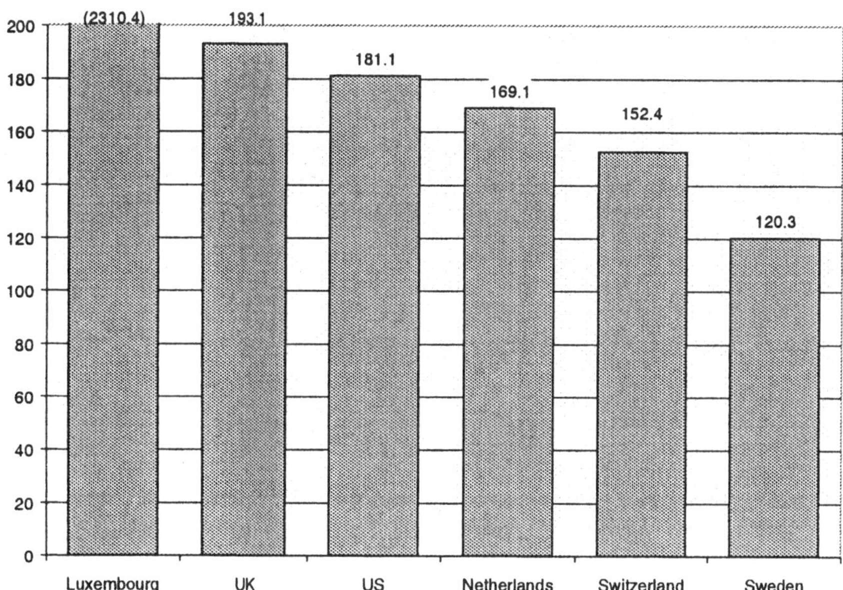

Figure I.1 Institutional investor base (1996) (percentage GDP).

Source: OECD – www.oecd.org.

Note
Countries with values over 100 per cent. Luxembourg not shown to scale.

We provide a more complete discussion on tax policies in Chapter 4, which focuses on a wide variety of policies towards SMEs on both sides of the Atlantic. Yet while taxation is more punitive in Europe than in the US, taxation is only part of the picture. Savings policies are even more diverse and perhaps more important.

Europe is faced with difficult policy choices as governments struggle to cut tax burdens. Early retirement, longer life expectancy and declining birth rates throughout the main economies in Europe are also forcing governments to address the refuelling of pension schemes that may be insufficiently funded in the future. Yet it is important to realise just how different the climate is – particularly for institutional investors and the savings that they agglomerate in different countries. This is one area of policy that is far-from-standardised by the EU.

As in the US, institutional investors are very active in the UK, Sweden, Switzerland, the Netherlands and Luxembourg, but not elsewhere. This is particularly true of pensions, whose methods of financial accumulation and investment patterns are very strongly determined by government policy. The countries that have the most dynamic institutional funding generally tend to be those with the most dynamic pension funds.

These issues matter for all investments, in large and small firms. But with more restrictive pensions and regulations governing them (without

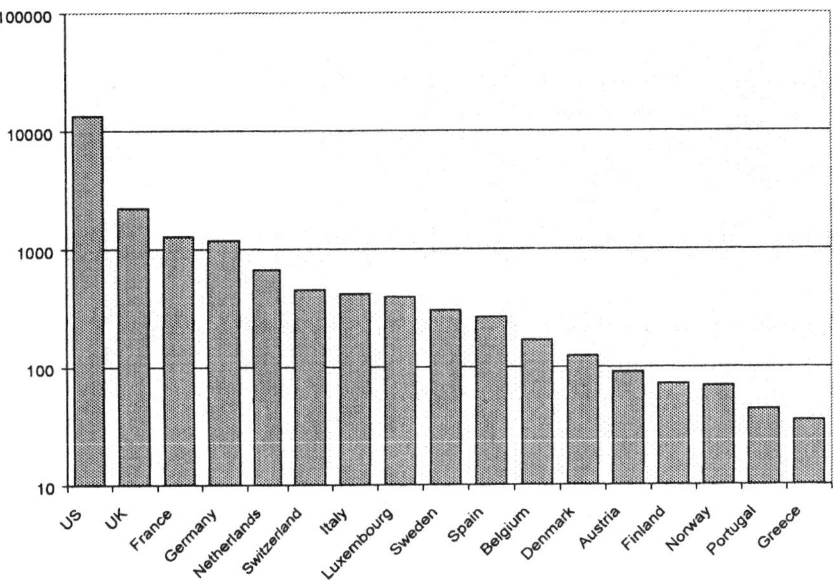

Figure I.2 Size of institutional investor base (1996) (US$).

Source: OECD – www.oecd.org.

Note
Logarithmic scale.

'prudent man' rules), even some places that do have moderately autonomous pension funding cannot use these funds to fuel SMEs through creating pools of risk capital. By contrast, SMEs can be fuelled by even modest pension funds, as long as 'prudent man' legislation is introduced, or institutions are encouraged or even required to buy SME equity. France's decision to effectively subsidise the Nouveau Marché with favourable legislation through introducing a tax efficient life insurance policy is likely to be overruled by the EU because of the exclusive focus of the tax breaks on French firms. Yet this did a great deal to increase value in that market and create a 'pull' effect that sparked increased venture capital activity. Successes were achieved despite the fact that France's private pensions, as evidenced by Figure I.3, are among the most poorly funded in Europe.

Yet on a more optimistic note, as European governments experiment with both tax breaks and more diverse savings institutions and pension schemes, European capital markets, for small-caps as well as others, become more dynamic and competitive. As examples, the countries of southern Europe formerly hosted no privately managed pensions to speak of, but in the 1990s they witnessed Europe's most rapid increases in institutional investment base, largely due to the introduction of new regulations.

Clearly, for Europe, it is important to free up not only savings and

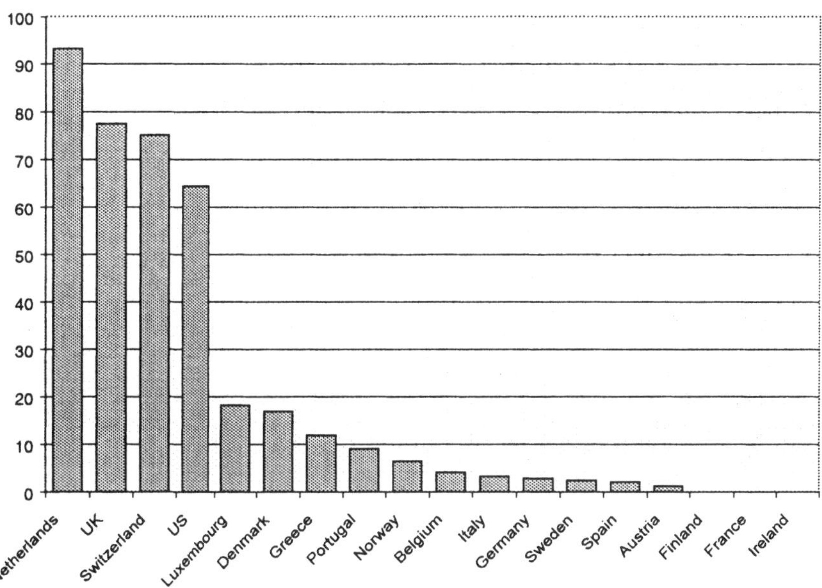

Figure I.3 Pension fund assets (1996) (percentage GDP).

Source: OECD – www.oecd.org.

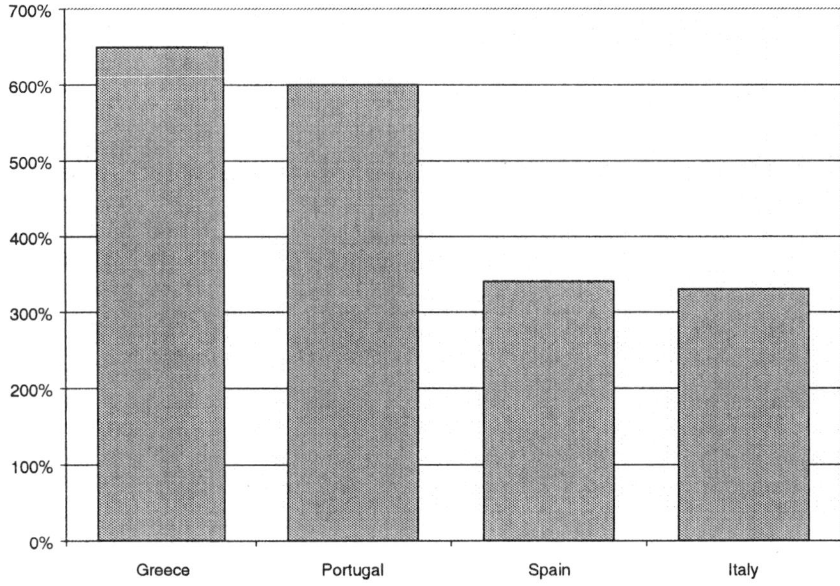

Figure I.4 Increase in size of institutional investor base (1990–6).
Source: OECD – www.oecd.org.

investment regulations for domestic investors, but also regulations on cross-border institutional holdings and pension schemes, so that truly international institutional powerhouses can emerge.

Single market

One of the clearest issues for Europe is the problem of disparate markets, with knowledge bases, technological and innovative centres, and markets for capital far less uniform, less centralised, and less unified than in the United States. The financial industry in general does appear to be one with extensive clustering of capital and services, where success breeds success. The completion of an internal free-trade zone and the launch of the Euro are both helpful for Europe's SME–equity links, but have not as yet eliminated many problems.

Decentralised, dispersed pockets of high-growth activity limit the involvement of the more active angel investment and VC firms, which in America tend to base themselves a 'stone's throw' from their funded companies in Silicon Valley, Massachusetts or New York, for better managerial consultation and information exchange. Dispersed small-cap markets also harm the potential to build a momentum of market makers and liquidity and therefore accommodate higher risk. The European small-cap markets themselves remain provincial, with listings primarily from the country in which the exchange is based. The result of provincial rules, trading systems, listings, and reporting requirements is that fund analysts require specialised country knowledge to make cross-border investments. Even then, they are only likely to expend their divided time on the largest companies in any market.

A possible solution would be greater efforts at clustering European SME, private equity and capital market support into already frenetic, already industrialised areas of significant national activity, rather than into depleted or declining regions. The 'level playing field' policy approach. Yet more important than this potentially unpopular policy shift would be continued steps towards greater coherence on regulations governing disclosure and exchange activity, and continued moves to consolidate small-cap exchanges. NASDAQ's proposed move into Europe should lead to more competition among small-cap exchanges and lead to new efficiencies. Hopefully, it will also create increased exchange alliances and perhaps even lead to mergers of exchanges across national boundaries. Finally, regulations limiting cross-border investments should be scrutinised. Whenever possible – based on 'prudent-man' principles – these regulations should be relaxed.

Cyclical effects

Cyclical effects are profound and should not be ignored. They create immense statistical distortions – in the exponentially increasing valuations of apparently 'high-growth' firms that may have very limited revenues or profits; in the apparent values of the funds that buy these firms; in the appetite for risk among investors generally; in the comparative values of currencies and hence stocks, turnover, and profits measured in those currencies; in the size of funds available for after-profit, after-tax re-investment; in the number of angel and venture capitalists who have money to spend; in the amounts of money they can spend; and in government policy. Recently, the Federal Reserve commented on a strong relationship between rising stock market values and consumer expenditure with there being strong evidence in the US of the latter leading the former.[6]

The US economy was booming to such an extent in the 1990s that its wealth levels again rose above those of Europe. The result was that US consumers had more money to boost both SME sales and SME valuations in private equity and small-cap markets. Among the largest economies in the OECD (discounting Luxembourg, Switzerland, Norway and Denmark), by the late 1990s the US was the richest.

So an underlying assumption of this study, that wealth levels on the two sides of the Atlantic are roughly similar, is less true in the year 2000 than it was at the beginning of the 1990s.

It should be noted that with recent improvements in many European

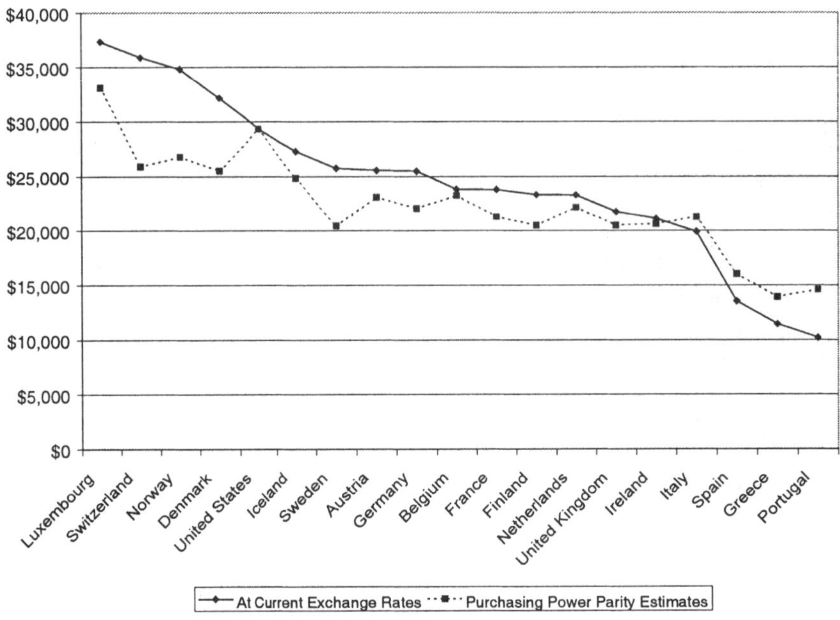

Figure I.5 Per capita income – Europe and the USA (1997) (US$).
Source: OECD – www.oecd.org.

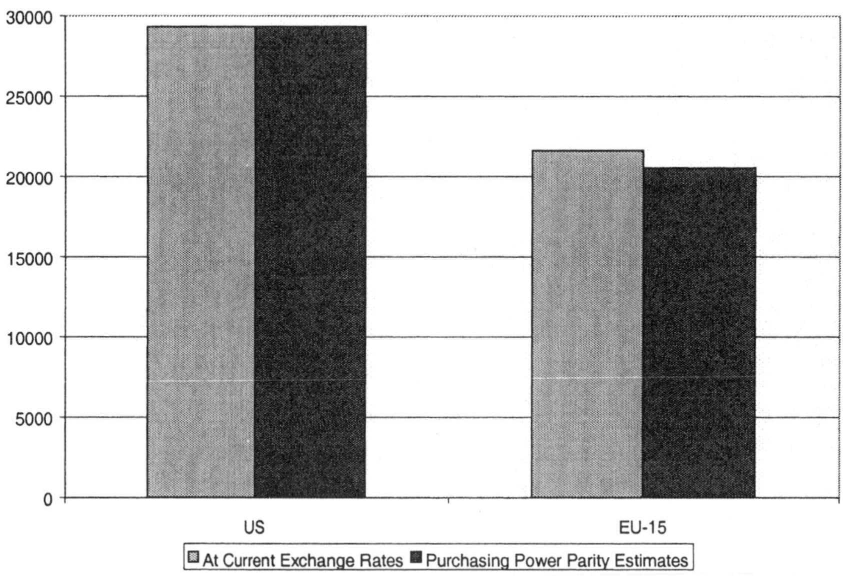

Figure I.6 Per capita income – Europe and the USA (1997) (US$).
Source: OECD – www.oecd.org.

economies, European VC and small-cap activity has picked up dramatically. Also, much of the energy in US capital markets for small-cap private and public equity is directed towards Internet businesses. These businesses grew first in the US, and at a more explosive rate than in Europe. But various sources are predicting quicker growth in the next few years in Europe. The same explosion that rocked the US may now head to the other side of the Atlantic to fuel a second boom.

At the same time, we would provide several caveats and counter-arguments for a hypothesis too strongly emphasising cyclical trends: (1) the laggard development and even decline in the activities of true SMEs on many European small-cap exchanges contradicts the idea that comparatively weak SME-high risk capital market links may be purely cyclical. Even in the current expansion in Europe, small-cap growth rates on the London Stock Exchange's Alternative Investment Market (AIM), for example, are actually declining;[7] (2) US VC and small-cap activity arguably has been more dynamic than in Europe since the early 1980s or before, through different boom–bust cycles; (3) even as European markets pick up, much of the highest-risk investment activity for SMEs is coming from US VCs, US funds and US investment banks that filter money and expertise and facilitate MBOs, MBIs and IPOs through London and other regional financial centres into Europe. European investment banks are facing increased competition and may be falling behind even on their

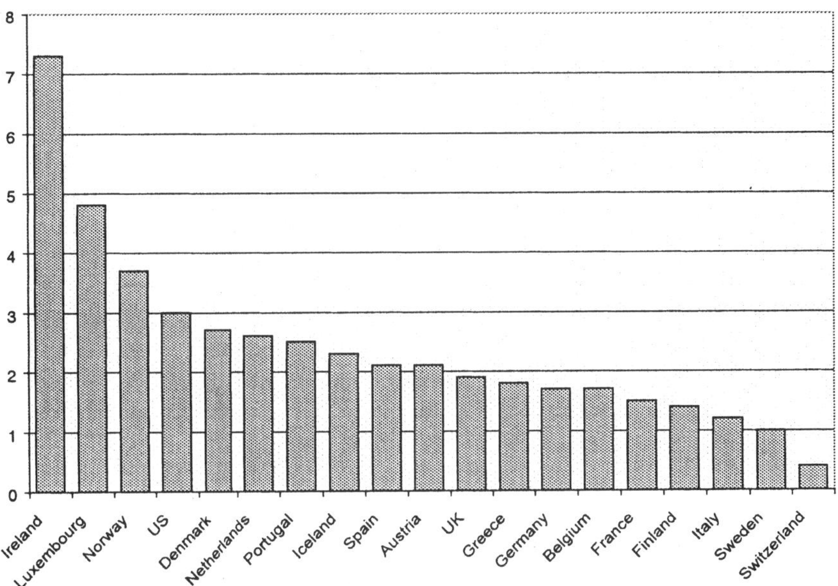

Figure I.7 Average annual change in GDP (1990–8).

Source: OECD – www.oecd.org.

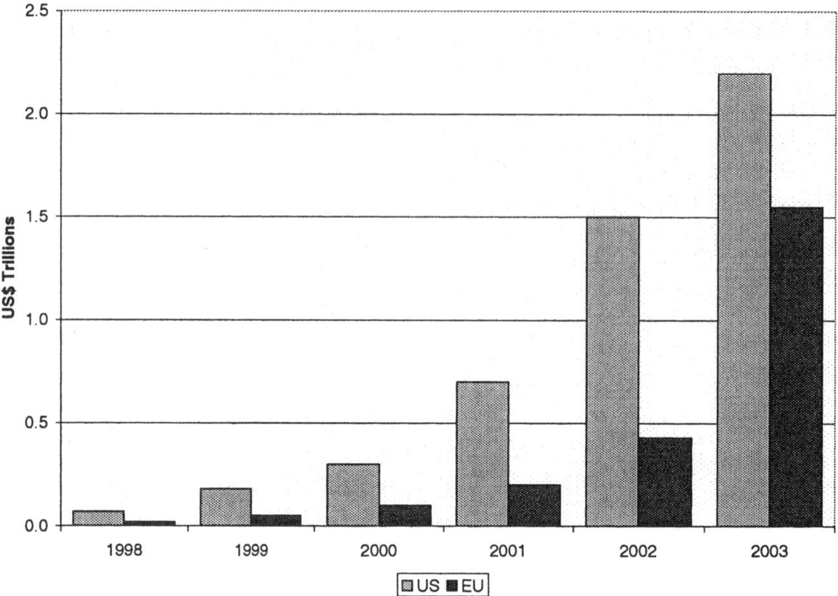

Figure I.8 US and EU Internet revenue forecast (1998–2003) (US$ trillion).

Sources: Forrester Research, European Commission, as cited in Glenn R. Simpson, 'Minding the Net,' *Wall Street Journal Europe* ('Networking' Section), 1 March 2000, p. 25.

home turf, within the confines of the same markets – so other factors must be at work.

Cultural differences

'Cultures of entrepreneurial dynamism' appear to provide a weaker explanation, or at least one that is very difficult to define and measure accurately. The culture of Silicon Valley might currently appear more exciting and dynamic than the Bavarian culture of Munich when it comes to enthralling VCs with a story over lunch, but applied economic analysis should not be overly influenced by fads and fashion. The literature on entrepreneurship is best seen when providing historical descriptions of isolated examples of creative thought and innovations – but worst when suggesting a valuation for particular cultural attributes or particular entrepreneurial activities. Problems result from definitions of 'entrepreneurial' business practice – from the fact that these variables can be highly qualitative rather than quantitative (measurable) – and those cultures appear to change with the times. For example, we can measure start-up activity in Sweden and find that there are fewer start-ups than in Spain and that SMEs are less important to Sweden's economy than to Italy's. But if we use start-up or SME ownership activity as a proxy for entrepreneurship, then we are ignoring entrepreneurial activity of executives heading new business divisions in Sweden's comparatively successful large enterprises. Isn't the successful 'head of strategy', or 'head of new business development' at a dynamic Swedish conglomerate likely to be as 'entrepreneurial' as a small shop-owner in Spain, Italy or for that matter Sweden? Considering a second illustration, German 'Mittelstand'[8] businesses are described as having an overly conservative leadership that is wary of outside ownership and managerial involvement which thereby suppresses supply of potential candidates to risk capital markets. This conclusion correlates both with polls of German owners who value independence and with VC activities in Germany that until very recently appeared anaemic. Yet not only are VCs in Germany experiencing an explosion of activity recently; their investments are also far less conservative than those of, for example, Tony Blair's 'Cool Britannia' are. In Germany, money is pouring into seed- and early-stage firms in pockets of success around Berlin, Munich and other cities. Germans also are notorious for placing their money in conservative savings institutions rather than stocks, but the current fad in Germany for high-risk warrants[9] (far more risky than ordinary equity) cannot be explained by cultural conservatism. Further, the largest VC funds throughout Europe (especially in the UK) are far more disposed towards Management Buy Outs (MBOs), and it is not clear why even the most conservative Mittelstand owners would oppose this instantaneous, well-defined, frequently cash-rich exit platform, where ownership is not shared but rather forfeited in exchange for a retirement of potentially vast wealth.

Similarly, culture is frequently not an 'independent variable', but rather is strongly influenced by comparative policy environments for taxes and savings. For example, Italian companies on average have a very high debt–equity ratio, three times that of UK companies and more than twice that of French and German companies.[10] One might conclude that this is because proud Italian owners of family firms want to control them at almost any cost. Whilst one can find evidence to support this stereotype about Italian owners, the problem is also a result of the Italian fiscal system, which has historically penalised equity over debt. Even after the removal of the 'double taxation' of dividends, problems remain. Interest expenses are almost fully tax deductible whilst dividends paid are not. The consequential typical financial structure of Italian SMEs has been to support expansion through internally generated funds and through borrowing – particularly short-term debt.

This is partly explained by the overall makeup of Italian industry. As can be seen from the figure below, Italy has a higher proportion of companies in 'old' economy industries such as primary and extraction, manufacturing and retail when compared to France, UK and Germany. Mature industries, where risks are better known, are capable of obtaining and

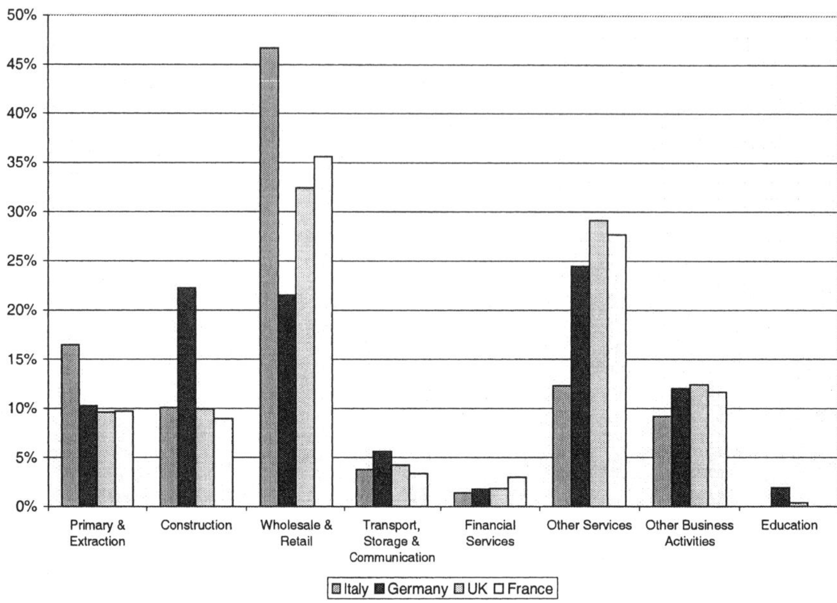

Figure I.9 Number of companies by major sector – Italy vs. Germany, the UK and France (1995).

Source: Eurostat.

sustaining greater debt proportions than in the 'new' economy sectors that have characterised the US and northern Europe.

This discussion also suggests new definitional problems with some of the terms that might define cultures. For example, the US appears to favour 'risk' (equity) investments rather than more the conservative 'fixed' debt or savings investments. Yet compared to the American firms, it would appear that Italian owners are actually taking on higher risks by assuming comparatively high debt – and so are the banks that lend to them. So definitions of 'risk-taking' cultures require caveats in their terms of debate: The Italian financial structure actually appears comparatively risky without including US-style 'risk' investments.

While culture is an important 'residual' variable in social sciences and economics, one would expect the cultures of business leaders to be particularly amenable to profit innovation and particularly subject to change when confronted with new operational procedures that work well. People throw out typewriters and buy computers when computers appear to yield efficiency savings. Much of the activity in financial markets can similarly be compared to the purchasing of new tools. Which is more efficient at a given rate and stage of growth: A relationship banker or an investment banker? Debt or equity? While savings methods are more conservative in Japan, somewhat conservative in Europe, and the least conservative in the US, culture seems to provide particularly 'residual' answers to these questions.

So what is the role of culture? Two unusual caveats to the above discussion help to show why culture, while perhaps a 'residual' variable, cannot be ignored.

First, one relevant difference on both sides of the Atlantic is the proclivity of US investors to invest in high-risk stakes of all kinds, including equity as opposed to interest-bearing savings accounts or debt, small stocks as opposed to blue chips, unlisted private equity as opposed to public equity, etc. This has a direct impact upon SMEs. For example, although small-cap indices are yielding unimpressive returns in the bourses on either side of the Atlantic, they are expanding more rapidly in America. And now they have begun to perform better there too. More importantly for all SMEs, even smaller firms without public equity issues tend to have more diversified, more high-risk funding sources at their disposal in the US than in Europe. In the US they therefore may be less tied down by mundane, tactical questions of cash flow, and this may influence the speed of development of truly high-growth firms. Again, equity/lending phenomena are partly cyclical and associated with the most recent 'exuberance' among US investors, and SMEs in Europe are moving towards more diversified financing. Yet the less conservative nature of the US investor is an established fact.

Second, there are no influential, powerful and rich institutions at the European level that can easily be compared with the vast US non-profit sector and particularly America's dynamic universities. Universities in the States have become institutional fund managers in their own right and also sources of scientific and managerial expertise. While these institutions and their importance to VC funding are discussed in the report, a more detailed study of non-profit and university investments is outside the bounds of this study.

More general findings

In addition to the findings above, we also provide the following significant conclusions and caveats for the comparative study of SMEs and capital markets generally:

SME development

It should be emphasised that while the vast majority of firms in the EU are SMEs and they provide the vast majority of the jobs, SMEs encompass a vast array of different firm types ranging from independent fishermen to urban, industrial firms employing hundreds of people. Those of interest to the private financial community are most likely to be in urban and suburban areas, and focused on a handful of high-growth firms with extensive capitalisation requirements. A long-term approach towards structural re-adjustment, employment on a national level, SME development of all types, and what is apparently a secondary issue politically – more vibrant capital markets – might consider a new policy emphasis.

SME importance

We have been able to find no clear link between the relative importance of SMEs in an economy and either wealth or economic growth rates in that economy. SMEs comprise over 95 per cent of the firms in existence on both sides of the Atlantic, and their importance is hailed on both sides as vehicles for job creation and as vehicles for growth. Further, SMEs grew in importance compared to large firms in all of the EU-15 nations and in the US from the post-war period through the early 1990s. Yet it is not clear that more SMEs, a greater percentage of an economy comprised of SMEs, or even faster rates of start-up activity necessarily imply greater wealth. Juggling the statistics, one finds either no correlation between SME importance and wealth or a negative correlation (see Chapter 1 on SMEs in Europe), meaning wealthier nations may emphasise production from larger enterprises rather than smaller ones.

In addition, the productivity of larger enterprises is now growing more quickly than the productivity of smaller ones, and their importance on capital markets is now greatly outpacing the importance of SMEs. So from the early 1990s, a post-war trend may have slowed or reversed. Generally, an absence of a clear wealth/SME correlation suggests that those hoping to build capital markets for the profits that they generate or for their obvious benefits to all industry may not wish to emphasise the building of dynamic or more 'entrepreneurial' SMEs as the central task. Instead, policies should be designed to benefit the entire industry.

Impact of dynamic capital markets

A related point is that we have found no clear link between very dynamic capital markets and very healthy SMEs at the national level. Indeed, SMEs are less important to the economies of the US and the UK than on continental Europe, and yet these are the two countries sporting the most dynamic capital markets in the world. So, although both healthy capital markets and healthy SMEs can be critical to economic success, and one can help to facilitate the other, the two are not linked in any obvious way if we study all SMEs in all sectors at a national level. Indeed, a very different link is far stronger. Markets for risk investments (equity) focus over 95 per cent of their resources (investments) on large enterprises even in places with dynamic VC and small-cap markets like the USA and Britain. So-called 'high-risk' capital markets have linked their fate far more to the success of lower-risk large firms than to higher-risk smaller firms, and large firms are in turn far more dependent upon capital markets than small firms. So while a study of the connection between SMEs and capital markets can be an important contribution to our understanding of modern economies, the stimulation of dynamic SMEs, again, should not be the first priority of capital market reformers. This is not to say that the opposite is incorrect. The 'pull' effect of efficient and dynamic capital markets are vital to act as a catalyst to create and maintain a vibrant private equity presence. Put another way, capital markets do not need SMEs as much as SMEs need capital markets.

Capital markets and productivity

There is also no clear link between the development of risk capital markets (equity) and the productivity of the private sector or its labour force. One would expect capital markets to promote more efficient labour practices, and 'Anglo-American' capitalism is often perceived as comparatively ruthless in its treatment of labour, with 'shareholder value' rather than worker relations at the centre of definitions of firm success. Yet a McKinsey Global Institute study on productivity in Britain helps to show that, of the four largest capital markets in this study, the US and Britain support the largest capital markets, but the total factor productivity of these two markets ranked first and last respectively. Britain, as the largest capital market in Europe, did not translate financial success into productivity success. Table I.1, using UK rates as a basis figure (100), demonstrates that while capital productivity is higher in the UK than on the continent, labour productivity is lower in the UK than among all of its largest competitors of relevance to this study.

Table I.1 Productivity comparisons (1997) (the UK, France, Germany and the US)

	Market sector total factor productivity	*Labour productivity*	*Capital productivity*
UK	100	100	100
France	113	126	92
Germany	114	126	93
US	126	137	110

Source: McKinsey Global Institute, *Driving Productivity and Growth in the UK Economy* (London: McKinsey and Company, 1998), p. 10.

Note
Regulations governing product use and especially land use are said to be much of the problem in the UK. A less skilled labour force and higher employment among low-skilled labour groups account for some of the rest.

Wealth

On correlations, there is a link between the size of securities markets (including small-cap markets) and levels of wealth, but the link is weak if we sample only the richest countries (especially within the EU-15). All of the richest countries in the OECD have institutions sufficiently reliable to support securities markets, and they all support these markets to some extent. Yet the UK in 1997 was poorer than 12 other European countries (measured by income per capita, OECD estimates; see Table I.1), and yet it has the largest securities markets in Europe. The development of small-cap markets tends to follow the development of large-cap ones far more closely than it follows wealth levels.

Capital market barriers

While risk equity markets have never been the primary source of SME funding generally, capital market barriers in Europe may represent a bottleneck to the development, more specifically, of high-growth SMEs in capital-hungry, high-tech sectors. Small-cap and VC markets in Europe remain comparatively small, apply a plethora of rules and regulations, lack liquidity and are backed by less adequate disclosure and cross-national development information, including industry benchmarking. Corresponding with this, there are fewer overnight, explosive success stories of comparatively new firms (e.g. Microsoft, Intel, Cisco, AOL) rising to astronomical valuations as brutish giants in their industry across every developed regional market. There are also fewer firms taking advantage of the opportunity to list, or go public. So too, there are fewer firms taking profits or enjoying restructuring advantages from buy-outs or mergers.

Some of the successes of high-tech, high-growth firms in the US definitely correlate with, and appear logically tied to, the stronger role and functions of its VC and junior public markets, with NASDAQ as the dramatic reference point. It is also important to note that NASDAQ, more than any European market, services an international clientele (over 500 foreign companies are listed out of a total of 5,000), including over 140 European firms. Further, NASDAQ has eyed the weaknesses in the European markets and is currently engaged in setting up a trading system on the continent with the same rules and regulations as the principal outfit in the United States. While Europe hardly needs one more small player serving a dispersed market, this is a welcome move if it grows in size and has teeth, shakes up European markets, and spurs them into action – especially with regard to regulatory harmonisation and SME information, distribution and disclosure. Some might also merge.

Similarity

It is important to point out, despite differences, the striking extent to which SMEs as a whole on both sides of the Atlantic are roughly similar. They are more or less equally important in terms of GDP contribution, employment creation and income generation.

Taking the point on rough similarities a bit further, it may even be that there is a very roughly natural rate of SME development at a given level of income and at a given stage in the development of capitalism, on both sides of the Atlantic. There is an extremely high correlation between the size of a country's population and the number of SMEs that it hosts. This correlation becomes even stronger when we look at levels of urbanisation and industrialisation. So, while SMEs are currently politically popular as employment vehicles and larger firms are frequently popular for industrial planning (Sweden) or as symbols of national pride (France), favouring one organisational form over another (independent proprietorships, small, medium, or large enterprises) may create unnecessary externalities and may yield negative results if indeed they yield any results at all. This study suggests that policies geared towards one enterprise size over another are likely to be far less productive than policies designed to change the overall investment environment (e.g. through tax breaks or changed pension and savings regulations) of the economy as a whole.

Regulatory environment and savings policies

Our discussion of policies and regulations emphasises the importance of tax and savings policies more than other policies on regulatory reform, standardisation or subsidisation. Yet one could also conclude that a key difference between the US and Europe is that the US has fewer but more focused policy support measures, with an emphasis on an open and rigorous regulatory environment rather than on financial support.

Admittedly, government subsidies have boasted key successes on both sides of the Atlantic. To provide two prominent examples, the European Commission was an early backer of EASDAQ (now NASDAQ Europe since the takeover by NASDAQ), and the US government the earliest backbone of the Internet, which has indirectly fuelled explosive small-cap growth and an entire industry for VCs to lavish with capital. But in both regions, official subsidies or investments tend to be a tiny portion of the total risk pool. Partly as a result, the US de-emphasises them completely in its policy efforts, and uses very limited public funds almost entirely to stimulate entrepreneurship among minority groups or in depressed areas. The European Commission also appears to emphasise subsidies more extensively in its policy pronouncements, and to rely upon them as a method to achieve a host of disparate and sometimes conflicting goals – despite this approach being bureaucratic and potentially inefficient and ineffectual. The discussion here is one of emphasis rather than one of fundamentally contrasting approaches, but the emphasis on the enabling environment, including harmonisation and disclosure in the EU, might be more productive.

Central assumptions tested

The underlying assumption of the central question of our study – 'Why do SME capital markets appear to have less momentum in Europe?' – is that they do, indeed, have less momentum in Europe. We tested hypotheses about an apparent European 'problem'. Yet first we had to test the assumption: Do these capital markets really have less momentum?

The first part of this study focuses in part on comparative statistics – a descriptive analysis of the state of both regions. Implications are drawn early on, but the authors hope that one major achievement of the book will be a more complete picture of the markets to date.

Our study divides evidence, and discussions of that evidence, four ways.

Evidence on small and medium sized enterprises

- Data from Eurostat (the EU's statistical office) on SMEs in the EU-15
- Data from the US Small Business Administration on SMEs in the US
- Data from Dun & Bradstreet, a leading commercial data warehouse and market research firm
- Academic monographs and articles focused on SMEs
- Business news and information sources

Evidence on private equity, angel capitalist and venture capitalist activity

- Angel capitalist associations in Europe and the US
- The European Venture Capitalist Association
- The US Venture Capital Association
- Venture capital associations of individual EU countries
- Financial news and information sources, academic journals and commercial websites

Evidence on public firms listing on stock exchanges and on the small-cap exchanges themselves

- Individual stock exchanges in many relevant countries
- Commercial indices and proprietary information from Morgan Stanley and other financial information sources

Evidence on public policy and the goals and concerns of EU, national European and US government bodies or leaders

- Extensive information downloads from websites of the EU and national governments
- Searches through reference materials on regional and national legislation, legal proceedings, and national statistical reference materials
- Outside views on policy and standardised statistical information from the World Bank, the IMF and commercial organisations like the Economist Intelligence Unit

The central assumption has been analysed taking account of SME definitions, employment and turnover on both sides of the Atlantic; sources of SME funding on both sides of the Atlantic; a comparative analysis of the size and dynamism of angel capitalist and VC firms, and a comparative analysis of the extent to which 'small-cap' public stock exchanges are both servicing true SMEs and doing so effectively.

Some of our comparative tasks are made considerably more difficult by definitional issues. For example: (1) SME definitions in the US and Europe are different; (2) VC firms frequently are not providing funds to SMEs but rather to very large firms; and (3) 'small-cap' markets primarily serve companies that are already huge by the standards of the average firm – and well outside the definitional boundaries of SMEs (although very small by the standards of the S&P 500 or the FTSE 250).

To provide a simple yet important statistical example of definitional difficulties, our statistics in Chapter 1 state that there are over 18 million incorporated SMEs in the European Union and only 15 million in the United States during one year of the late 1990s.[11] So this helps to demonstrate the central paradox that needs an explanation in this study: Although there are more businesses in Europe, why are their links to capital markets more anaemic? Yet the US Small Business Administration (SBA) in 1999 claimed that the US actually hosted 24 million 'small businesses', considerably more than our most up-to-date figures for Europe.[12] This is because the US adopts a 'broad definition' of SMEs which includes self-employed non-incorporated concerns, whereas our statistics through necessity only focus on incorporated enterprises that are required to file information that is in the public domain.

Our methodology has been, whenever possible, to use comparative statistics provided by international commercial organisations using similar measurements in their calculations (e.g. Dun & Bradstreet and Eurostat), but we note discrepancies in our statistics and definitions whenever possible. In this case, the US definition encompasses a much wider range of businesses in terms of employee base, and we believe the Dun & Bradstreet figures provide superior comparisons.

Despite the difficulties of measurement across-borders, we conclude more broadly that the primary assumption of the study is currently correct. European SMEs are quite successful, even more successful than US ones in many respects, but the capital markets that serve them are indeed less well-developed. We analyse how, where, why and to what extent this is the case.

Definitions

Small and medium sized enterprises

The USA and Europe use similar criteria to define SMEs. The institutions driving the definitions are the European Commission and the US Small Business Administration. However, both within Europe and the US, there are many working definitions that differ from these 'official' benchmarks – depending upon the objectives of the institution and the availability of information.

Key benchmarking criteria include:

- Number of employees
- Turnover
- Total assets
- Independence of the enterprise

The thresholds for turnover and balance sheet are adjusted on a regular basis by both the European Commission and the SBA, to take account of changing economic circumstances in the country – normally leading to revisions every four years. At the time of this writing, the European Commission is considering modifying substantially upwards the balance sheet threshold.[13] This change would actually be of major importance to many thousands of companies. The first tangible benefit will be to bring about immediate dispensations on financial reporting, a considerable financial and administrative burden on most SMEs at present.

Although the official benchmarks within the two trading blocs use similar criteria, their thresholds and application differ markedly. A summary of the definitions is shown below.

The EU definition of an SME

The EU definition of micro, small and medium enterprises was incorporated within a recommendation to the Commission of April 1996 and came into full effect, after a transition period, on 1 January 1998. The definition uses criteria covering employees, turnover, total assets and independence, and replaced the original definition that was contained in the Fourth Council Directive (78/660/EEC).

An SME in Europe is a company that

- has fewer than 250 employees
- has either an annual turnover not exceeding €40 million, or an annual balance sheet total not exceeding €27 million
- is independent. This means that less than 25 per cent of the capital or voting rights are owned by one enterprise, or jointly by several enterprises, falling outside the definitions of an SME.

The definition also distinguishes between 'micro', 'small', and 'medium sized' enterprises based principally upon number of employees.

- Micro enterprises have fewer than 10 employees
- Small fewer than 50
- Medium sized fewer than 250.

The US definition of an SME

The US defines SMEs dependent upon the industrial sector in which the company operates. By sector, the SBA determines varying thresholds that generally encompass the following:

- Fewer than 500 employees; or
- A turnover of less than €5 million (converted from dollars).

The range within a sector can vary extensively, with the number of employees being in the range 100 to 1,500 and turnover in the range €1.5 million to €20.5 million.

While both sets of definitions are logical, the European one is easier to use and provides simpler comparisons across countries. It is therefore the one that is almost always used in this report.

Development/financing stages

Companies can also be categorised according to their stage of development or financing stages, the most important of which are as follows:

- *Seed*: Companies included in this category inevitably tend to have a relatively short corporate memory, i.e. most would have been in business for only a short period of time. These are formative stage companies requiring financing primarily for research, business plan preparation and business concept development. These activities/phases are requisites to move the business into a start-up stage. These companies normally have a high-risk profile. But their financing needs are great, albeit not in actual amount terms. The mortality rate of these companies is obviously higher than for other categories. Official and commercial co-financing might be a solution to address this problem.

- *Start-up*: These are SMEs requiring financing primarily for product development and initial marketing. Companies included in this category inevitably tend to have a relatively short corporate memory i.e. most would have been in business for only a short period of time. Some may have products that have yet to be sold commercially. Others may have started production and sales but without actual profit generation. Their risk profile is high, but less so than with seed entities. The importance of equity financing cannot be underestimated. The latter opens the doors to debt financing. Many 'winners' are identified at this stage. Indeed, this is the experience in the US venture capital industry, which since the mid-1980s has made this category one of the key target investments (alongside expansion stage companies).
- *Expansion*: Companies in this group require financing for growth and expansion. Typically this type of company may be operating at a break-even point or perhaps even trade profitably. Capital injections are often required to increase production capacity and/or additional market or product development. A large number of these companies also have an acute need for working capital finance. Quite often this finance is limited on account of narrow capital structures. Expansion SMEs can involve management buy-out and management buy-ins
- *Replacement capital and later-stage funding*: These are companies capable of entertaining secondary share purchases. Another equity fund provider may undertake the purchase of shares. This purchase may also be executed by business angels and/or from existing shareholders.

Risk capital

Risk capital is defined as money provided by investors to make equity investments, especially in unquoted companies. The risk element is characterised by the relatively illiquid and long-term nature of the investment. Investors typically look to invest over a 3 to 7 year period in these companies. Investors look for a superior return from their investment to mitigate the risk – 'high risk equates to high return'.

Sources of risk capital

- *Individuals*: Risk capital is provided by individuals, either acting along or together with other like minded 'business angels', to companies in which the individuals then take an active management role. These individuals will mentor a company and provide capital and expertise to help develop companies. Angel investors may either be wealthy people with management expertise or retired businessmen who are looking to assist with business development first-hand.

- *Institutions*: Risk capital is provided by institutions, principally through investing in venture capital funds. The type and nature of the institutions is very wide, and can include pension funds, insurance companies, commercial banks, endowment funds, charities, foundations and wealthy private individuals.
- *Governments*: The US Government, European Union and several individual member state governments have state-backed investment funds aimed at providing risk capital to SMEs.

Venture capital

- *Venture capital (VC) funds* are created and managed by professionals to channel state, institutional, corporate or individual risk capital into companies. These funds typically have a clear strategic goal in terms of geographical focus, investment stage and industrial sector in which they will operate. The funds also usually have a finite life of 7 to 10 years and a pre-agreed capital limit. The norm is for them to be organised as limited partnerships, with the general partner being a professional venture capital company with up to 100 limited partners providing the investment capital.
- *Venture capitalists* are professional fund managers who invest alongside, government, institutional, corporate and private investors in venture capital funds. They are responsible for the management of the funds – including the selection of the investment portfolio. A successful venture capitalist may well manage several funds simultaneously.

Success

In comparing and contrasting SMEs in Europe and the USA, we have considered several variables for measuring SME development and success. We have also differentiated between the incorporated self-employed (non-agricultural self-employed or NASE) and employer businesses (SMEs).

Some of the statistics considered include:

- NASE and SME density as a proportion of total population
- *Birth rates*: business incorporations, business formations and active new businesses.
- *Death rates*: business bankruptcies and terminations
- SMEs as a percentage of all businesses in an economy
- Employment rates
- Turnover
- Mortality

Success can also be measured by the extent to which 'entrepreneurial activity' is promoted by SMEs, private equity and the capital markets that serve them, or the employees that work in them. 'Entrepreneurship' is sometimes defined statistically through proxies, such as the number of people starting up new firms, or the number of leaders of high-growth firms. By contrast, it is defined in one European Commission report more qualitatively as

> a dynamic process by which individuals constantly identify economic opportunities and act upon them by developing, producing and selling goods and services. This process requires qualities such as self-reliance, a capacity for risk-taking and a sense of personal commitment.[14]

A qualitative definition makes comparisons difficult, but in a dynamic work environment, it is probably a more accurate approximation of a process that is not easily confined to one statistical measurement of success.

Outline

In addition to the preface, acknowledgements, sponsors, contributors and introduction, the study contains two main parts.

The first half, (Chapters 1 through 4) provides an introduction to the difficulties of comparative analysis. To offer an example, readers already familiar with capital markets know that NASDAQ has not been a small-cap exchange for some time, but it might be less obvious that even the market cap of the NASDAQ small-cap listings is also primarily comprised of firms that the EU, for example, would characterise as large.

With a focus on the available data, this part compares the situation in the EU and the US, and homes in on four subjects that comprise its chapters: (1) SME development, (2) angel capitalist and VC development, (3) capital markets development, and (4) institutional policy towards SMEs.

The second half of the book (Chapters 5 through 7) provides far more detailed analysis of differences within Europe – particularly the European Union, to gain a better sense of the extent to which our assumptions and arguments are valid country-by-country.

This part accepts that the European market is less unified than the US one, and concentrates on many of the same issues as they apply exclusively within the European Union (with occasional references to Switzerland and other European countries): (5) SME development, with comparisons and analyses of differences across countries within Europe; (6) angel capitalist and VC development, country-by-country; and (7) capital markets development across countries.

The conclusion reiterates some of the main themes and provides a few policy recommendations. A glossary of terms used within the book is included to aid understanding.

Notes

1 Sources: Panorama of the European Union – Enterprises in Europe – SME Database, 1999 Edition, Eurostat; The European Observatory for SMEs Fifth Annual Report, 1997, European Network for SME Research, Executive Summary; US Small Business Administration Office of Advocacy 1997 Small Business Economic Indicators, 1998, SBA; US Small Business Administration Office of Advocacy, 1997 Report of the President The State of Small Business, 1998, SBA.
2 Organisation for Economic Co-operation and Development (OECD) – www.oecd.org
3 The Second World War, 1939–45.
4 The exception being during the American Civil War, when the Confederacy produced its own currency.
5 See glossary.
6 'The New Economy: Unanswered Questions for 2000'. Speech by Roger Ferguson, Vice Chairman of Federal Open Market Committee to Downtown Economists Club, New York, 17 February 2000.
7 London Stock Exchange – www.londonstockex.co.uk
8 See glossary.
9 See glossary.
10 OECD – www.oecd.org
11 Dun & Bradstreet, Eurostat, European Observatory, Small Business Administration.
12 Aida Alvarez (US Small Business Administrator – SBA), New Data Show Small Business will Drive Exports in 21st Century, 10 November 1999 – www.sba.gov
13 European Commission Discussion Papers – www.europa.eu.int/comm/enterprise
14 Fostering Entrepreneurship in Europe: Communication from the Commission to the Council (7 April 1998). Reference COM (98) 222 Final, page 1.

1 An overview of SMEs in Europe and the USA

This chapter provides an overview of SME development on both sides of the Atlantic. Similarities are noted and differences between the two regions highlighted. Starting from the proposition that SMEs are Europe's backbone, it considers the role played by SMEs in recent history and goes on to look at overall numbers of firms, the importance of SMEs as a source of employment and their contribution in economic terms.

This chapter acts as a backdrop to the central premise – that *capital markets for SMEs appear to have much more momentum and relevance to their growth in the US than in Europe.* Finally it attempts to conclude on linkages between SME activity and overall country wealth and between SME demographics and capital market activity.

Theories on comparative advantages of large firms vs. SMEs

Since the 1970s, rates of growth in the number of SMEs have been higher than in the immediate post-war periods. Within the EU, the number of self-employed and SMEs has increased from 11.6 million in 1988 to over 18 million, employing two-thirds of the employed work force in the late 1990s.[1,2] In the US, small business accounts for about 53 per cent of total employment.[3]

In the words of *The Economist*:

> Despite ever-larger and noisier mergers, the bigger change coming over the world of business is that firms are getting smaller. The trend of a century is being reversed. Until the mid-1970s, the size of firms everywhere grew; the number of self-employed fell ... No longer. Now it is the big firms that are shrinking and small ones that are on the rise. The trend is unmistakable – and businessmen and policy-makers will ignore it at their peril.[4]

Of course the trend is, in fact, mistakable and complex. Larger firms gained productivity and higher market caps much more quickly than smaller firms in the late 1990s, and it may be that the tides are turning once again. But it is clear that SMEs are central to any post-war OECD economy, and that their influence has grown dramatically in the post-war period.

It might be tempting to attribute the rise of small firms to a fall in the importance of manufacturing to the GDP of post-industrial, service-based economies. For example, employment in US manufacturing fell from 40 per cent of the total workforce in 1959 to 27.7 per cent of the workforce in 1984. However, the shift in economic activity from large to small firms has been greater in manufacturing than in services or finance. The small firm share of employment is growing faster in the goods-producing sector than for the economy as a whole.[5]

Hence, by the early 1980s, 80 per cent of employees in Italian manufacturing worked in SMEs – a high-mark for the developed world, whereas 37 per cent did in the US by the mid-1980s, a low mark.[6] But in both cases, the percentage of employees working in small firms even in manufacturing was rising from the late 1970s.

Since the 1930s, large firms have been viewed as having several advantages over smaller ones:

- Innovative activity requires a high fixed cost; R&D work typically involves scale economies.
- Supposedly, only firms large enough to attain market power will choose innovation as a means for maximisation, because only these firms will be big enough to exploit any discovered gains.
- R&D is risky, and smaller firms take the most risk. Larger ones can diversify their risk by diversifying their R&D efforts, increasing the likelihood of at least some successes.[7]

Yet small firms also have advantages, some of which grow more pronounced with the 'information revolution':

- Smaller firms may be less bureaucratic, and may have less 'inertia' in their operating structures.
- Innovative activities may flourish more in the small or 'start-up' environment.
- Smaller firms frequently place innovation (rather than market presence) at the centre of their strategy for advancement.[8]
- Intensified global competition due to transportation, information and communication improvements has led large diversified manufacturers to sell off less competitive holdings and has forced all producers into leaner manufacturing.
- Significant increases in the degree of uncertainty due to high rates of interest, inflation, unemployment, exchange rate volatility and growth slowdown in industrialised countries may have favoured smaller, more versatile firms in the 1970s and 1980s.

- Intensified market fragmentation due to growing consumer demand for differentiated products may have favoured smaller, more versatile firms.
- New mechanisation methods and computerisation may have further provoked more differentiation and specialisation of products and 'leaner' manufacturing.[9]

The result is that since the 1970s, small firms have been of increasing importance both to EU and US economies generally and to their investors and capital markets in particular.

Number of SMEs in Europe and the USA

According to recent statistics from the Small Business Administration and the European Commission, coupled with our own independent research in collaboration with Dun & Bradstreet, there are over 18 million SMEs in the European Union[10,11,12] and 15 million in the United States.[13] The self-employed, small and medium sized enterprises make up 99.8 per cent of all enterprises in the EU and 99.7 per cent of all enterprises in the USA.[14,15]

In both the EU and USA, the total number of self-employed is stable in absolute terms and declining in terms of the proportion of the workforce.

One interesting comparison is the self-employed proportion of total enterprises. In the US, it has remained relatively stable at around 60 per cent of total enterprises. In the EU it is around 50 per cent of total enterprises. Both trading blocs are exhibiting a declining trend in the self-employed proportion. This is a reflection of the better general economic

Table 1.1 Non-agricultural self-employment (NASE) (1993–7) (million)

	1993	*1994*	*1995*	*1996*	*1997*
EU	9.2	9.1	9.3	9.3	9.4
USA	9.0	9.0	8.9	9.0	9.1
Total	18.2	18.1	18.2	18.3	18.5

Source: Dun & Bradstreet, Eurostat, SME Observatory, SBA.

Table 1.2 NASE as a proportion of total enterprises (1993–7) (percentage)

	1993	*1994*	*1995*	*1996*	*1997*
EU	53	52	52	50	50
USA	60	60	59	59	59

Source: Dun & Bradstreet, Eurostat, SME Observatory, SBA.

Table 1.3 Total SME numbers (1993–7) (million)

	1993	*1994*	*1995*	*1996*	*1997*
EU	8.2	8.6	8.7	9.2	9.3
USA	5.9	6.0	6.1	6.2	6.3

Source: Dun & Bradstreet, Eurostat, SME Observatory, SBA.

well-being and feeling of more job security encouraging labour to join or remain part of a company rather than going it alone. The trend is more marked in the EU, reflecting the greater economic change.

Focusing on small and medium sized enterprises, there are over nine million in EU and 6 million in the USA.

The number of SMEs in both trading blocs is increasing, but the rate of growth in Europe is higher than that of the US, reflecting to a large extent the recovery of the EU from recession. During the same period, the EU records a 13 per cent increase in the number of SMEs whilst the US only records a 7 per cent growth.

The difference between the two blocs appears in part to be one of timing. A comparison of SME density, calculated as the ratio of population to number of SMEs, reveals a narrowing of the differences over the time period and the EU 'overtaking the US' at the end.

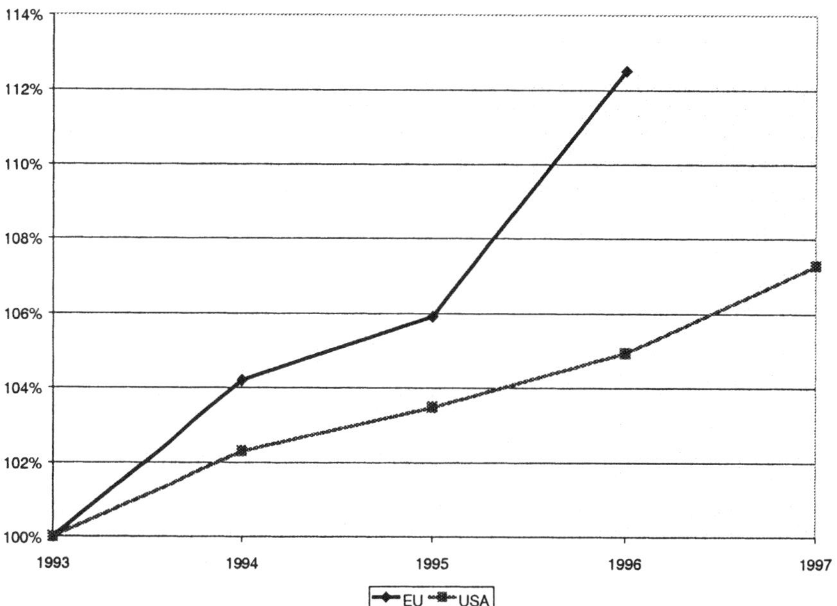

Figure 1.1 Rate of growth in number of SMEs (1993–7) (percentage).

Source: Dun & Bradstreet, Eurostat, SME Observatory, SBA.

Table 1.4 SME density (1993–7) (SMEs/thousands)

	1993	*1994*	*1995*	*1996*	*1997*
EU	22.2	23.1	23.4	24.8	25.0
USA	22.9	23.2	23.2	23.3	23.6

Source: Dun & Bradstreet, Eurostat, SME Observatory, SBA, US Bureau of Census.

At a regional level, within Europe, most NASE and SMEs are concentrated within a few countries. Eighty per cent of all SMEs are located in the five countries of France, Germany, Italy, Spain and the UK. This trend is unlikely to have changed much recently.

This is to be expected, as these are the five largest countries by population. However, what is more interesting, is the spread in NASE density[16] and SME density[17] between countries as can be seen in the table below.

The countries with the highest NASE density statistics are those such as the UK, Spain and Belgium, which have a tradition, coupled with a friendlier fiscal and tax regime of encouraging self-employment. There are also the lesser-industrialised countries such as Portugal and Greece. Ireland is an exception, where there has been a tradition of working abroad. Sweden and Austria have a more socialist/corporatist approach, resulting in a greater number of large enterprises rather than SMEs, as do to a lesser extent France and Germany.

A slightly different pattern emerges from considering European SME densities. Here we see that SMEs form the backbone of the economy in

Table 1.5 NASE and SMEs in Europe by country (1995)

Country	*NASE*	*SME*	*% Total*	*LE*	*Total*
Luxembourg	6,887	11,037	0	65	17,989
Ireland	23,817	46,730	1	317	70,864
Finland	97,584	82,504	1	489	180,577
Denmark	152,165	83,045	1	519	235,729
Austria	78,764	157,260	2	1,363	237,387
Sweden	104,242	138,486	2	825	243,553
Netherlands	223,532	272,166	3	2,212	497,910
Belgium	418,427	176,957	2	992	596,376
Portugal	300,443	355,520	4	794	656,757
Greece	399,489	347,007	4	360	746,856
France	1,091,940	1,019,639	12	4,657	2,116,236
Spain	1,366,388	996,110	12	2,473	2,364,971
Italy	1,530,996	1,713,039	20	2,544	3,246,579
Germany	1,209,277	2,113,671	24	11,836	3,334,784
UK	2,351,568	1,137,781	13	6,574	3,495,923
Total	9,355,519	8,650,952	100	36,020	18,042,491

Source: Eurostat.

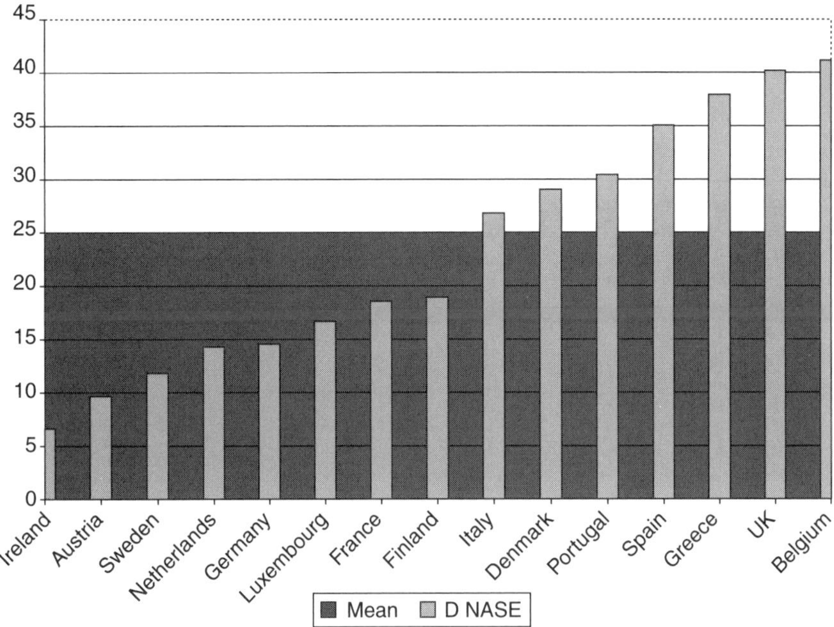

Figure 1.2 Europe NASE density (1995) (per '000 capita).

Source: Eurostat, US Bureau of Census.

the main continental European countries of France, Germany, Italy, Spain and the Netherlands. This is further borne out by the later economic contribution analysis. However, the United Kingdom is similar to the US with a much lower density of SMEs.

In the US, there is much less of a differentiation between regions. The north west has the highest density of SMEs, followed by the north east and the west.

Business start-ups in Europe and the USA

According to recent statistics available from Eurostat and the SME Observatory, business start-ups in the ten European countries for which the information is recorded reached a level of just over 1.8 million. As these countries represent over 90 per cent of total businesses in Europe, it is reasonable to extrapolate the information to impute a Europe-wide statistic. On this basis, Europe-wide, business start-ups topped 2 million in 1995.

Most start-ups (71 per cent) were the self-employed and a further 26 per cent of all start-ups were SMEs with four employees or less. Only 3 per cent of all European start-ups had more than five employees.

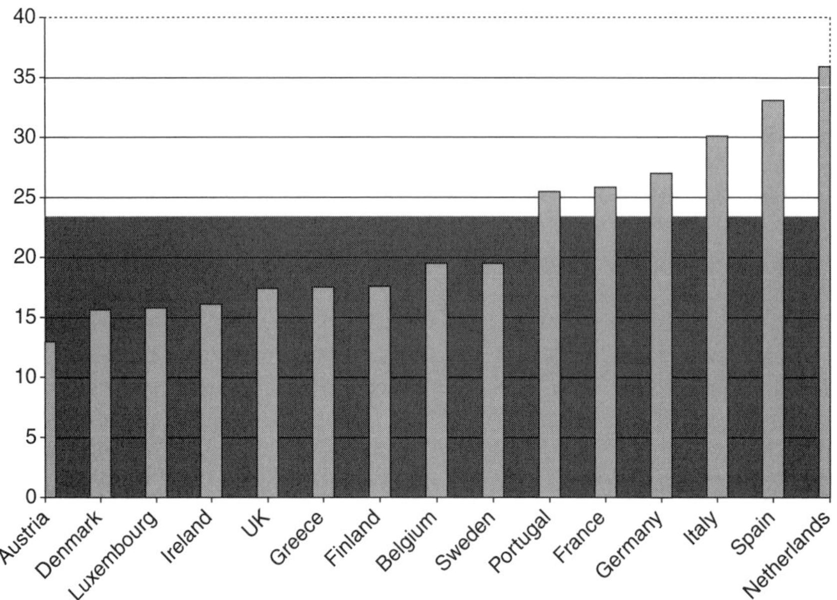

Figure 1.3 Europe SME density (1995) (per '000 capita).

Source: Eurostat, US Bureau of Census.

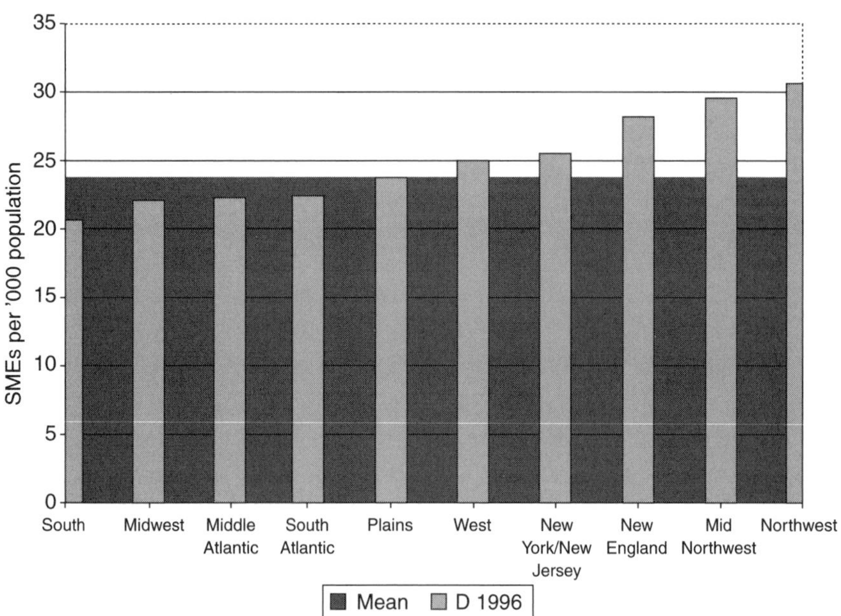

Figure 1.4 US SME density (1996) (per '000 capita).

Source: US SBA, US Bureau of Census.

Table 1.6 European start-ups (1995)

Country	*Start-ups ('000s)*	*Number of employees at start-up (%)*			
		0	*1–4*	*5–9*	*10+*
Denmark	16	90	10	0	0
Finland	31	78	19	1	1
France	285	76	21	2	1
Germany	528	n/a	n/a	n/a	n/a
Italy	287	74	26	0	0
Netherlands	25	61	36	2	1
Portugal	96	78	18	2	1
Spain	365	73	22	3	2
Sweden	51	87	10	1	1
UK	161	43	48	6	3
Total	1,845	71	25	2	1

Source: Eurostat, SME Observatory.

Note

Totals may not sum exactly due to rounding differences.

When viewed in terms of activity,[18] there was a wide variation between the EU countries reviewed. Most start-up activity occurred in Germany, the Iberian Peninsula and Scandinavia. Surprisingly, the Netherlands, which has the highest density of SMEs in the EU, reported the lowest start-up activity.

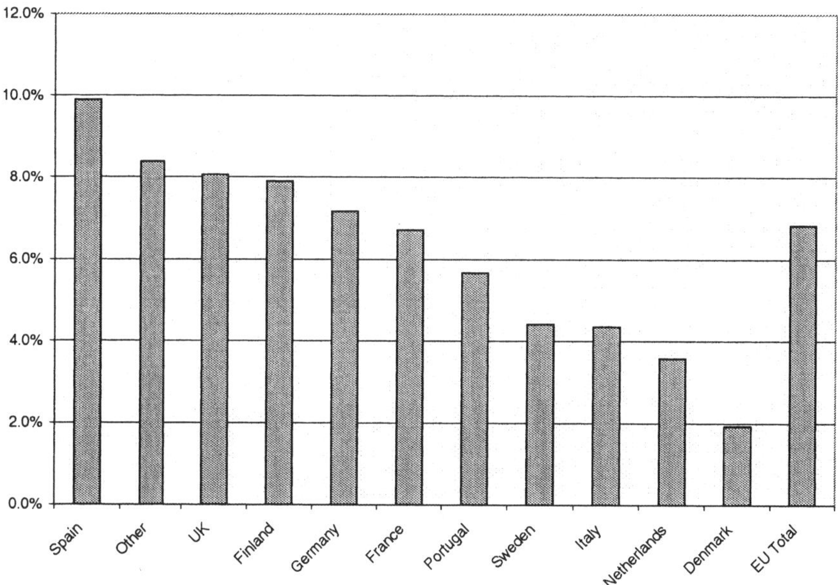

Figure 1.5 European business start-up activity (1995) (percentage stock).

Source: Eurostat, SME Observatory.

Considering SMEs, a total of 378,000 were created amongst the countries considered. Extrapolating this to the EU as a whole, 591,000 new SMEs were created in 1995. In relation to the total of 8.7 million SMEs in the EU, this represents an activity level of 6.8 per cent.

When viewed in terms of SME start-up activity, there was a wide variation between the EU countries reviewed. Most start-up activity occurred in the Iberian Peninsula and other smaller countries. Surprisingly, the Netherlands, which has the highest density of SMEs in the EU, has amongst the lowest SME start-up activity.

Amongst the biggest differences in patterns within Europe emerges when considering only non-agricultural self-employed (NASE) start-up activity. Countries with relatively low SME start-up activity register significant NASE levels. This complex picture can be interpreted as both the influences of the fiscal regimes in northern European countries offering better terms for incorporated entities and traditional employment practices in southern European countries.

In the USA, SME active business start-ups recorded by Dun & Bradstreet were 168,000 in 1995.[19] This represents an SME activity level of 2.8 per cent. New business formations were 820,000[20] and new business incorporations were 770,000 for the same period.[21] These also include non-agricultural self-employed and represent an activity level of 5.5 per cent and 5.1 per cent respectively.

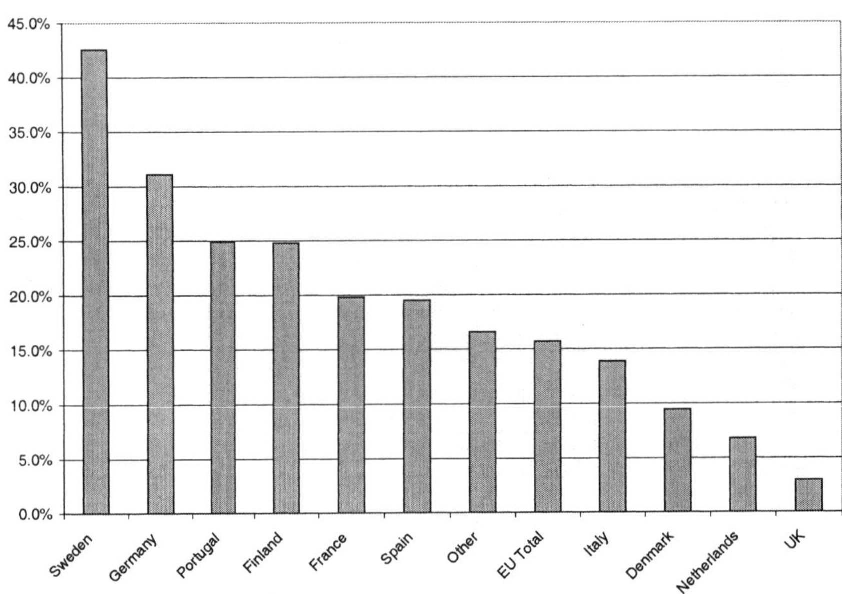

Figure 1.6 European NASE start-up activity (1995) (percentage stock).

Source: Eurostat, SME Observatory.

Table 1.7 US business start-ups by sector (1995)[a]

Sector	*1995*	%
Agriculture	2,199	1
Mining	564	0
Construction	16,980	10
Manufacturing	12,172	7
Transportation and utilities	7,161	4
Wholesale trade	14,956	9
Retail trade	36,381	22
Finance and real estate	10,362	6
Services	44,586	27
Other	22,797	14
Total	168,158	100

Source: Dun & Bradstreet.

Note
a 1995 statistics have been used for the USA to provide a direct comparison with Europe.

As in Europe, most SME starts have few employees. Eighty-three per cent of all new SME starts had less than five employees. This compares with the EU where 88 per cent of all new SME starts had less than five employees.

In the US, as in Europe, there is a concentration of new start-ups within certain regions. Over two-thirds of new formations were located on the Eastern Seaboard (East North Central, Middle Atlantic, South Atlantic) and the Pacific.

From Table 1.7, it can be seen that new business ventures tend to be concentrated in the service type business sectors. Services and retail make up three-quarters of all new business creations.

US statistics from 1995 have been taken to enable a direct comparison with Europe, for which later statistics were not available at the time of writing. Empirically, the furore over the Internet and the 'new economy' might suggest that there has been a change in this mix since the mid-1990s.

Grouping the data by major sector, we see similar patterns between business start-ups in the US and in Europe. US service and retail sectors make up 77 per cent of all start-ups.

In Europe, amongst the nine countries for which the data is monitored, the similar statistic was 75 per cent. Amongst the 'old' economy, although in the US and Europe start-ups represented 23 per cent and 25 per cent of the total respectively, construction represented 10 per cent in the US as compared with 14 per cent in Europe.

We attempted to create a more recent data set using the company information made available by Dun & Bradstreet. However, we were constrained by the relative opaqueness of the NACE codes which have not been substantially updated since 1992 – the start of the Internet boom. Although the SME data is primarily taken from 1995, our information on

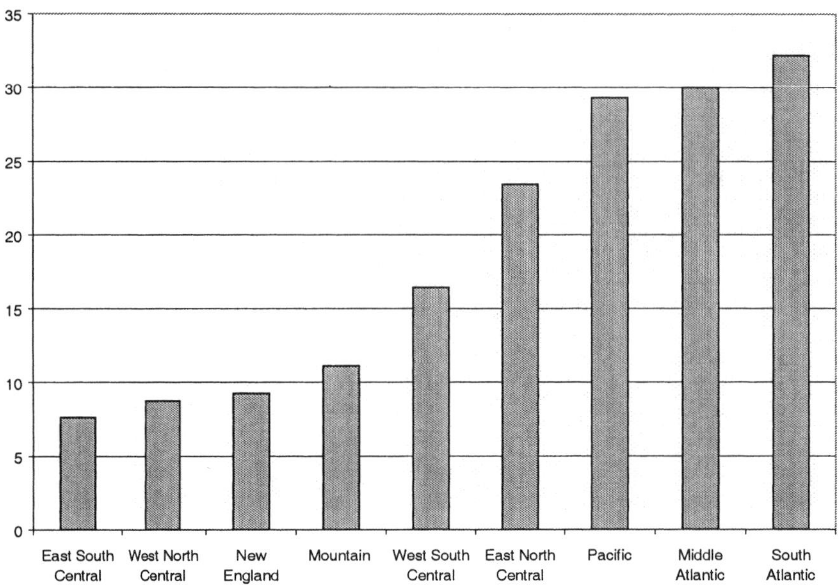

Figure 1.7 US business start-ups by region (1995) ('000s).

Source: Dun & Bradstreet.

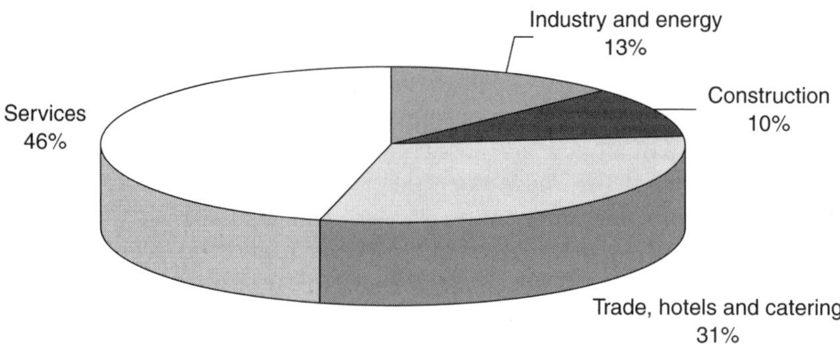

Figure 1.8 US business start-ups by sector (1995).

Source: Dun & Bradstreet.

capital markets, private equity and venture capital is much more current and dates between 1998 and 2000.

To test the impact of the Internet boom on overall start-ups, we have analysed over 10 million companies in the US and Europe using 1998/9 data provided by Dun & Bradstreet. Given constraints in establishing commonalties between the available datasets, a proxy for high growth companies was adopted under which they were defined as being companies formed since 1995 that were independent and had achieved a turnover of at

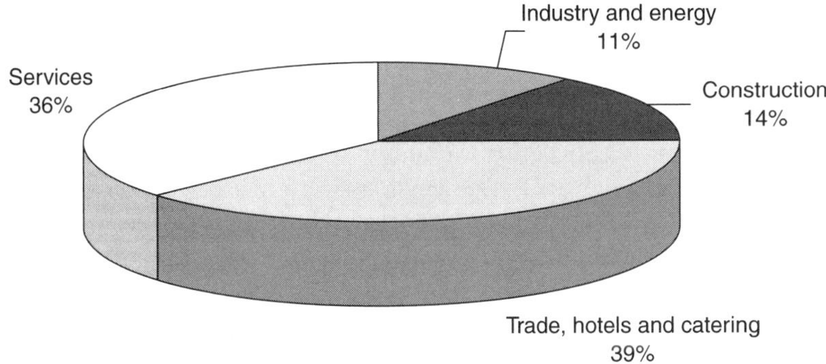

Figure 1.9 EU business start-ups by sector (1995)[a].

Source: EU SME Observatory, Eurostat.

Note

a EU sectoral start-up statistics compiled using country data from Denmark, Finland, France, Italy, the Netherlands, Portugal, Spain, Sweden and the UK. The data is only available for these nine countries.

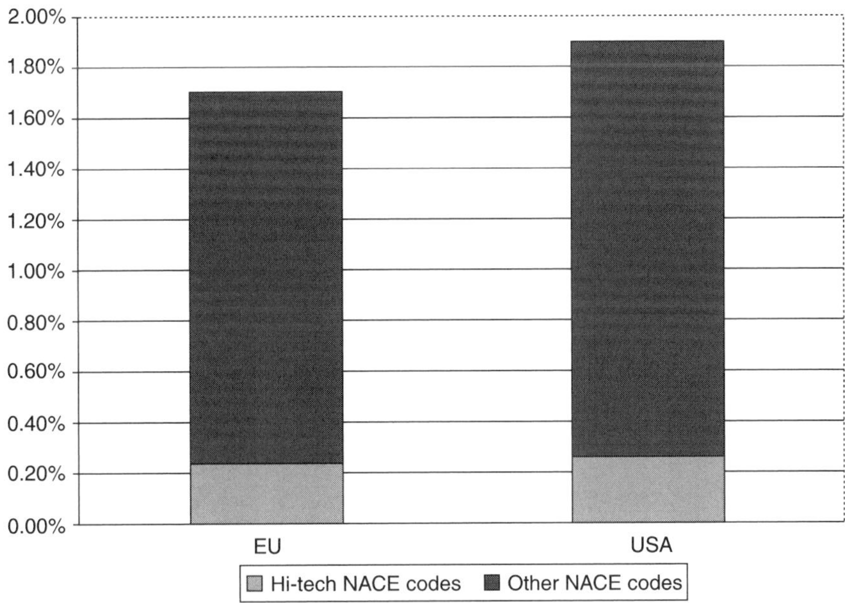

Figure 1.10 High growth companies in the EU and the USA (1998/9) (percentage total).

Source: Dun & Bradstreet.

Note

'Hi-tech' NACE codes selected by authors based on NACE code allocated to known 'new' economy companies.

least €1 million by 1998/9. This definition does not significantly skew the analysis due to the small number of large independent company start-ups (see above). High-growth companies were selected and analysed by NACE sector. Amongst the total sample, 1.7 per cent in Europe and 1.9 per cent in the US met our high-growth criteria. From within this sample, there was no noticeable difference between the number of high-tech SME start-ups in the US and the EU. High-tech NACE codes were chosen based upon comparing codes applied to a sample of known high-tech companies in Europe and the US. This further research revealed that approximately 0.25 per cent of all companies could be categorised as high-growth, high-tech 'gazelles', with no significant difference between the two regions.

This research however must be qualified in that the NACE codes used to categorise companies have not been revised since 1992 – or roughly since the beginning of the Internet boom. As a consequence, many high-tech companies are categorised within the 'miscellaneous' or 'other' categories that are available – with the result that the data may be skewed by genuine other – but low-tech – high-growth start-ups. There is suggestive evidence that the Internet boom has had a significant impact on the type of start-up.

Business failures in Europe and the USA

Extrapolating the countries within the EU for which there is data available, business failures topped 1.7 million in 1995, the latest year for which EU wide data is available. As with business start-ups, there is a wide disparity in failure activity throughout Europe. However, with the notable exception of the UK, all other countries recorded less business failures than starts during the year. Comparing total business starts and failures (see Figure 1.11), two patterns and one exception emerge. The patterns are:

- The high business start countries have equally high business failure rankings. Sweden, for example, tops both leagues, and the other regions are also high in both rankings.
- The low business start countries have equally low business failure rankings. The Netherlands for example has the lowest activity under both measures.

The exception is Spain. Although it has a high business start ranking, it has a low business failure ranking.

In absolute terms, Spain has the second highest net increase in small businesses. An analysis of starts and failures at a sector level, which are then compared with Sweden, indicates the following. The main start-up areas in Spain are in the high value-added sunrise industry sectors, including the manufacture of computers, computing, research and development, financial services and telecommunications. In Sweden it is tobacco, recycling, education and recreational and sporting activities which, other than tobacco, are sectors that are sensitive to cyclical factors.[22]

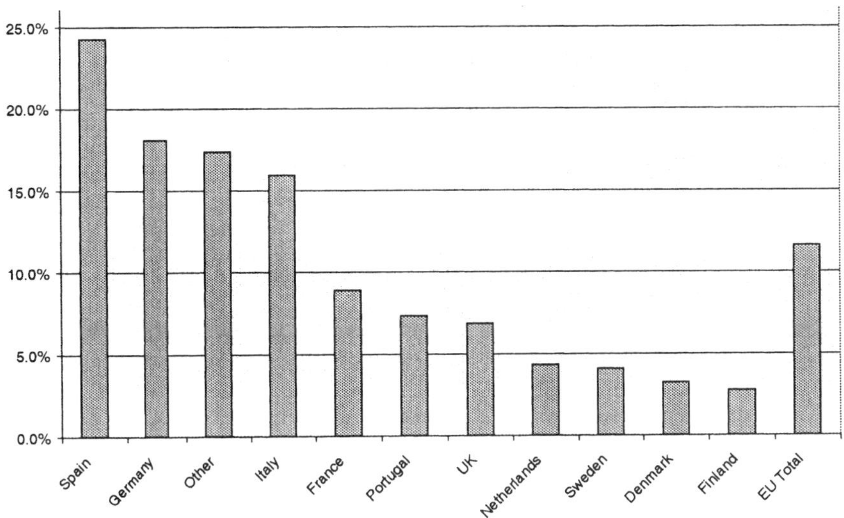

Figure 1.11 EU combined NASE and SME start-ups (1995) (percentage stock).

Source: Eurostat, EU SME Observatory.

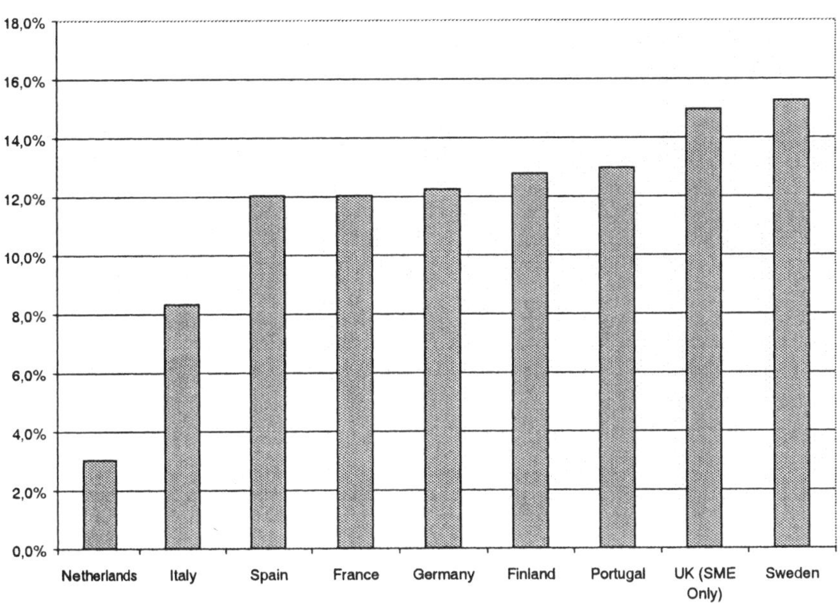

Figure 1.12 European combined NASE and SME failure activity (1995) (percentage stock).

Source: Eurostat, SME Observatory.

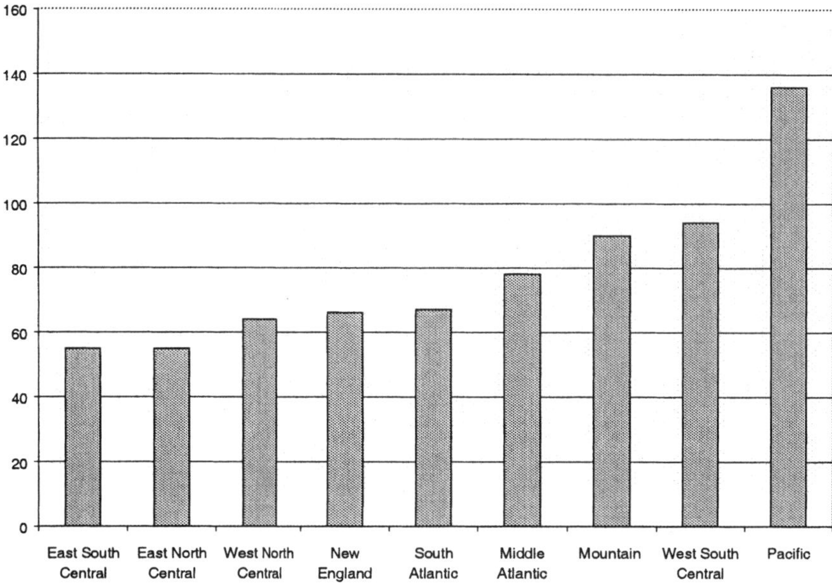

Figure 1.13 US business failure activity by region (1995) (per 10,000 businesses).
Source: Dun & Bradstreet.

In the US, SME business failures according to the Dun & Bradstreet survey topped 71,000 in 1995. Figure 1.13 shows the number of small business failures per 10,000 small businesses. As can be seen, most failures are either in the developed pacific region or in the less-developed and poorer West South Central and mountain regions of the US.

In terms of sector, US failures, like European ones, are concentrated in the high-risk sectors of construction, transportation and manufacturing. However, unlike Europe, the lowest business failure sector is represented by services. Figure 1.14 shows the range of business failures by sector.

In Europe, most failures are in the wholesale trade, retail trade, hotels and catering, followed by services. Construction is ranked only as the third business failure sector.[23]

The US all-business failure profile below shows the failure likelihood for small businesses in the US peaks in the third year of activity. Within Europe, the diversity of legal and political systems have resulted in various definitions of bankruptcy which as a consequence make the collation of business failure statistics extremely difficult. Apart from definitional differences, data is not nationally available for certain countries such as Germany, where it is available only at a state level.

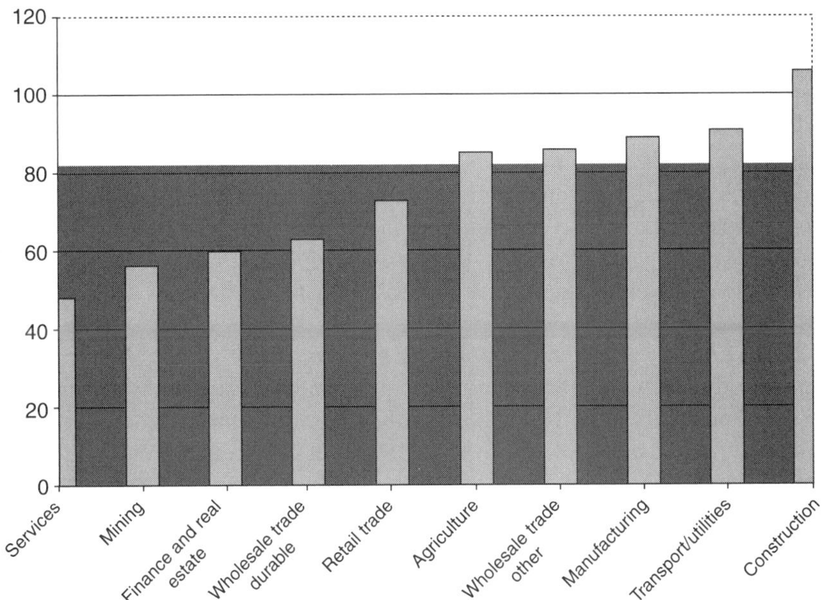

Figure 1.14 US business failure activity by sector (1995) (per 10,000 businesses).

Source: Dun & Bradstreet.

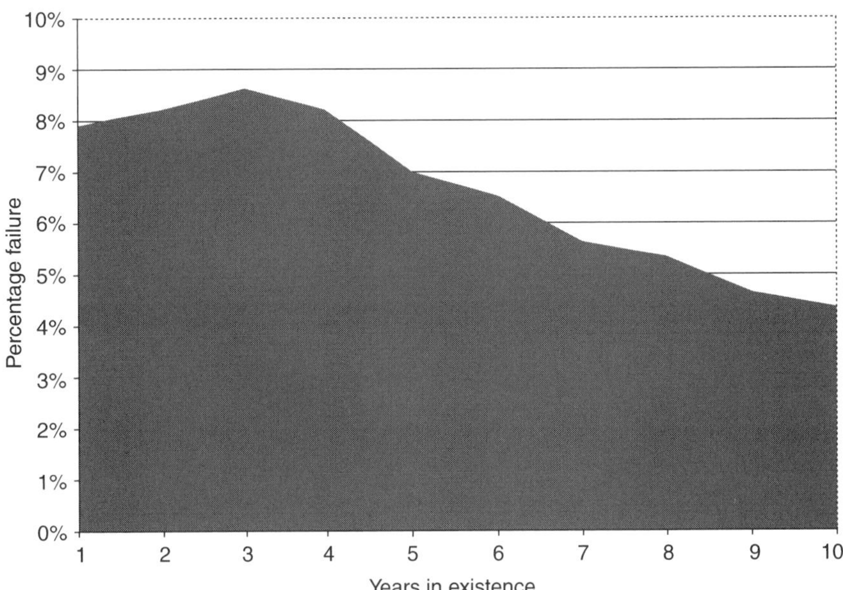

Figure 1.15 US all-business failure profile (1995).

Source: Dun & Bradstreet.

Small business employment in Europe and the USA

There is a wide variation in self-employment within Europe. At one extreme, there is Germany and Austria, where self-employment is less than 3 per cent of the total workforce. At the other extreme, there is Belgium, Spain and Greece, where self-employment is at twice the European average.

As with the US, self-employment represents approximately 10 per cent of the workforce, with the numbers of NASE reported at just over 10 million.[24] There is a similar pattern to Europe, with the self-employed being concentrated in the traditional NASE regions, or those that are less developed.

Table 1.9 shows how important SMEs are for employment. Again, there is a wide disparity between the more industrialised economies of the UK, France, Germany, the Netherlands and Scandinavia and the Mediterranean and Iberian countries. In the latter, there is a much greater reliance upon SMEs for employment.

Combining NASE and SME statistics, as shown in Figure 1.16, gives a much clearer picture of this disparity. The US as a whole is similar to the European industrialised nations, with SMEs representing just 53 per cent of total employment.

Looking at both NASE and SME employment figures combined, the EU and the USA are similar with an average employment of 66 per cent and 64 per cent respectively.

Ranking SME employment by sector into 'heavy' (above average) and

Table 1.8 EU NASE employment by country (1995)

Country	*Total*	*NASE*	*NASE (%)*
Germany	30,032,770	816,757	3
Austria	2,586,923	86,116	3
Ireland	695,832	29,731	4
Luxembourg	179,967	9,322	5
Sweden	2,109,808	109,910	5
Finland	1,066,169	56,797	5
Netherlands	5,218,848	316,549	6
Denmark	1,552,039	100,243	6
Italy	13,979,206	1,522,651	11
France	15,335,260	1,688,764	11
Portugal	2,857,252	318,582	11
United Kingdom	20,124,117	2,481,731	12
Belgium	3,678,610	725,381	20
Spain	10,933,530	2,189,097	20
Greece	1,731,406	476,133	27
Total	112,081,737	10,927,764	10

Source: Eurostat, SME Observatory.

Table 1.9 EU SME employment by country (1995)

Country	*Total*	*SME*	*SME (%)*
United Kingdom	20,124,117	8,959,812	45
Finland	1,066,169	554,796	52
Belgium	3,678,610	1,945,235	53
Netherlands	5,218,848	2,847,078	55
France	15,335,260	8,419,862	55
Germany	30,032,770	16,510,935	55
Sweden	2,109,808	1,177,019	56
Greece	1,731,406	1,022,257	59
Spain	10,933,530	6,488,994	59
Austria	2,586,923	1,583,627	61
Denmark	1,552,039	978,468	63
Ireland	695,832	446,853	64
Luxembourg	179,967	119,455	66
Portugal	2,857,252	1,953,954	68
Italy	13,979,206	9,649,400	69
Total	112,081,737	62,657,745	56

Source: Eurostat, SME Observatory.

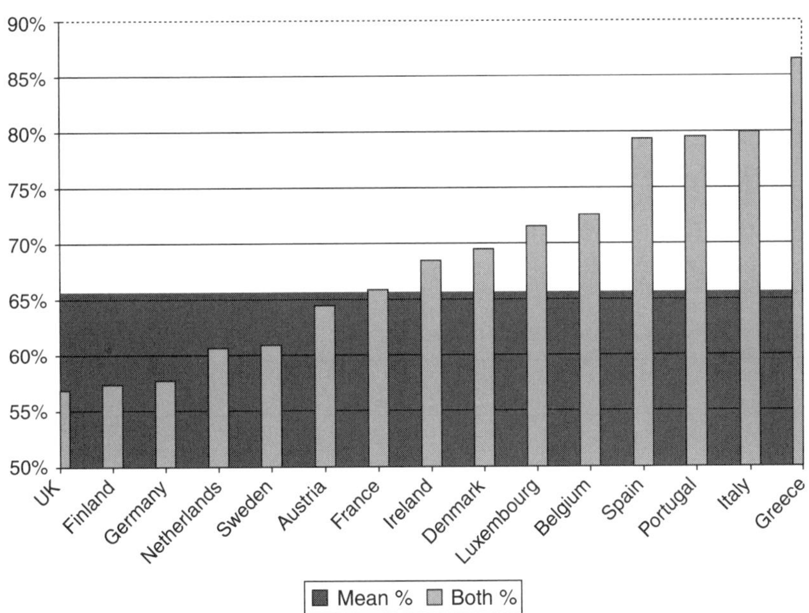

Figure 1.16 EU NASE and SME employment by country (1995).

Source: Eurostat, SME Observatory.

Table 1.10 SME employment by sector (1995) (thousands and SME percentage of total employment)

Sector	*EU-15*	*%*	*USA*	*%*
Agriculture	n/a	n/a	557	89
Mining	105	51	222	39
Construction	7,228	71	5,037	89
Manufacturing	16,820	51	7,197	39
Transport, telecoms and utilities	3,139	37	2,381	36
Wholesale and retail trade	19,563	65	16,540	55
Financial and real estate	1,105	24	3,066	43
Commercial services	14,697	58	19,982	56
Total	62,657	56	54,982	53

Source: Eurostat, SME Observatory.

Note
Percentage indicates proportion of workforce employed by SMEs.

'light' (below average) concentrations, we see that there is no difference between the US and Europe. 'Heavy' sectors for employment include construction, wholesale and retail trade and commercial services. The rest are 'light' sectors – mining, manufacturing, transport and financial services. The lack of dominance in these latter sectors reflects a combination of their capital/labour intensive nature and maturity.

Economic impact of SMEs

SMEs are more important in Europe than in the US when measured in terms of economic activity. A direct comparison of the share of GDP contributed by SMEs in Europe and the US is difficult due to differences in the way statistics are compiled. A reasonable proxy is the turnover generated by SMEs. In 1995, SMEs within Europe contributed just over 55 per cent of sales (see Table 1.11) as compared with just over 47 per cent in the

Table 1.11 Sales/receipts by region (1995)

	SME	*LE*	*SME (%)*	*LE (%)*
US receipts (US$ billion)				
1993	6,679,975	7,418,597	47.4	52.6
1994	7,023,980	7,816,472	47.3	52.7
1995	7,404,386	8,346,979	47.0	53.0
EU Receipts (€ billion)				
1993	8,703,048	7,215,353	54.7	45.3
1994	9,137,434	6,969,449	56.7	43.3
1995	9,366,812	7,742,004	54.7	45.3

Source: Eurostat, SBA.

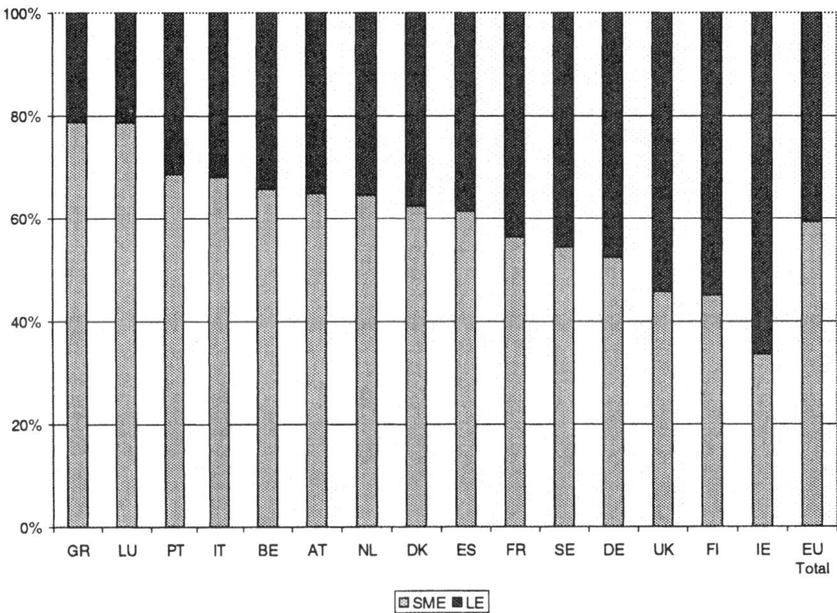

Figure 1.17 EU share of turnover by country (1995).

Source: Eurostat.

US for the same period. As a corollary, large enterprises are significantly more important in the US.

Over time, the contribution is relatively static, staying at around 47 per cent in the US and 55 per cent in the EU.

Within the EU, there is a wide variation in the importance of SMEs when considered in terms of their economic contribution. Sixty per cent of countries are above the EU average.

These are mainly the southern European countries such as Greece, Portugal and Italy, or the smaller countries such as Luxembourg or Belgium. At the other extreme are the European economic powerhouses of Germany, the UK and France, along with Scandinavia.

Financing of SMEs

Although SME liquidity information at a European level is not available, it is compiled for certain countries. Such data is collated for Germany, which with its significant number of SMEs represents a reasonable proxy for Europe.

As can be seen from Figure 1.18, total debt–equity ratios for SMEs in Germany was 187 per cent. As might be expected, it is construction and

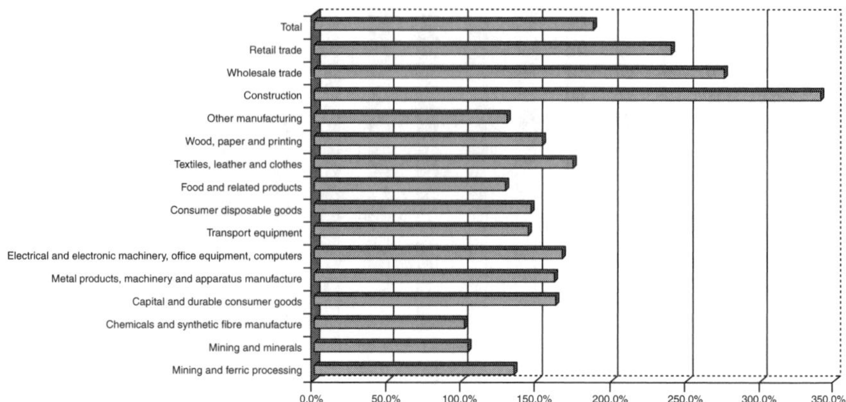

Figure 1.18 Debt–equity ratios for German SMEs (1994) (percentage).

Source: Institut Für Mittelstandsforschung, Bonn, 1998, *SMEs in Germany – Facts and Figures 1998*, Hans-Eduard Haouser, IfM Bonn, p. 42, Table 18.

Note

Data calculated for German enterprises with between €7 and 40 million turnover.

the services sectors that have the highest leverage. There is a significant difference between the two regions. The debt/equity ratio for the USA is half that of Germany at 91 per cent.

Analysis of SMEs on a sectoral basis has shown that there is little difference between Europe and the USA. Thus it is reasonable to assume that funding requirements are similar. The difference between the ratios reinforces the perception of the maturity of US capital markets and the availability of private equity reducing the requirement for debt financing in the US.

Conclusions on SME development

SMEs are more important in Europe than in the US when measured in terms of numbers and economic importance. But SMEs in the United States were more successful in terms of 'graduation' track record in the 1990s.

The birth rates (newly founded start-ups) of European SMEs are higher than in the USA, but so are mortality rates (bankruptcies). Statistics on births and deaths are affected by a variety of factors, especially cycles of the economy (with rising rates of foundation at the beginning of a boom and rising rates of death both during recession and towards the end of a boom. Politics also plays a part; encouragement of new firm growth in Britain just before a recession in the late 1980s and early 1990s, for example, led to artificially high start-up rates and then very high bankruptcy rates during that recession.

Table 1.12 SME debt–equity ratios for Germany and the USA (1994) (percentage)

Country	*Debt–equity ratio (%)*
Germany[a]	187.7
USA[b]	90.9

Sources

a Institut Für Mittelstandsforschung, Bonn, 1998, *SMEs in Germany: Facts and Figures 1998*, Hans-Eduard Haouser, IfM Bonn, p. 42, Table 18.

b Small Business Administration, Washington DC, 1997, *The State of Small Business 1996: A Report of the President*, US Government Printing Office, Washington DC, Chapter 2, p. 42, Table 2.1.

Notes

a Data calculated for German enterprises with between €7 and 40 million turnover.

b US Estimates by Federal Reserve Board for non-farm, non-financial corporations and non-farm non-corporate businesses. Total assets and debt for small corporations were estimated by applying 17.5 per cent and 19 per cent respectively to that of all corporations. Net worth is treated as a residual. These ratios were estimated by using corporate tax return data published by the US Department of Treasury, Internal Revenue Service. Assumed that SMEs are entities that fit the selection criteria and have less than US$ 25 million in assets.

There are significant differences between SMEs within the EU itself. The northern countries have more successful SMEs measured by size and turnover. The southern countries have a greater share of their economies in the hands of smaller firms.

The capital base of European SMEs appears to be narrower than their counterparts in the US. There is also a greater emphasis and reliance on working capital finance than in the US. This constrains growth, particularly in the case of earlier stage development companies.

US companies are more familiar with VCs and capital market operators. This leads to a better understanding of funding and post-funding criteria and needs.

European SME management skills are comparable with those in the US. Nonetheless, day-to-day activities in Europe focus more on short-term than on development or strategic work. European companies are more concerned with obtaining and managing working capital finance.

Generally, it can be said that SMEs have become more significant to virtually all OECD economies, and their importance grew dramatically from the 1970s through to the mid-1990s. Yet we should remember that there is no clear tie between the importance of SMEs in an economy and wealth in that economy. And, from the perspective of capital markets, it is not all SMEs that are of interest, only those that are particularly high-growth and particularly in need of financing – a small subset of the total. Especially in the 1990s, the US boasted more firms of interest to angel and VC funding institutions, more firms listed on small-cap exchanges, and more dynamic growth in sectors currently particularly fashionable among equity investors, including computers and the Internet.

We close this chapter with a focus on the issue of cultural 'entrepreneurship' – an issue that is not regarded as a strong causal variable in this study, but is nevertheless a central focus of the European Commission.

While Europe appears to have more of its economy based in small firms than the US, Europe has been criticised by many scholars and businesspeople as being insufficiently 'entrepreneurial', and this may limit start-up activity and prevent small firms from becoming larger ones of interest to capital markets.

The European Commission itself has apparently endorsed a hypothesis on insufficient 'entrepreneurialism' in Europe:

> A strong entrepreneurial culture is also essential for the future competitiveness of the European economy and for generating growth ... Although in Europe there is a high level of entrepreneurial dynamism, it is not so high compared with the main competitors, particularly the United States. Therefore, we need to create a strong and vibrant business community and we must develop a spirit of enterprise and risk-taking ... We need to provide business starters with the skills for starting and managing a business in an increasingly competitive environment.[25]

While we agree that culture matters, we would again look to institutions to understand cultural differences. On entrepreneurship, in the US it is encouraged throughout the managerial board of companies. Smaller companies pay their boards less, but offer more stock options, according to a study by Grant Thornton Accountancy. Their study, comparing smaller NASDAQ companies to larger NYSE companies found that the smaller companies that granted stock options granted more than four times the medium current-year stock option grants that large companies do (4,750 shares vs. 1,000 shares, respectively). Directors of small-to-medium companies hold nine times as many total stock options as directors of large companies (18,000 vs. 2,000). The median for total shares owned by directors at the smaller NASDAQ companies is 51,080; at larger companies, only 15,674.[26]

Many European governments, as we shall see elsewhere, treat stock options as ordinary income. Taxing unrealised income in this way ignores the considerable risks that they entail for their owners. Additionally, as capital gains are frequently heavily taxed in Europe, this can make options an even more expensive form of remuneration. Finally, company boards in some European countries (e.g. Germany) provide less generous packages to executives and more power to labour bodies than in America.

Thus, the management incentives that have proved most effective for US small firms are, due to institutional frameworks, therefore less effective for European firms. Of course, legal changes on taxes and the rewards of board membership could immediately provoke changes in 'entrepreneurship'.

Notes

1 Eurostat, Panorama of the European Union, Enterprises in Europe SME Database, 1999 Edition.
2 European Observatory for SMEs Fifth Annual Report, 1997, Executive Summary.
3 Small Business Administration Small Business Economic Indicators, 1997, Executive Summary.
4 A 1989 quotation from *The Economist* contained in Zoltan J. Acs, 'Small Firms and Economic Growth', Zoltan J. Acs, Bo Carlsson and Roy Thurik, *Small Business in the Modern Economy*. Cambridge, MA: Blackwell, 1996, p. 11.
5 Zoltan J. Acs, Bo Carlsson and Roy Thurik, ibid., p. 46.
6 Ibid., p. 13.
7 Ibid., pp. 25–8.
8 Ibid., pp. 25–8.
9 Ibid., pp. 63–125.
10 Dun & Bradstreet proprietary database Small Business Administration.
11 Panorama of the European Union Enterprises in Europe SME database 1999 Edition, 1999, Eurostat.
12 The European Observatory for SMEs Fifth Annual Report 1997, 1999, European Network for SME Research, Executive Summary.
13 1997 Small Business Economic Indicators, 1998, US Small Business Administration Office of Advocacy, Executive Summary.
14 The European Observatory for SMEs Fifth Annual Report 1997, ibid., Executive Summary.
15 1997 Small Business Economic Indicators, ibid., Executive Summary.
16 Definition: Calculated as the number of non-agricultural self-employed divided by the total mid-year population expressed per 1,000 capita.
17 Definition: Calculated as the number of small- and medium-sized enterprises divided by the total mid-year population expressed per 1,000 capita
18 See glossary.
19 1995 used to provide direct comparison with latest statistics available from the EU. Although later statistics available for the USA, this is not the case for the European Union.
20 See glossary.
21 See glossary.
22 European SME Observatory Fifth Annual Report 1997.
23 The EU SME Observatory Annual Report 1997.
24 Small Business Administration, Small Business Economic Indicators, 1996, Small Business Administration Office of Advocacy.
25 EU Commission DG XXIII (Enterprise). Fostering Entrepreneurship.
26 Grant Thornton Accountants. *Annual Study of Small-to-Midsize and Large Public Company Boards*, 1998.

2 Private equity and venture capital in Europe and the USA

Venture capitalism has undergone revolutionary changes since the first days that it achieved recognition in the early 1950s. With respect to the US, the industry started in earnest in the 1950s and 1960s. Individual investors – business angels – were the archetypal venture investors. While this type of individual investment did not totally disappear, the modern 'professional' venture firm quickly emerged as the dominant venture investment vehicle. This trend has reversed in the last few years, with individuals once again becoming a potent force and increasingly taking a larger role in the early stage/start-up parts of the venture life cycle. These 'angel investors' will mentor a company and provide needed capital and expertise to help develop companies. Angel investors may either be wealthy people with management expertise or retired businessmen and women who seek the opportunity for first-hand business development.[1] These days, institutions are much bigger players than individuals in terms of the assets that they manage. Despite a resurgence of the individual investor described above, institutions remain the dominant investment sources in the industry.

Yet on an individual level, the venture capital industry in the US has benefited greatly from a higher and higher public appetite for new stocks. This has traditionally been one of the significant differences between the US and Europe, although the situation is changing in Europe. The fact that US investors are less risk-adverse is influenced by tax and savings policy, but it is also cultural: US consumers are aggressive spenders and even avid gamblers (a multi-billion dollar industry in America), and they are not afraid to invest surplus capital, even their primary retirement accounts, into higher-risk investments than Europeans. Because of greater inequalities of wealth, despite similarities in GDP per capita, there are also more people in the US who are very wealthy. These rich people have a greater ability to diversify their assets (and therefore their risks) by allowing a portion of their savings to form a large pool of high-risk investment in new firms or new industries with less-tested valuation methodologies.

Comparing markets in the US, Europe and other countries, VC funding

Table 2.1 Private equity under management by region (1998–9)

Country/Region	*Capital managed (US$ billion)*	
	1998[a]	*1999*[b]
USA	332.3	400.0
UK and Europe	79.0	92.0
Asia	29.1	38.3
Canada	5.4	11.2
Israel	5.0	10.4
Latin America	4.9	6.0

Notes

a *National Venture Capital Association Yearbook 1999*, Venture Economics Information Services, p. 13.

b *National Venture Capital Association Yearbook 2000*, Venture Economics Information Services, p. 20.

in the US is the largest by far, but Europe, led by funds flowing through London, also sports a vibrant market, more than double the size of the markets of all of Asia and Latin America combined.

What are the sources of US leadership and what does leadership imply for SMEs?

In the US, an institutional investor will usually allocate 2 to 3 per cent of giant institutional portfolios – for example, public and private pension funds each comprising the savings of tens or even hundreds of thousands of people – for investment in alternative assets such as private equity or venture capital as part of overall asset allocation. This helps to explain why 50 per cent of investments in VC/private equity come from public and private pension funds. Far more than those in Europe, VC markets in the US are fuelled by pension funds willing to take risks, or diversify them, through private companies and other VC investments. This is a force that is suppressed in Europe by pay-as-you-go public pension/social security systems and also conservative regulations on how the public manages money. If Europe is to compete with the US as a force for VC activity, a primary priority will be changing the nature of pension/social security savings and how it is managed.

Indeed, US state pension funds' support for high-risk markets is probably the greatest support that the government provides to these markets outside the rigorous regulatory framework. In the US, 46 of 50 state governments sponsor local venture capital funds and in at least 19 states, local public pension funds also channel funds into VC vehicles. Total funds under management by state-sponsored local VC funds are near US$ 2.25 billion, roughly 50 per cent greater than the UK equivalent figure after adjusting for GDP differences. US regional funds, both sponsored and not, favour earlier stage and high-tech investments. With respect to support from government pension funds, according to a survey commissioned by Aberdeen Asset Management, only 15 out of 80 UK local authority pension funds invest in venture capital.[2]

With respect to taxes, even in liberal Britain, capital gains tax receipts totalled £1.3 billion in 1997–8, forming only 1 per cent of the government budget,[3] but with tax rates well over 30 per cent. Tax rates are lower for long-term investments, with the aim of discouraging shorter-term investments by pension funds. Although this fiscal framework might, prima facie, encourage private equity, rather the low number of funds amongst public institutions reflects their viewpoint of private equity and venture capital being a short-term investment, rather than a longer-term commitment.

Many countries in Europe, not just the UK, are beginning to develop quite vibrant markets. But the markets in the UK (also discussed in detail in a later chapter) most resemble those of the US, and are most tied to US capital. Also, despite successes on the continent, in the late 1990s the US venture capital industry was not only almost three times larger than the rest of the world's combined (figures above); it was growing at a faster rate and pulling ahead. Here, the 'cyclical' explanation seems important to understand why US leadership is actually growing so rapidly, but differences in tax and savings methodologies help to demonstrate a continuous source of strength in US markets.

In terms of SME funding, it is also important to remember that the US leadership is in part the result of VC activities at later stages of funding that have essentially blended the distinction between the VC industry and investment banking. As with 'small-cap' exchanges, the lion's share of the VC funds is not actually going towards SMEs. Still, the link between this industry and the explosive start-ups in California, Massachusetts and New York is clear. And the trend suggests that Europe's new-found interest in VC funding could be encouraged far more thoroughly. This would provide fuel for more dynamism in the high-tech, high-growth sectors most likely to attract substantial funding.

On US angel and venture capital activity

The US definition of 'venture-backed' firms has different meanings depending on the context, according to the US National Venture Capital Association. Three working definitions are used, depending on the nature of the investor, and the timing and nature of their exit.[4]

Other terms of relevance to 'stages of investment' also include 'seed', 'early', or 'expansion stage' financing (see also introduction).[5]

Table 2.2 Definition of venture-backed firms

Definition	*Investor*	*Exit*
Venture Capital Journal Statistical definition	Non-buy-out venture capital fund	At or post IPO
Tight definition	Non-buy-out venture capital fund	At any time – through trade sale or IPO
Broad definition	Buy-out or non-buy-out venture capital fund	At any time – through trade sale or IPO

Source: National Venture Capital Association.

The dominance and size of US firms and funding

The dominance of US firms in the global markets is illustrated in Figure 2.1.

Figure 2.1 actually under-emphasises US leadership because much of the European activity is US-based money channelled through Europe (see below). But while US investments have helped to fuel the MBO/MBI[6] activities in European, especially British markets, the same cannot be said of foreign capital in the US, which forms only a very small fraction of venture funding (around 1 per cent).

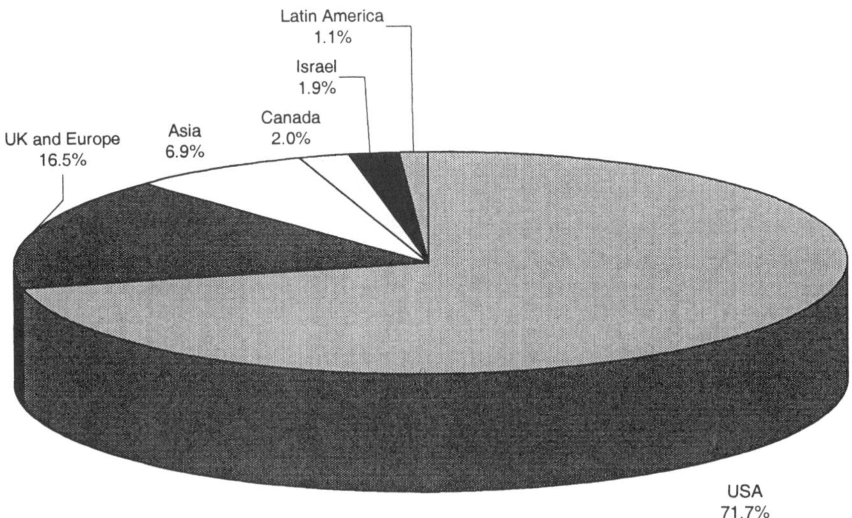

Figure 2.1 Private equity under management by country (1998).

Source: *National Venture Capital Association Yearbook 2000*, Thomson Financial Securities Data/Venture Economics, p. 20.

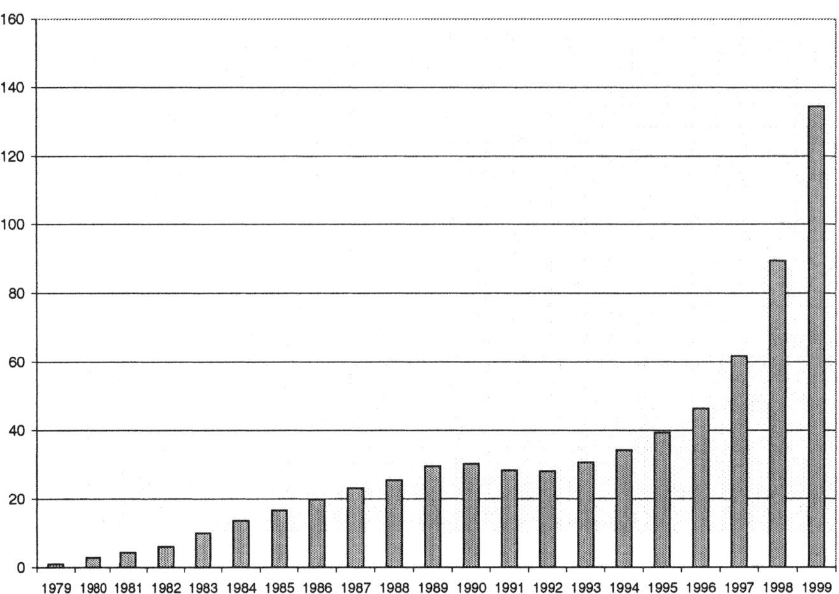

Figure 2.2 Capital under management (1979–99) (US$ billion).

Source: *National Venture Capital Association Yearbook 2000*, Thomson Financial Securities Data/Venture Economics, p. 15, Figure 1.01.

Figure 2.2 shows the incredible pace of growth for US VC markets, with $135 billion under management by 1999.[7] Despite the large number of firms liquidated in the early 1990s, this increase in funds has also fuelled an increase in the number of firms in operation; there are 620 in operation compared with 387 in the late 1980s.[8]

The NVCA lists as the two primary factors for the success of the US VC funds in the late 1990s.[9]

- In the favourable economic climate, VC firms were able to return considerable amounts of distributions to their limited partners, and partners chose to re-invest the money.
- High stock market values have caused institutions to rebalance their portfolios, reallocating investment assets into areas such as private equity.

Both of these factors are uninteresting from a comparative perspective, in that they are essentially describing the benefits of cycles rather than favourable regulatory and organisational frameworks. Capital breeds capital and success breeds success, but we think that this is hardly the full story. One can add to the cyclical discussion the incredibly fortunate

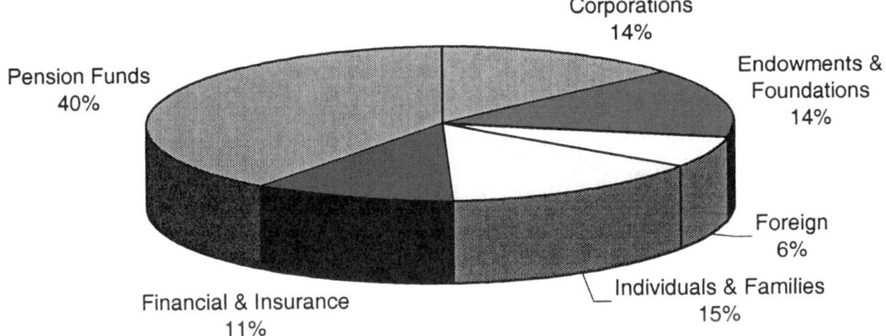

Figure 2.3 US accumulated capital commitments by type (1979–99) (percentage).

Source: *National Venture Capital Association Yearbook 1999*, US: Venture Economics Information Services, NVCA, p. 1.

investment climate that investors are operating in generally; the incredible valuations attributed to VC-funded industries regardless of firm size and sometimes regardless of revenues or profits; the reduced 'crowding out' problem of US government deficits, which have disappeared; low inflation; and a host of other factors. More and more money from more and more sources exists to blow wind into the sails of the more resourceful VC firms.

Yet again, a favourable regulatory and organisational climate explains a great deal of the story. Much of this money is coming from the largest institutions that blend traditional VC activities with investment banking; almost one-quarter of the money is actually from investment banks, but much of the rest of it is from giant institutions behaving like the merchant arms of a traditional investment bank and making similar types of purchases, with heavy participation in MBOs, for example.

Analysis by firm type: the comparative importance of aggressively managed pensions, endowments and financial institutions

Historically, pension funds account for 40 per cent of venture capital finance in the US, compared with around 27 per cent in Europe. One of the reasons for the increase in pension fund finance is the rise in the pension assets of financial and industrial corporations. The latter group ranks second in the US in terms of venture capital fundraising. Other fund providers include:

- Endowments and foundations
- Foreign investors
- Individuals and families
- Financial and insurance companies.

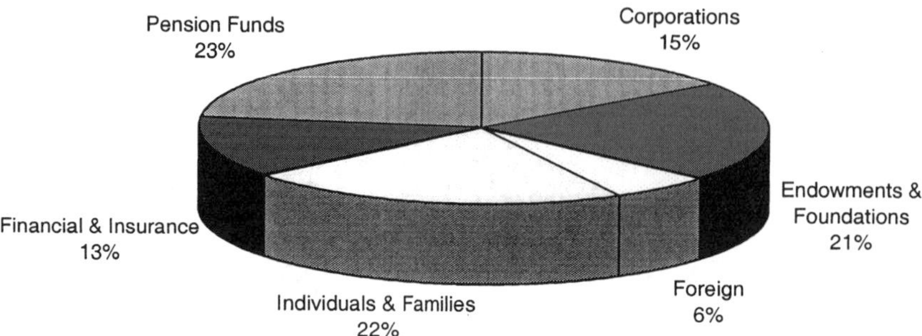

Figure 2.4 US capital commitments by type (1999) (percentage).

Source: *National Venture Capital Association Yearbook 2000*, Thomson Financial Securities Data/Venture Economics, p. 22, Figure 2.04.

However 1999 was somewhat different. The industry raised US$ 46 billion Although pension funds increased their amount of capital, their share fell to 23 per cent.

This is due to a dramatic increase in contributions from individuals and families, corporations and endowments, and foundations looking to take advantage of the spectacular short-term gains that the Internet boom had been delivering. While pension funds are growing in importance to European VCs, in the EU banks and insurance companies are still the principal finance providers.

Buy-out funds raised the majority of the private equity money invested in 1999, but the industry as a whole grew at an impressive pace.

Table 2.3 demonstrates that the bulk of US venture capital is managed

Table 2.3 Capital under management by US venture funds (1980–99)

Statistic	*1980*	*1989*	*1999*
Number of firms in existence	95	387	620
Number of funds in existence	142	847	1,237
Number of professionals	719	2,053	3,658
Number of first-time funds	20	18	99
Number of funds raised	51	103	344
Capital raised this year (US$ billion)	2.1	5.4	46.1
Capital under management (US$ billion)	2.9	29.5	134.5
Average firm size to date (US$ million)	42.9	86.5	217.3
Average fund size to date (US$ million)	28.7	39.5	108.9
Average fund raised (US$ million)	39.3	53.1	135.3
Largest fund raised to date (US$ million)	1,000	1,775	5,000
Largest 10% firms manage (US$ billion)	2.8	13.3	70.3
Largest 10% firms manage (%)	69	45	52

Source: *National Venture Capital Association Yearbook 2000*, Thomson Financial Securities Data/Venture Economics, p. 9, Figure 1.0; p. 17, Figure 1.03.

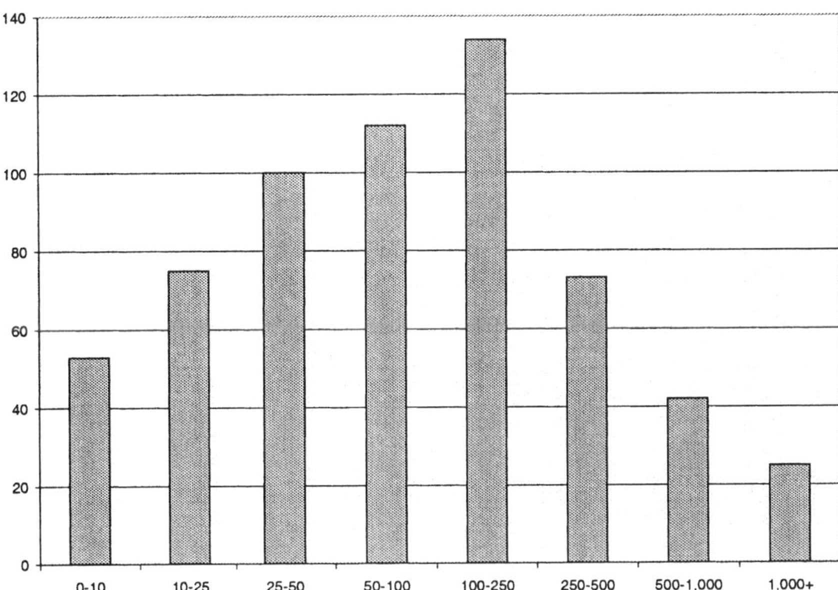

Figure 2.5 Distribution of firms by capital managed (1999) (US$ million).

Source: *National Venture Capital Association Yearbook 2000*, Thomson Financial Securities Data/Venture Economics, p. 17, Figure 1.03.

by a relatively small number of firms with a large-capital base. This is not quite the case in Europe, where the capital base is narrower and the number of operators making investments more evenly distributed.

In the US a total of 67 firms manage more than US$500 million (up from 28 in 1998). About 128 firms, however, managed funds within the US$ 10 million range. It is estimated that 134 firms managed funds valued at US$ 100 to US$ 250 million. Still, the averaged capital managed is increasing faster than the number of firms. The latter grew by 13 per cent since 1998 while the former rose 41 per cent.

NVCA's classification scheme for these operators embraces six categories: independent firms, investment banks, corporate financial firms, SBIC,[10] corporate industrial firms and other. Independent firms comprise both private and publicly quoted companies, including institutionally and non-institutionally funded firms, family groups and affiliates (and non-affiliates) of SBICs. Investment banks include affiliate and non-affiliate and/or subsidiaries of investment banks. Non-investment bank financial entities, including commercial banks and insurance companies, are grouped as corporate financial groups. Corporate industrial groups include venture capital subsidiaries and affiliates of industrial corporations, as well as their associated SBICs.

Independent firms dominate the market with US$ 105 billion under

Table 2.4 Capital under management by firm type (US$ billion) (1980–99)

Firm Type	*1980*	*1985*	*1990*	*1996*	*1997*	*1998*	*1999*
Independent	2.2	12.4	21.8	36.6	49.7	67.5	105.0
Investment Bank	0.4	2.6	6.0	7.2	7.5	15.7	19.5
Corporate Financial	0.2	1.0	1.7	1.6	2.6	3.5	4.4
Corporate Industrial	0.1	0.5	0.6	0.8	1.4	1.9	4.2
Other	0.0	0.1	0.2	0.3	0.5	0.9	1.4
Total	2.9	16.6	30.3	46.5	61.7	89.5	134.5

Source: *National Venture Capital Association Yearbook 2000*, Thomson Financial Securities Data/Venture Economics, p. 16, Figure 1.02.

management, equivalent to 78 per cent of the total venture capital under management in the United States. Capital under management increased in all categories of companies. Investment banks registered a large jump in 1997–9.

Clustering around the coast of California and the north-eastern corridor

In terms of regional bases of funding, it is important to note that funding sources, VC firms, and funded companies are in much more concentrated locations than in Europe. This is a market that logically may naturally create clusters of capital, expertise, and high-growth, funded firms. In Europe, that natural concentration by region is blocked by regulatory hurdles limiting, for example, pension investments across-borders, hurdles in education and expertise, hurdles of taxation methodologies, and perhaps also a less serious concentration of industry focus and expertise.

US investors are most willing to invest close to their offices in part so

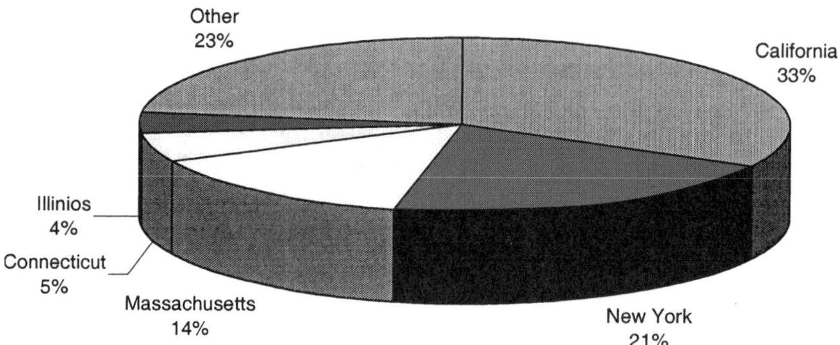

Figure 2.6 Capital under management by major state (1999) (US$ billion).

Source: *National Venture Capital Association Yearbook 2000*, Thomson Financial Securities Data/Venture Economics, p. 17, Figures 1.04 and 1.05.

that they can play a more active role in managerial decisions. This helps to explain the clustering of VC money and companies receiving VC investments. In Europe, VCs tend to be less active managers, and the industry is less clustered in particular countries or regions (except London).

Most of the US private equity and venture capital groups are based in the Northern and West Coast regions. The key centres are California, New York, Massachusetts, Connecticut and Illinois. These areas combined account for US$ 103.4 billion (77 per cent) of funds under management.

Northern California in particular is a phenomenon unto itself, with record-breaking VC funds providing larger-than-ever individual investments into a record-breaking number of firms.

Figures 2.7 and 2.8 from a commercial source suggests incredibly rapid growth, which would only be magnified if the 1999 figures were complete; and this information discusses Northern California alone, not the state as a whole.

Generally, in terms of where the funds come from at a national level, most of the money is also raised in New York, California, and Massachusetts, Connecticut and Illinois (79 per cent) and, in the case of 1999 significant fundraising also occurred in Washington DC and Texas.

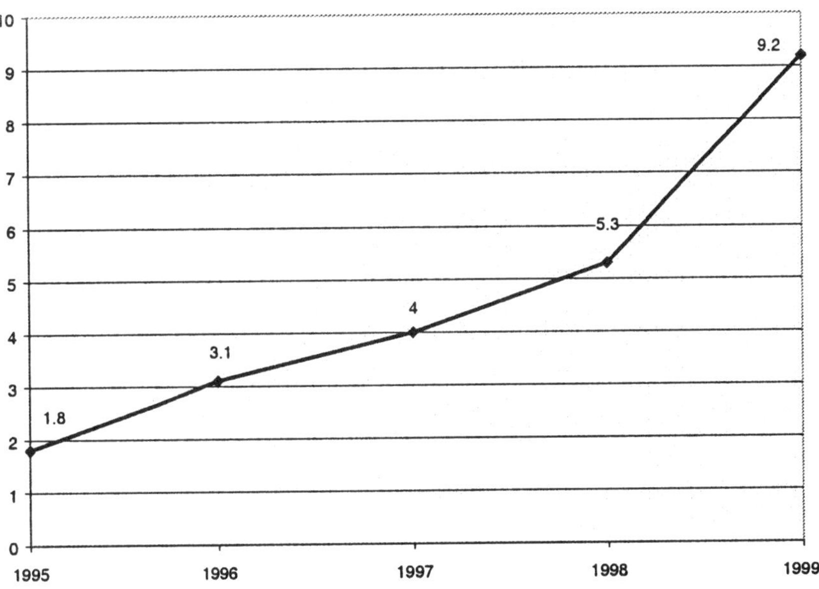

Figure 2.7 Northern California venture capital investments (1996–9) (US$ billion).

Source: Monica McGlinchey, 'Average Venture Capital deal size expands rapidly in Northern California,' 1 November, 1999 news release, www.ventureeconomics.com.

Note

* 1999 data covers only three quarters.

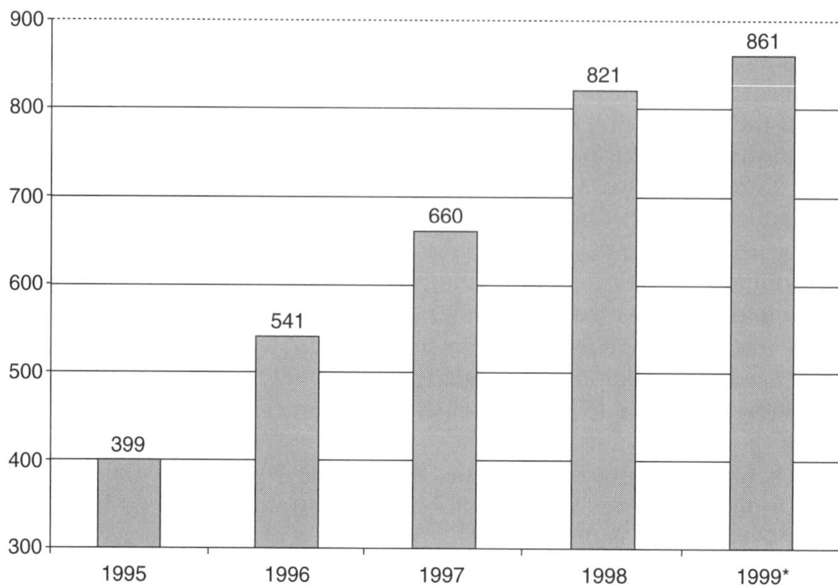

Figure 2.8 Companies funded in Northern California by year (1995–9).

Source: Monica McGlinchey, 'Average Venture Capital deal size expands rapidly in Northern California,' 1 November, 1999 news release, www.ventureeconomics.com.

Note
* 1999 data covers only three quarters.

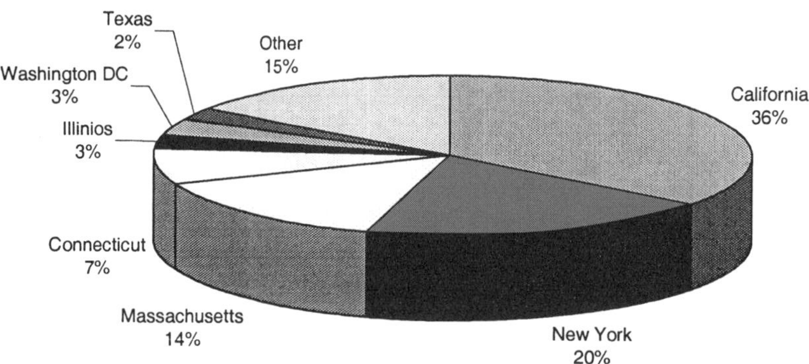

Figure 2.9 Capital commitments by location (1999) (percentage).

Source: *National Venture Capital Association Yearbook 2000*, Thomson Financial Securities Data/Venture Economics, p. 23, Figures 2.05 and 2.07.

Perhaps most important in the regional discussion is where the money goes: California and Massachusetts are the key destination points for venture capital investment in the US with over 52 per cent of the total. Traditionally, California is the leading recipient of venture capital. It is

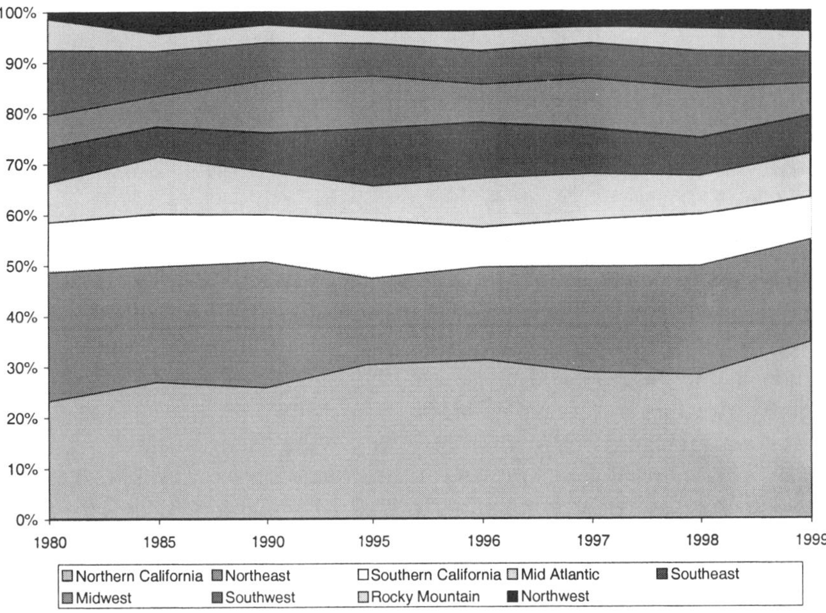

Figure 2.10 Investments by region (1980–99) (percentage).

Source: *National Venture Capital Association Yearbook 2000*, Thomson Financial Securities Data/Venture Economics, p. 28, Figure 3.08.

also the state that shows the greatest increases in dollar terms year in and year out – with increases of US$ 13.4 billion in 1999 alone. Texas, New York and Colorado are the other hot spots for venture capital. This is different from the chart above, describing where the capital is managed. Although the locations of funds under management and of firms receiving investments are usually very closely linked.

Within the West Coast, Northern California received US$ 16.6 billion in investment in 1999, compared with US$ 4.1 billion by Southern California. For five years in a row, Northern California has attracted the highest share of investment in the state and country.

Investments by stage of funding and industrial sector

The VC industry is moving away from early-round investments compared to the past. In 1980, the majority of venture capital disbursements went to first-round investments in the US, but this is no longer the case.

VC firms are going after more established players than in the past, and this reinforces the point that a large percentage of the money is not necessarily going to SMEs. Indeed, the financing stages in the US are changing. Since the 1980s, the leading stages have been either earlier stage or expansion, and early stage financing used to be most popular. But 1999

Table 2.5 Venture capital disbursements (1980–99) (first/follow-on US$ million)

Year	*First*	*Follow-on*
1980	397	305
1999	19,037	29,009

Source: *National Venture Capital Association Yearbook 2000*, Thomson Financial Securities Data/Venture Economics, p. 30, Figure 3.13.

was the third year in a row that expansion SMEs received the lion's share of financing. Investment in all financing stages of SMEs increased except later stage financing. Expansion stage investments rose from US$ 8.0 billion to US$ 26.4 billion in 1999, or 55 per cent of the total capital outlays in the industry and a rise on 1998 of 230 per cent. This too is a major contrasting feature with Europe.

But early stage investments are also on the increase in the United States. The value of funds moving in this direction rose by 104 per cent between 1998 and 1999, amounting to US$ 10.8 billion in 1999. This is an important development, led as in Europe by IT-based companies. Buy-out financing fell by 7 per cent and later stage rose by 139 per cent.

On the other hand, the incredibly heavy weighting towards so-called high-growth tech stocks of any size provides a more aggressive image of

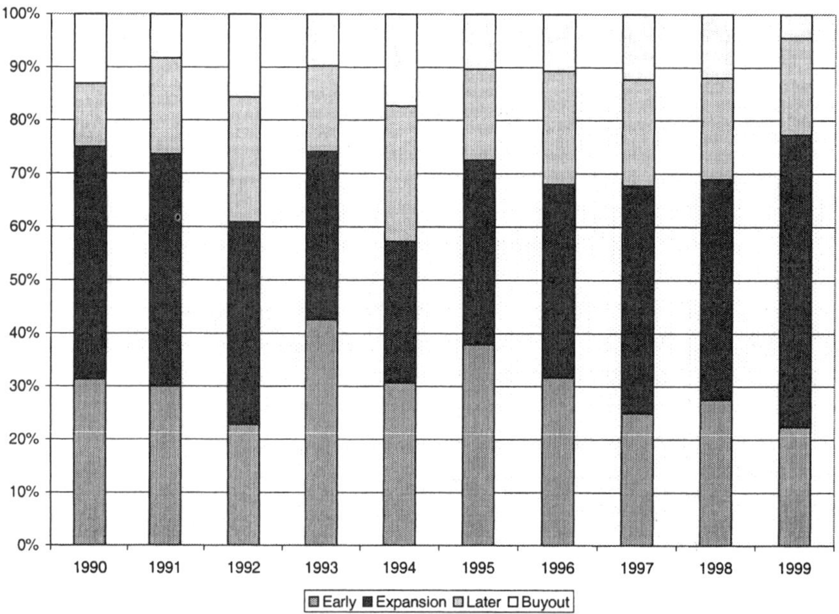

Figure 2.11 Investments by stage (1990–8) (percentage).

Source: *National Venture Capital Association Yearbook 2000*, Thomson Financial Securities Data/Venture Economics, p. 28, Figure 3.09.

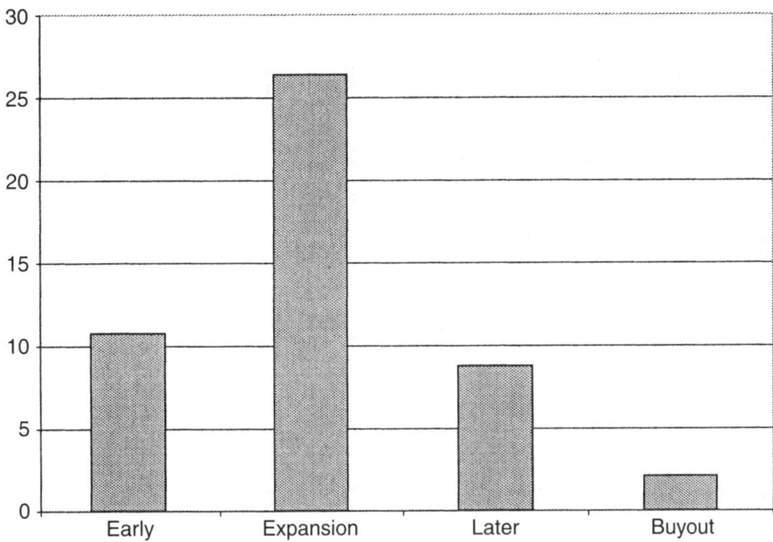

Figure 2.12 Investments by stage (1999) (US$ billion).

Source: *National Venture Capital Association Yearbook 2000*, Thomson Financial Securities Data/Venture Economics, p. 28, Figure 3.09.

these funds and demonstrates their importance to SMEs especially in this sector.

For example, Internet investments rose over 30,000 per cent in six years, from US$ 60.9 million in 1994 to US$ 18.5 billion in 1998.[11] Online specific ventures dominate the investments into the IT sector, representing 50 per cent of disbursements.

Out of the total investment placed during 1999, US$ 37.4 billion went into the information technology sector. Some 2,558 companies benefited

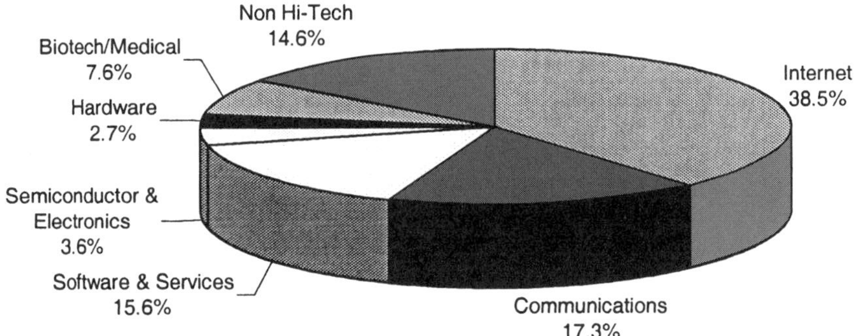

Figure 2.13 Investments by sector (1999) (US$ billion).

Source: *National Venture Capital Association Yearbook 2000*, Thomson Financial Securities Data/Venture Economics, p. 28, Figure 3.10.

Table 2.6 IT related investments by stage (1999)

Disbursements	*Number of companies*	*Total US$ billion*	*Average US$ million*
Initial	1,707	14.0	8.2
Follow-on	851	23.4	27.5
Total	2,558	37.4	14.6

Source: *National Venture Capital Association Yearbook 2000*, Thomson Financial Securities Data/Venture Economics, p. 25, Figure 3.02.

from this outlay. A significant share (33 per cent) of IT investments were repeat business or follow-on investments. Although two-thirds of the IT companies receiving funding (1,707 out of the total of 2,558) were first-round candidates, these were only extended investments of US$ 14.0 billion. The average initial investment was US$ 8.2 million. This compares with the follow-on investments, which averaged US$ 27.5 million – over three times as much.

As can be seen from Table 2.7, the next most important sector is the medical, health and life sciences industry. About 586 companies received US$ 3.4 billion in new finance in 1998. Over half of these were existing clients and 239 represented new deals (with a total outlay of US$ 1 billion).

The non-high-technology sector is also an important recipient of venture capital funds in the US with US$ 7.0 billion in 1999. In total, some 684 companies benefited from capital injections. More than 400 of these were new clients. A more detailed analysis of disbursements by sector is provided in Table 2.8.

On VC-backed IPOs

The next chapter deals more with IPO-related information than this one. But it should at least be noted that of the almost 544 IPOs that took place in the US in 1999, 270 were VC funded. According to the Venture Economics group of Thomson Financial Securities Data, nearly 50 per cent of

Table 2.7 Medical, health and life science related investments by stage (1999)

Disbursements	*Number of companies*	*Total US$ billion*	*Average US$ million*
Initial	216	1.1	5.1
Follow-on	274	2.5	9.1
Total	490	3.6	7.3

Source: *National Venture Capital Association Yearbook 2000*, Thomson Financial Securities Data/Venture Economics, p. 25, Figure 3.02.

Table 2.8 High-tech related investments by subsector (1999) (US$ million)

Subsector	*US$ million*	*% total*	*% sector*
Internet	18,513.1	39	50
Communications	8,335.4	17	22
Software and services	7,500.9	16	20
Semiconductor and electronics	1,740.2	4	5
Hardware	1,303.8	3	3
Total IT	37,393.4	78	100
Medical/Health	2,457.0	5	68
Biotechnology	1,182.2	2	32
Total medical/health/biotech	3,639.2	8	100
Other products	4,551.9	9	65
Consumer related	1,710.4	4	24
Industrial energy	751.1	2	11
Total other	7,013.4	15	100
Total	48,046.0	100	100

Source: *National Venture Capital Association Yearbook 2000*, Thomson Financial Securities Data/Venture Economics, p. 28, Figure 3.10.

all IPOs in 1999 were venture backed. ‘Never before has venture backing been so important for the success of the sometime shaky confidence in the IPO market. Venture-backed IPOs helped fuel the growth of a record-setting year for the NASDAQ Stock Market in 1999.’[12] This was not a record year for the number of venture-backed IPOs, but it was for their value.

Table 2.9 US venture-backed IPOs (1995–9)

			Relating to venture-backed IPOs			
Period	*Total IPOs*	*Number venture backed*	*Total raised at IPO (US$ bn)*	*Market cap 31 Dec. 99 (US$ bn)*	*Average offer size (US$ m)*	*Average market cap 31 Dec. 99 (US$ m)*
1999	544	271	23.6	136.2	87.2	502.6
1998	373	78	3.8	17.8	49.2	228.2
1997	629	138	4.9	22.6	39.5	163.8
1996	868	280	12.2	58.6	43.6	209.3
1995	580	204	8.2	33.2	40.6	162.7

Source: *Venture Economics and National Venture Capital Association (NVCA)*, as quoted in the website of the Venture Economics group of Thomson Financial Securities Data – www.ventureeconomics.com

While again, many VC-backed IPOs do not fund start-ups or SMEs, venture-backed companies are not only raising more dollars; they are also going public at an earlier age. The average offer size for a venture-backed IPO was up 75 per cent from the previous year to $87.2 million along with an unprecedented average post-offer valuation of $502.7 million – more than twice as much as the prior year. So this suggests that these were not small companies. On the other hand, the median company age of venture-backed IPOs was 4.0 years in 1999, versus 4.5 in 1998 and 5.5 years in 1997.[13]

These statistics also have to take into account the listing requirements of the particular markets. NASDAQ has no minimum float-listing requirement. VCs exercise tight control over the placement of the stock in the market. Bill Smith, who runs Renaissance Capital, a research and fund-management firm, reckons the actual float for any IPO is less than half the shares that are offered.[14] In recent flagship offers, such as Terra Networks and Palm Computing, less than 15 per cent and 5 per cent of the stock has been listed respectively. This has become common practice. Of the stocks listed in the first half of March 2000, only one listed more than 20 per cent. In fact, under the 'preferred placement' system operated for VC-backed IPOs, whereby shares are effectively placed with a club of investors, less is more – less float leads to high market capitalisation. An analysis of IPOs that have taken place during 2000 shows that those that have the largest float have performed the worst. Supply-side management has the effect of forcing up stock prices. This contrasts with Europe where the most successful high-growth exchanges all have minimum float requirements that make such practices more difficult to achieve.

Comparisons of different funds are difficult, and annual returns may be over-inflated by current stock valuations. But it also appears that those with the stomach to invest in the earlier stages have reaped the highest rewards when they successfully take their funded companies to market.

Table 2.10 Best and worst performing IPOs in the US (2000)

Company	*Float (%)*	*Total return (%)*
724 Solutions	16	731
WebMethods	11	700
Quantum Effect Devices	12	521
Diversal	20	520
Avanex	9	516
VarsityBooks.com	24	−13
VantageMed	34	−17
Beasley Broadcast	28	−20
Sawis Communications	18	−22
Pets.com	28	−39

Source: Renaissance Capital, *The Economist*.

Table 2.11 Venture economics PEPI returns (12/99) (percentage)

Fund type	*1 year*	*3 year*	*5 year*	*10 year*	*20 year*
Early seed	247.9	75.6	63.2	31.5	22.7
Balanced[a]	122.0	46.8	39.8	21.9	16.9
Later stage	70.2	33.8	36.4	26.5	18.7
All venture	146.2	53.8	46.4	25.2	18.8
All buy-outs	25.9	19.0	18.6	16.6	20.0
Mezzanine	8.0	8.9	10.0	11.0	11.4
All private equity	61.1	31.4	28.5	20.3	19.3

Source: Press Release, Thomson Financial Securities Data, 1 May 2000, 'Triple Digit Returns for 1999 Year End: Have VCs Seen the Top?', Monica McGlinchey.

Early/seed stage venture capital funds averaged 91.2 per cent 1-year returns as of Q3 1999. Performance of buy-out funds improved as well, but 'buy-out returns paled in comparison to venture capital performance since exits via IPO has a more direct effect on venture capital returns than on buy-outs.'[15] These results represent the net return to investors in private equity funds and represent both realised and unrealised performance.

Venture Economics' Private Equity Performance Index (PEPI)[16] Returns for investment horizons ending on 31 December 1999 are shown in Table 2.11.

Generally, we can see that while the vast majority of VC-funded companies do not manage to IPO, those that do have recently generated enormous rewards for the VC firms participating in this market.

The NVCA's policy priorities

In terms of policy, the National Venture Capital Association focuses to the most limited extent on government policies other than promoting return on investment for economic organisations like pension funds. Most of the 'legislative report card' on its website focuses on the VC tax burden. For example, it salutes Congress for the reduction in the capital gains tax of August, 1997 – 'the largest tax victory ever for the venture capital and entrepreneurial communities. For the first time, AMT taxpayers will be treated the same as ordinary income taxpayers for capital gains purposes.' Other issues include the ability to list or exclude stock options on annual reports granted to employees in a way that is favourable to employees or companies; and several legal issues related to liability claims and asset protection. Government support for the industry, beyond 'fair' taxes and regulatory burdens, simply does not figure as an issue that members care much about.[17]

Angel and VC activity in Europe

The European private equity and venture capital industries as a whole are becoming larger, healthier, and more diverse, but it must be remembered that its greatest successes frequently have little to do with SMEs. For example, a great percentage of the private equity and VC money is going to buy-outs, and most of the buy-out money heads towards the largest firms. Meanwhile, the largest firms are receiving the highest valuations by far as measured by P/E ratios in these deals. Even in the current boom, while P/E ratios for buy-outs of the largest firms are rising quickly and are the highest by far, P/E ratios for smaller firms are actually declining.

The European Private Equity and Venture Capital Association (EVCA) includes in its membership most of the region's top operators. Our review of the industry is based largely on information provided by them.

EVCA was set up in 1983 with 43 members. Today's membership numbers 600.[18] The association acts as lobby for the industry and is responsible for the preparation and dissemination of development initiatives for the sector. Its key objectives are to promote an entrepreneurial environment; reach institutional investors; enhance the knowledge and acceptability of MBOs and MBIs; facilitate investment in technology in early-stage ventures; propose policy and follow-up action measures at the level of government; promote the use of standards for portfolio performance measurement; encourage the publication of pan-European investment benchmarks to support investors with better and more accurate information; advise and promote the establishment of new stock markets for growth companies; and help develop the industry in the new transition economies of Eastern Europe and CIS.

Current performance

The industry managed to raise some €25.4 billion during the 1999 financial year. This represents an increase of 25 per cent on funds raised in 1998, a previous record high.[19]

Note that in Europe, the definition of VC funds is broader than that used in the US. They include funds devoted to leveraged buy-outs, MBOs and MBIs. The reason for this is partly due to the nascent quality of the European VC industry – where there are few if any funds that just specialise in these areas of activity, unlike in the US.

The bulk of the new funds were raised in the UK, Germany and France, three of Europe's leading private equity and venture capital bases. The UK, for instance, contributed 10 per cent more in 1999 than in 1998, whilst Italy increased 103 per cent over the same period. Germany, France, Italy and the Netherlands are also important contributors, all with over €1 billion each in new funding, yet Germany is the most disappointing

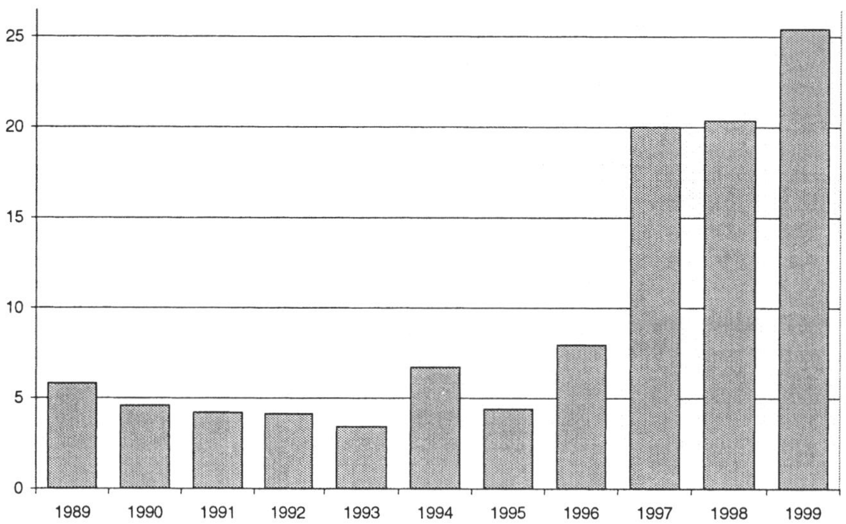

Figure 2.14 European new funds raised (1989–99) (€ billion).

Source: *EVCA Yearbook 2000*, European Private Equity and Venture Capital Association, Luxembourg, p. 9.

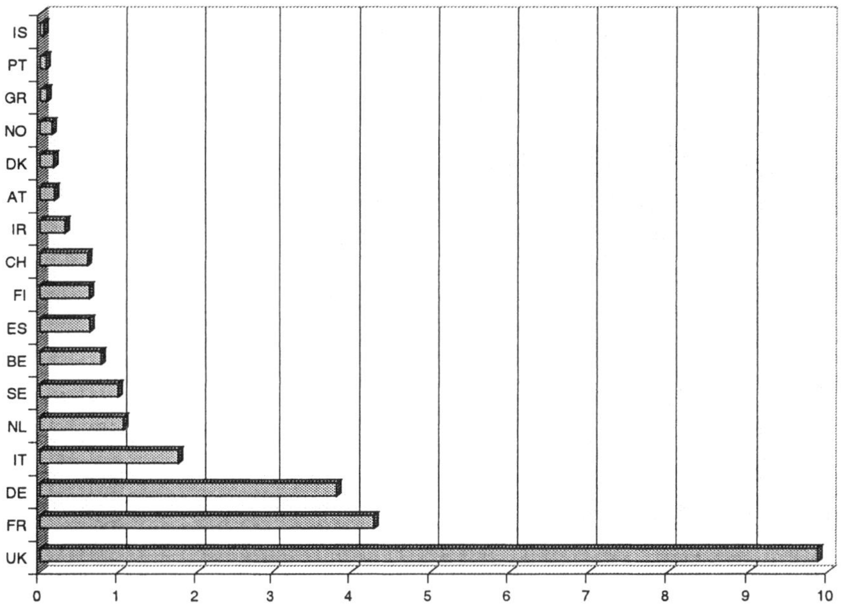

Figure 2.15 New funds raised by country (1999) (€ billion)

Source: *EVCA Yearbook 2000*, European Private Equity and Venture Capital Association, Luxembourg, p. 9.

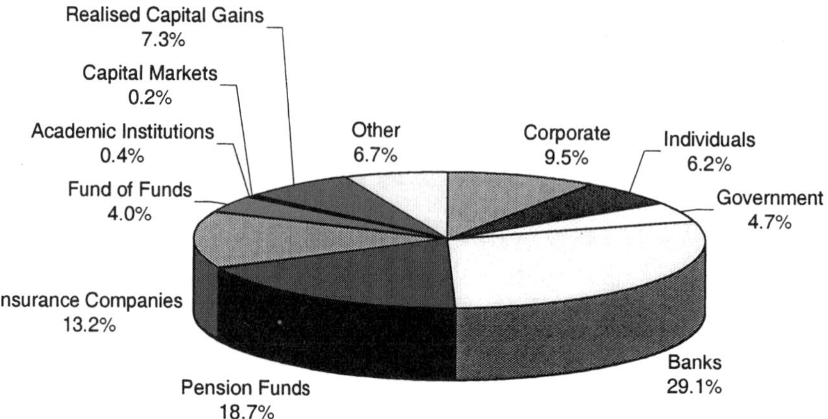

Figure 2.16 Private equity raised by type of investor (1999) (percentage).

Source: *EVCA Yearbook 2000*, European Private Equity and Venture Capital Association, Luxembourg, p. 28.

performer considering the size of its economy. More about that will be discussed in Chapter 6. The Netherlands is one of the most impressive success stories, with private equity under management approaching German and French levels.

The largest sources of capital within Europe are banks (about 29 per cent in 1999) and pension funds (19 per cent). Insurance companies represent the next most important category with 13 per cent of the total. The balance is from a wide range of sources including capital markets, individuals, academic institutions and corporate investors.

While the categories differ somewhat from those provided by the US's NVCA, some important contrasts include especially the decreased importance of pensions and also the increased importance of banks in European VC funding.

The bulk of private equity and venture capital funds are raised in the country where the venture is based. European cross-boarder fundraising is still surprisingly constrained, representing on average around 20 per cent of the total, though there has been an improving trend with 1999 representing the first year it has been greater than 20 per cent. Non-European finance providers have been historically more important, accounting for around 30 per cent of the total. This trend has been declining for the past few years, with them accounting for only just over 20 per cent of funds raised in 1999.

Independent funds account for just under three-quarters of the funds raised (about €18.2 billion in 1999). Captive funds[20] are becoming increasingly important. At present, these represent almost 20 per cent of the total

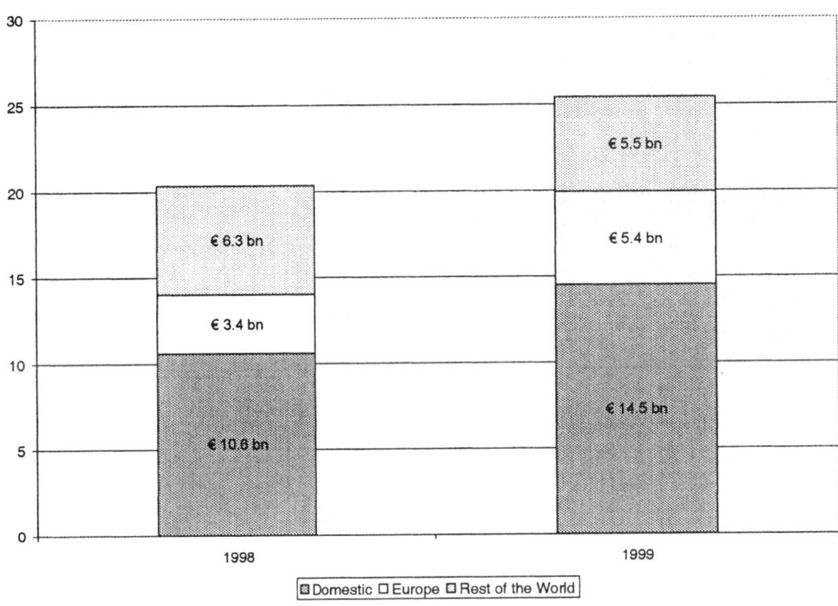

Figure 2.17 Geographic origin of new funds raised (1998–9) (€ billion).

Source: *EVCA Yearbook 2000*, European Private Equity and Venture Capital Association, Luxembourg, p. 28.

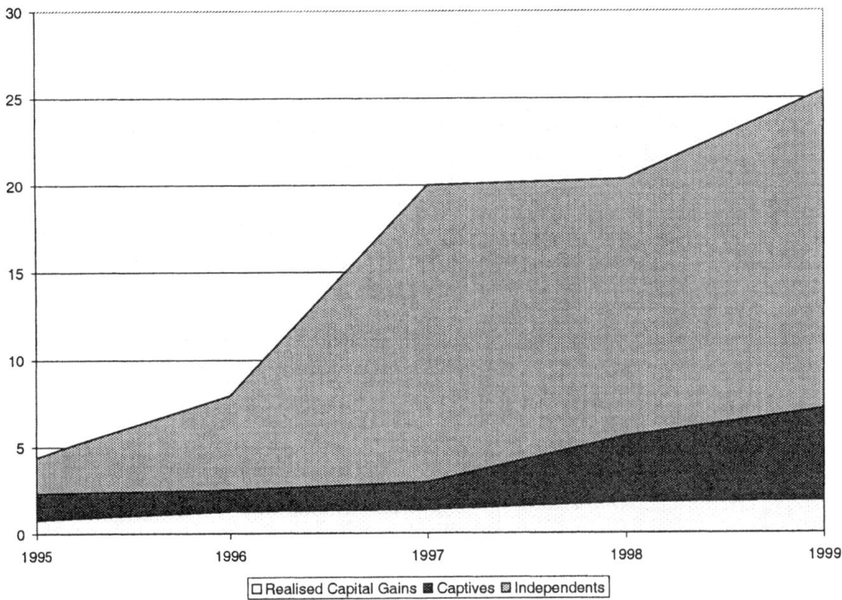

Figure 2.18 Change in source of new funds raised (1995–9) (€ billion).

Source: *EVCA Yearbook 2000*, European Private Equity and Venture Capital Association, Luxembourg, p. 29.

funding raised by the industry. Re-investments from capital gains amount to less than €2 billion a year (9 per cent).

Investment patterns

The European private equity and venture capital industry tends to invest the bulk of its funds in management buy-outs and management buy-ins (close to 52 per cent). This represents a significant difference with the US, where buy-outs and buy-ins represent less than 9 per cent of total venture capital disbursements.

In a recent survey of the European sector, investors suggested less than half of the funds raised would be placed in 'pure' venture capital. This is a somewhat startling fact, accentuated still further by rather disproportionate differences between countries within Europe. In the UK, MBOs and MBIs are expected to absorb some 72 per cent of the funds during 1999.

Total investment by operators in 1999 reached €25.1 billion, a staggering increase of 74 per cent per cent on 1998. This level of investment is actually an all-time high.

The amount invested has been on the increase, recently rising by more than 36 per cent annually. The number of investments has also increased, rising by 48 per cent in 1999.

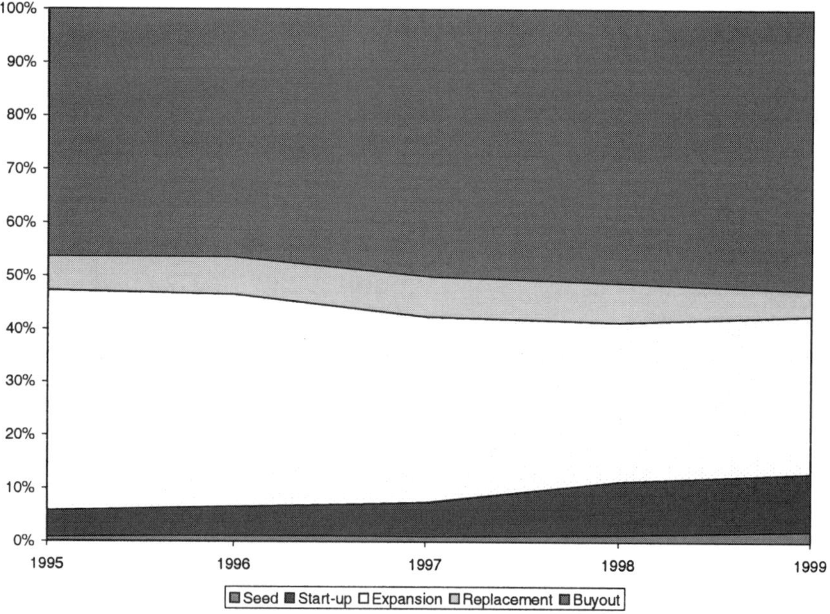

Figure 2.19 European investments by stage (1995–9) (percentage).

Source: *EVCA Yearbook 2000*, European Private Equity and Venture Capital Association, Luxembourg, p. 36.

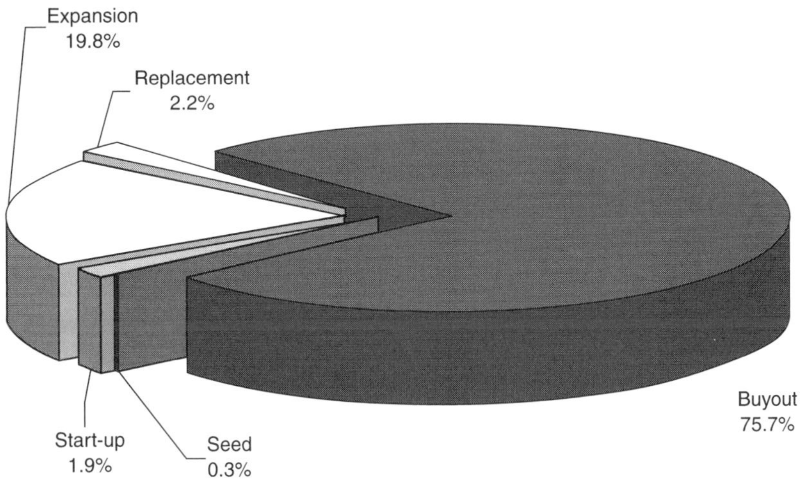

Figure 2.20 UK investments by stage (1999) (percentage).

Source: *EVCA Yearbook 2000*, European Private Equity and Venture Capital Association, Luxembourg, p. 39.

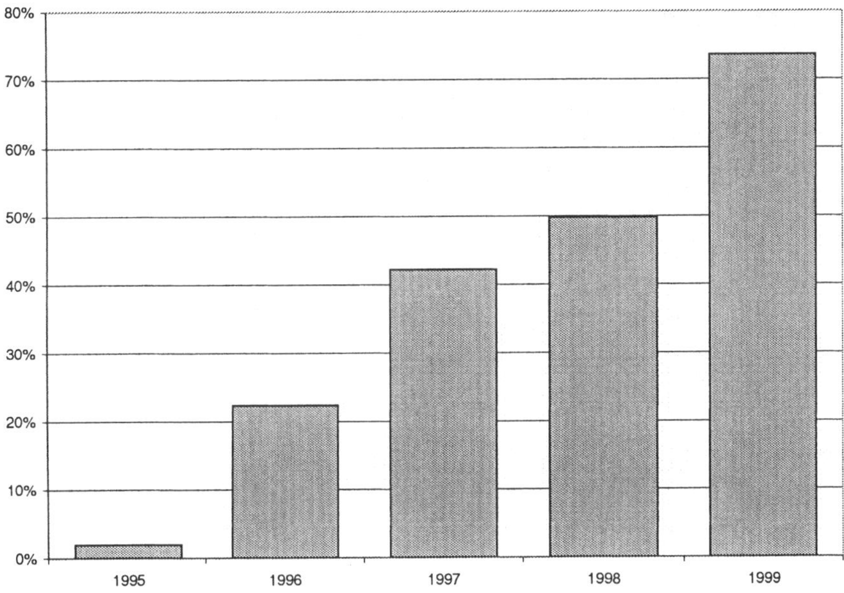

Figure 2.21 Growth in amount invested (1995–9) (percentage).

Source: *EVCA Yearbook 2000*, European Private Equity and Venture Capital Association, Luxembourg, p. 39.

Table 2.12 Number of European investments (1999)

Country	*1998*	*1999*	*%*
UK	2,018	2,309	14
DE	1,513	2,081	38
FR	1,544	2,545	65
IT	267	390	46
NL	707	872	23
SE	115	819	612
ES	244	314	29
BE	233	504	116
CH	86	254	195
NO	161	172	7
FI	274	364	33
PT	68	95	40
DK	50	150	200
IR	106	173	63
AT	93	91	−2
GR	29	45	55
IS	120	75	−38
Total	7,628	11,253	48

Source: *EVCA Yearbook 2000*, European Private Equity and Venture Capital Association, Luxembourg, p. 32.

The average size of each investment has also risen during the period (from €1.9 million to €2.2 million). Since investments took place in 8,536 companies, the average size of each company investment was actually €2.9 million.

The single largest market for private equity and venture capital investments is the UK. The latter registered an increase in investments in 1999 in excess of 60 per cent (equivalent now to €11.5 billion). This is a trend started some time ago and reflects the longer-standing venture capital tradition.

The other key markets in Europe are Germany and France. Countries with rapidly increasing venture capital profiles are Austria, Iceland, Switzerland, Spain and Italy.

Independent organisations are the most important players within the venture capital industry in Europe with about 60 per cent of the business. This performance varies between country and year. Captive and semi-captives are the next most important players. The role of government agencies is also important, although its market share stands at only 5 per cent.

One other feature of the European private equity and venture capital industry is its tendency to act alone with target companies receiving investment. Syndication/co-financing is uncommon. However, recently, in no small part due to the incredible amounts of money being invested by private equity, coupled with some worries about high-technology investments, the proportion of syndications increased to almost one-third.

Table 2.13 Average deal size (1998–9) (€ million)

Country	*1998*	*1999*	*% change*
UK	3.5	5.0	41
DE	1.3	1.5	18
FR	1.2	1.1	−4
IT	3.5	4.6	31
NL	1.5	2.0	31
SE	1.8	1.6	−12
ES	1.5	2.3	55
BE	1.1	1.3	20
CH	2.5	1.7	−31
NO	1.0	1.5	50
FI	0.7	0.7	−1
PT	0.7	1.3	70
DK	0.8	0.8	−3
IR	0.6	0.6	1
AT	0.5	1.0	82
GR	0.7	1.6	129
IS	0.2	0.3	75
Total	1.9	2.2	18

Source: *EVCA Yearbook 2000*, European Private Equity and Venture Capital Association, Luxembourg, p. 32.

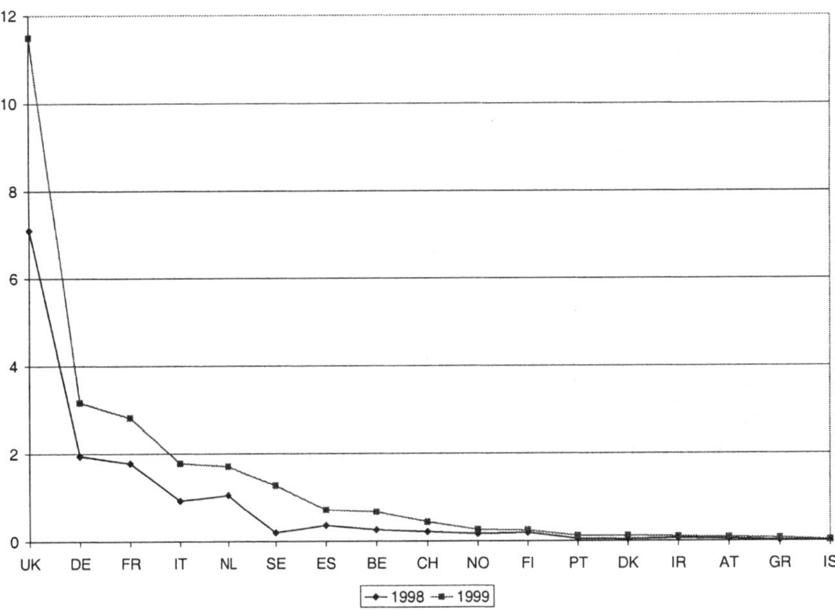

Figure 2.22 Investment by country (1998–9) (€ billion).

Source: *EVCA Yearbook 2000*, European Private Equity and Venture Capital Association, Luxembourg, p. 32.

Table 2.14 Investments by investor type (1997)

	Amount € m		*No. investments*		*No. companies*	
1998						
Independent	6,870	48%	3,200	42%	2,659	43%
Captive	3,950	27%	2,298	30%	1,960	31%
Semi-captive	2,813	19%	1,186	16%	812	13%
Public Sector	827	6%	943	12%	796	13%
Total	14,460	100%	7,627	100%	6,227	100%
1999						
Independent	15,659	62%	5,717	51%	4,474	52%
Captive	4,761	19%	2,301	20%	1,859	22%
Semi-captive	3,466	14%	1,612	14%	1,203	14%
Public Sector	1,230	5%	1,623	15%	1,000	12%
Total	25,116	100%	11,253	100%	8,536	100%

Source: *EVCA Yearbook 2000*, European Private Equity and Venture Capital Association, Luxembourg, p. 33.

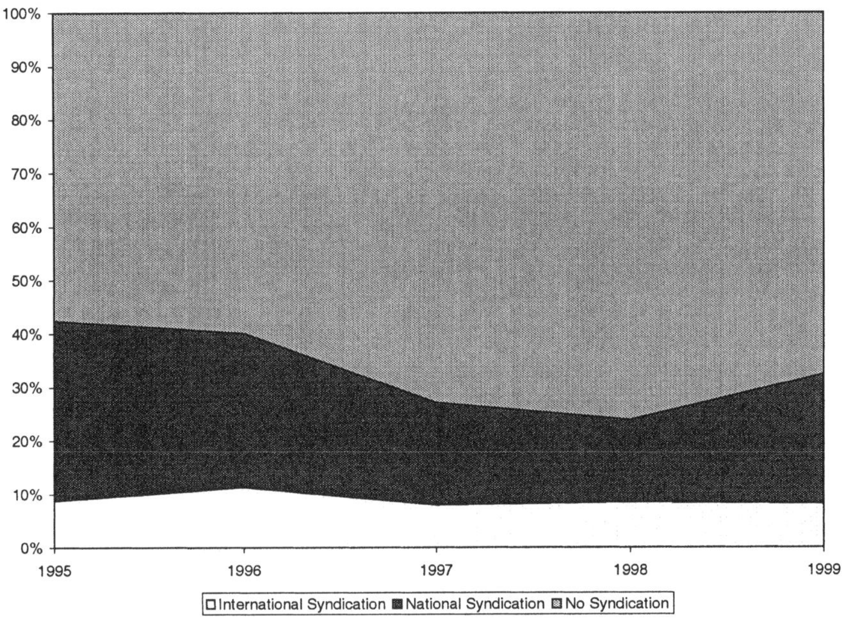

Figure 2.23 Syndication of investments (1995–9) (€ billion).

Source: *EVCA Yearbook 2000*, European Private Equity and Venture Capital Association, Luxembourg, p. 36.

This contrasts starkly with the USA where syndication and co-investment are commonplace. However in Europe, co-financing, when it takes place, tends to involve other private equity partners. Bank co-financing in Europe is not common, although capital investments do pave the way for credit facilities, especially working capital finance. Cross-boarder syndications and co-financing with banks and other institutions within the EU are generally uncommon. This is a reflection of the different investment rules and conditions in the member countries. Only 8 per cent of the investments represent EU cross-border syndications and co-financing at present. Non-EU co-investment is more than double that from EU member countries. This is a startling figure. Most of the non-EU funding comes from US investors.

Sectoral allocation of placements

Europe and the USA share a common portfolio classification. The largest subsector is high-tech.

In Europe, this sector has been growing rapidly from a relatively low base a few years ago. Just over 30 per cent of all investments are directed at companies operating here. The figure is considerably higher in the USA

Table 2.15 Investments by sector (1999)

Sector	*Investment*	*%*	*No. firms*	*Average*
Communications	2,915	11.6	1,317	2.2
Computer related	2,718	10.8	1,537	1.8
Other electronics related	518	2.1	313	1.7
Biotechnology	644	2.6	417	1.5
Medical/health related	1,006	4.0	524	1.9
Energy	202	0.8	78	2.6
Consumer related	4,727	18.8	789	6.0
Industrial products and services	2,915	11.6	1,009	2.9
Chemicals and materials	1,342	5.3	187	7.2
Industrial automation	219	0.9	147	1.5
Other manufacturing	2,276	9.1	478	4.8
Transportation	842	3.4	111	7.6
Financial services	453	1.8	199	2.3
Other services	2,049	8.2	622	3.3
Agriculture	95	0.4	72	1.3
Construction	639	2.5	210	3.0
Other	1,556	6.1	525	3.0
Total	25,116	100.0	8,535	2.9
High-tech	6,418	25.6	3,702	1.7

Source: *EVCA Yearbook 2000*, European Private Equity and Venture Capital Association, Luxembourg, p. 34.

Table 2.16 Average size of European high-tech investment (1995–9)

High-tech	*1995*	*1996*	*1997*	*1998*	*1999*
Investments (€ million)	1,328	2,105	2,307	4,027	6,418
Companies (no.)	1,387	1,580	1,592	2,402	3,702
Average (€ million)	0.96	1.33	1.45	1.68	1.73

Source: *EVCA Yearbook 2000*, European Private Equity and Venture Capital Association, Luxembourg, p. 34.

but its market is more mature (although also much more heavily concentrated in Silicon Valley). The high-tech sector includes communications, computer related companies, electronic industry SMEs, biotechnology and medical/health care related operations.

As can be seen from Table 2.16, the number of investments in this sector has been rising almost as rapidly as the value of placements, estimated currently at 3,702 transactions. The average value of each investment has been rising over the past few years from around €1.0 million in 1994 to €1.7 million by 1999. Although this increase is impressive, it still lags way behind the average funding provided by US counterparts – where the average size of investment is almost three times as much.

Although comprehensive statistics are not available, there is strong empirical evidence that individual investments made by funds do not differ greatly between the two regions. Rather, this statistic probably reflects a combination of factors – not least of which is the level of co-investing and syndications that takes place in the US.

There are signs of economic activity and clustering springing up all over Europe. Barcelona is a centre for high-tech start-ups, Munich now has over US$ 10 billion under management and invested locally, Ireland is a world leader in Software exports (second only to the US). Where it differs from the US is in the number of centres that still demonstrate a nationalistic approach. Munich is Germany's software centre, Barcelona is Spain's etc. There is not a pan-European focus. A recent article in *Business Week* provided a resume of the clustering in Europe.[21]

Company size

The average size of companies receiving investments from private equity and venture capital companies in Europe has actually been decreasing. Of the portfolio investments in 1998, for instance, 68 per cent were effected in companies with less than 100 employees This figure rose to over 72 per cent during 1999.

Over 80 per cent of the companies, receiving almost 40 per cent of the funds, employ fewer than 200 people. The EU definition of an SME includes companies with under 250 employees and under a certain equity

Table 2.17 European high technology clusters (1999)

Ireland	World's no. 2 exporter of software after US GDP grew over 9% last year. Unemployment is down to 5.1%.
Southeast England	Thanks to London's financial markets and a surge in Internet start-ups, the region is one of the richest in Europe.
Cambridge	The area around this university town is a centre of biotech and software start-ups. Microsoft has a research centre here.
Paris	A vibrant centre for venture capital. New entrepreneurs' lobby is improving conditions for start-ups.
Grenoble	Telecoms and microelectronics research institutes have spawned spin-offs.
Strasbourg	A major European centre for biotech start-ups.
Nice	The Côte d'Azure has become a centre for software and electronics start-ups, thanks to R&D centres set up by multinationals such as Texas Instruments and IBM.
Toulouse	With aerospace giant Airbus Industries' headquarters here the region is an incubator for electronics and aerospace start-ups.
Barcelona	Flourishing software and Internet start-ups, technical universities, and local government policy have pushed unemployment down to 6.5%, less than half the national average.
Ypres	The Flemish heartland is home of 42 language software companies, led by Lernout & Hauspie Speech Products. GDP grew 3.1% last year, vs. 2.3% for Belgium overall.
Netherlands	Internet start-ups are flourishing in one of the world's most heavily cabled nations.
Frankfurt Region	Software giant SAP is located in nearby Walldorf, while biotech start-ups are dotted around Heidelberg.
Munich	This hot spot for venture capital, with $10 billion in funds under management, is now attracting both American and British venture capitalists.
Denmark	The world leader in hearing aids and audio technology – key elements in cell phones.
Norway	Some 80% of Norwegians, 13–20, use cell phones. Joblessness is 3.2%.
Stockholm	About 80% of the city's residents have access to the Internet, vs. 30% for Europe as a whole. Computer literacy has pushed up incomes 15% above the national average.
Helsinki	Home to Europe's most valuable company, Nokia. Here, 65% of residents own cell phones.
Oulu	This Arctic city is a major manufacturing centre for Nokia and a research hub, thanks to a technical university and a government-backed science park. The local economy is growing 9% annually.

Source: 'Business Week International Europe: Work in Progress', *Business Week*, 31 January 2000.

Table 2.18 Investment by company size (1999)

No. of employees	*€ million*	*%*	*No.*	*%*	*Average*
0–9	1,231	9.1	1,237	24.0	1.0
10–19	588	4.4	761	14.8	0.8
20–99	2,156	16.0	1,728	33.6	1.2
100–199	1,180	8.7	542	10.5	2.2
200–499	2,044	15.1	440	8.6	4.6
500–999	1,330	9.9	185	3.6	7.2
1,000–4,999	2,670	19.8	218	4.2	12.2
5,000+	2,298	17.0	35	0.7	65.7
Total	13,497	100.0	5,146	100.0	2.6
Unknown	11,619	0	6,107		1.9
Total	25,116		11,253		2.4

Source: *EVCA Yearbook 2000*, European Private Equity and Venture Capital Association, Luxembourg, p. 35.

valuation; so these figures (employee numbers somewhat low; equity value unknown) serve as an incomplete, rough approximation for the number of SMEs receiving funding.

European exits

The European private equity and venture capital industry has a reputation for being *better at investing than exiting*. This contrasts with the United States and is largely a reflection of poorer liquidity in the markets.

The EVCA database provides information on the exits realised in 1999. The amounts of divestments measured at cost (as opposed to in terms of the amounts realised at sale) reached €8.6 billion in 1999, an increase of 24 per cent on 1998. The bulk of these divestments were trade sales (€3.2 billion).

Public offerings, although on the increase, still only amounted to €1.8 billion. Most observers suggest the limited number of IPOs as one of the key obstacles to private equity and venture capital industry growth and performance. Other typical exit forms in Europe include write-offs (falling in importance in recent years), management buy-backs and redemption of preference shares.

Investment portfolio

The total investment portfolio of the industry is now estimated at €58.4 billion of net investments. The UK represents 48 per cent of the total portfolio value, with France and Germany a further 23 per cent. The remaining

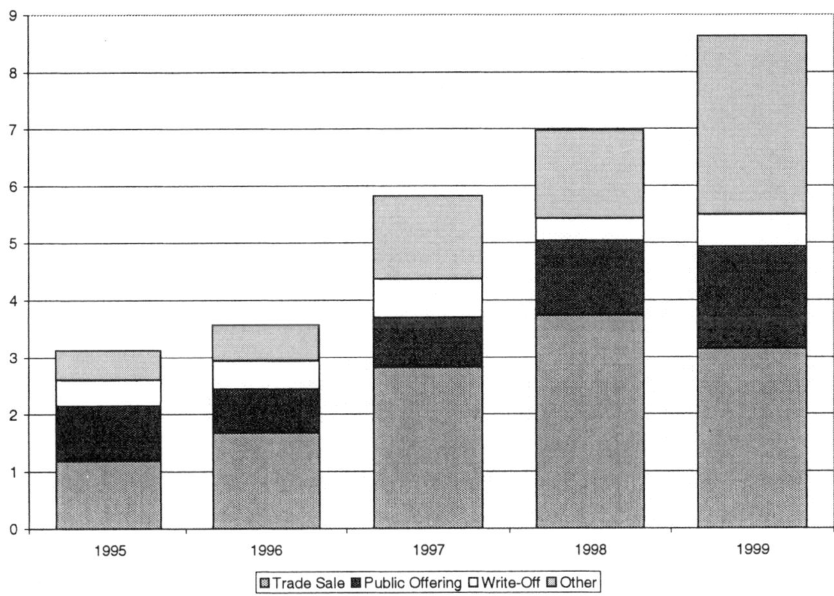

Figure 2.24 Divestments (1995–9) (€ billion).

Source: *EVCA Yearbook 2000*, European Private Equity and Venture Capital Association, Luxembourg, p. 43.

countries hold just 29 per cent of the total portfolio. Spain has just 2.6 per cent of the total.

In terms of reflecting the maturity or penetration of private equity within Europe, we considered the per-capita portfolio ratio. This shows clearly the lead in private equity enjoyed by Northern Europe – particularly Scandinavia and the UK, as compared with Southern Europe which has some catching up to do.

In terms of policy, the European Commission has concerned itself more than the US government and NVCA with seed capital projects designed to improve *not* return on investment (ROI) but rather the environment for start-up companies and the entrepreneurial culture and jobs that they help to create. In 1989, the Commission launched a pilot European Seed Capital Scheme and subsequently supported the establishment of 23 Seed Capital Funds. The objective is to make capital available to new businesses which would normally have extreme difficulty in raising funds from the market and to improve the quality of seed-stage projects.

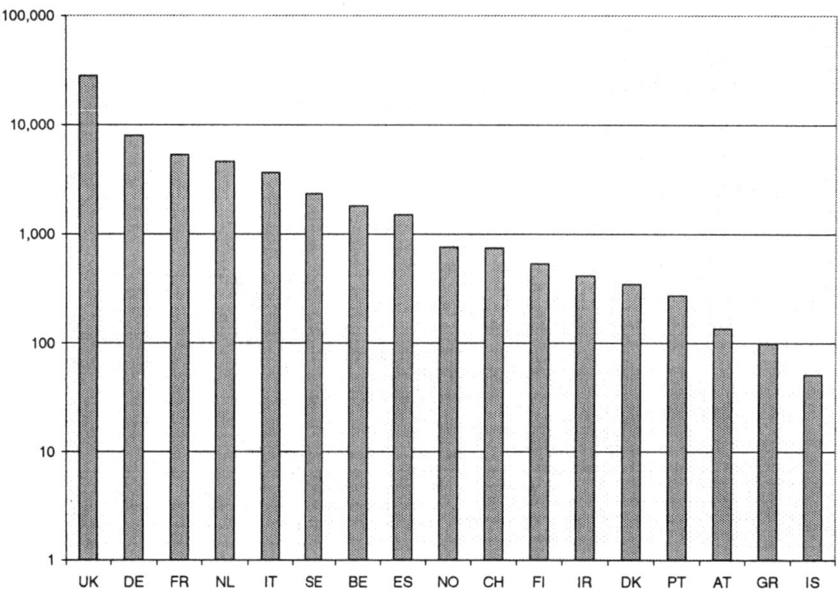

Figure 2.25 European investment portfolio (December 1999) (€ million log scale).

Source: *EVCA Yearbook 2000*, European Private Equity and Venture Capital Association, Luxembourg, p. 46.

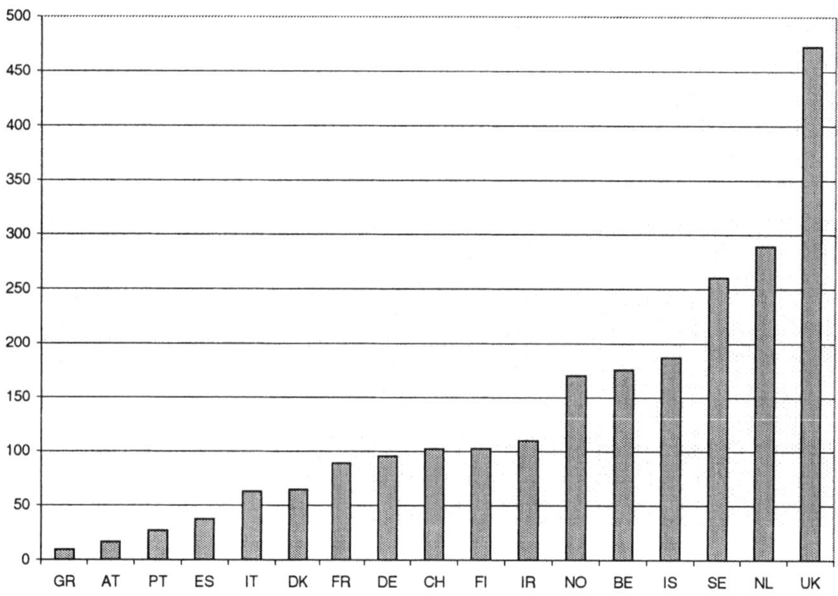

Figure 2.26 Private equity under management per capita (1999) (€).

Source: *EVCA Yearbook 2000*, European Private Equity and Venture Capital Association, Luxembourg, p. 46; US Bureau of Census, www.census.gov – Mid-1999 population statistics.

Conclusion: common denominators and differences

Fundraising

There are more common denominators than differences between VCs in the US and Europe. One common feature is their fundraising process. The main difference lies with the actual amount involved and the size of the funds. US venture capital companies dwarf their European counterparts. In terms of funding, Europe raises annually about €20 billion compared with US$ 84 billion in the US.

Funds on both sides of the Atlantic rely more or less equally on institutional and individual investors for their resources. Pension funds are a more important source in the US, whilst banks dominate the scene in Europe. Insurance companies, captive, semi-captive and independent funds are major players too; but their contributions vary quite significantly from year to year. Individual investors play a more important role in the US than in Europe. On the whole, institutional investors are more important in the US venture capital industry than in Europe's. Most of the fundraising takes place in the country of the fund. This is natural in the case of the US. But in Europe this represents a lost opportunity. The development of the VC industry would benefit from greater cross-border fundraising and investment. Different rules and regulations militate against that. In any event, the fundraising profile and practice in Europe is changing. In the medium term it will have more common features with that in the US than differences.

Investment pattern

US investment funds finance a lower number of deals per year than their European counterparts. But the average size of each investment is higher. Companies in the US make more value investments per year. This situation translates into higher productivity rates and profitability. On the whole, deal-processing costs tend to be more of less the same irrespective of transaction size, i.e. it takes the same time and due diligence effort. Deal size in Europe is increasing. But this is on account of higher outlays on management buy-outs, as opposed to funding seed and early-stage investments. An interesting scenario is that Europe has a higher SME 'birth rate' than the US. In the absence of a change in the pattern of investment, this means that an increasing number of new SMEs will be without access to capital finance from VCs. US private equity and venture capital firms are much more specialised. This means that they have a greater capability to bet on start-ups within a particular sector, thus spreading portfolio risk – a contrasting feature with the more generalist European counterparts. US firms also gave a higher level of repeat business. This is especially the case in the IT sector.

Sectoral investments

The sectoral allocation of investments is broadly the same. High-tech sectors dominate the scene in both cases. The US companies have a higher success 'hit rate' in this area. However, some European countries (e.g. Spain) have high SME 'birth rates' and low 'mortality rates' in IT, a development that will pave the way for a substantial deal flow over the medium term.

Investment criteria and process

European and US private equity and venture capital companies have similar investment criteria and decision-making processes. As stated, US companies are more specialised than their counterparts in Europe. This means that their ability to understand and reach decisions on a transaction is better. Their due diligence requirement is generally narrower on account of this specialisation. This saves time and money to the target SMEs. But it also translates into lower cost to the VC. The due diligence process in all instances involves the following matters:

- *Legal*: title to assets and corporate governance
- *Technical*: investment plans, operating cost structures, etc.
- *Commercial*: market, competition and competitors
- *Management*: operations, sales and finance
- *Environmental*: audits and action plans
- *Financial*: audited accounts and pro-forma statements.

The deal processing cycle is also quite similar. Most firms require a business plan, the basis for the preparation of an internal concept paper and various management investment reviews. Deal processing can take between 4–8 months, depending on viability, market and company risk.

Support to SMEs

Risk capital operators provide two basic services – capital and knowhow. The strategy they adopt with regard to both can sometimes mean the difference between success and failure. In general, our observations suggest that US firms have a greater involvement with the target investment companies than the European ones. Their specialised skill base aids this strategy. European counterparts focus more on management buy-ins. In the worst-case scenario, they simply concentrate their post-investment effort on deal monitoring and financial control. Management buys-ins can often be a positive contribution to SMEs (especially those in the product launch stage). But it is also a fact that most entrepreneurs resist the proposal since it takes away considerable control and a share of the 'upside'. On several recent fundraising mandates undertaken by Morgan Stanley Dean Witter, the management buy-in conditionality by VCs tended to reflect more their lack of knowhow of the industry concerned than the risk profile of the investment itself.

Divestment

One of our hypotheses was that *US* financiers have a greater opportunity to IPO their investments (and to do so more quickly) than their European counterparts. Our research confirms this to be the case. The issue is treated separately elsewhere. However, for the purposes of this comparative analysis, the main conclusion is that US firms are able to exit much more smoothly and successfully. This has a strong ‘pull effect’ on the SME market as a whole. But it also encourages the recycling of funds into new investments. European companies rely quite heavily on trade sales. These can be lucrative but more difficult and costly to strike. Sales to other funds are also restricted. Cross-boarder sales are uncommon. In addition, there are too many differences in the area of incentives and exit options within Europe, with varying rules and regulations, including those applying to ‘stock options’.

The results of a 1996 Price Waterhouse survey in Europe interviewing 30 VCs in 14 countries was that ‘exiting’ an investment was usually more onerous or lengthy than expected. Venture capitalists had a target life for their investments of between three and six years, but they frequently dragged on through eight years or more. Seventy per cent said that they had at some time experienced difficulties in exiting their investments. They identified the following as causes for their problems:

- Stock trading sentiment.
- Lack of institutional buyers for IPOs
- Lack of trade buyers for a particular investment
- Uncooperative managers or co-investors
- Due diligence results
- Poor performance by the business.[22]

By far the largest number of exits took place through trade sales.

Financial products

Another of our hypothesis was that US financiers utilise a greater range of financial instruments with lower cost when investing in SMEs than the European companies.

We are of the view that this is the case, with US firms appearing to combine equity and quasi-equity financial instruments with debt from banks much more frequently than their European counterparts. This co-financing (and greater willingness to undertake co-investments with industry peers) strengthens the overall financial package to SMEs. It also spreads information and risk.

US companies also include in their financing scheme cumulative preference shares and stock options. These can cut back quite considerably on the need to raise additional debt, thus easing the cost structure of companies. Cross-border deals are common in the US. They are seldom executed in Europe. Also, traditional venture capital funds are more visible than other forms of investment. But in the US at least, private equity is also a major SME financier. Indeed venture capital funds represent about one-third of what is termed private equity. Buy-out funds or 'leveraged acquisition funds' account for the largest share of the private equity pool. Total funds raised amounted to US$ 79 billion in 1998 and US$ 96 billion in 1999. Venture funds represent 48 per cent of the total private equity funds raised in the US in 1999 – a record high, up from the historic levels of 20 to 30 per cent.[23]

The US private equity industry remains the world's largest by some considerable margin. However, comparisons with Europe can be difficult. One of the reasons is a definition problem. In the UK, for instance, later stage, buy-out and corporate captive investment vehicles dominate venture capital. These are in fact more akin to the US buy-out market than to traditional US venture capital operators. Continental Europe has a significant amount of traditional venture capital and buy-out investment activity. The total capitalisation of US private equity funds amount to US$ 96 billion in 1999, compared with the €25 billion raised by European and UK private equity investment fund and vehicles.

Of private equity venture capital investments, in the US they rose by more than 150 per cent between 1998 and 1999 to reach US$ 48 billion. This is significantly higher than the corresponding amount in Europe. The total number of companies receiving funds rose quite considerably by 11 per cent to 3,638. Financing rounds increased to 4,941 from 3,744 a year earlier. Monies raised in the first rounds increased by more than 145 per cent over the same period. Follow-on investments also rose with 1,955 companies getting more than US$ 29 billion. This represents a major difference with respect to Europe, where the follow-on rate is much lower. Average financing per company in the US is more than four times that in Europe at US$ 13.2 million. The average deal size is rising, thus making venture capitalists more efficient. SME in the States are, however, larger, especially those in the 'expansion' and 'developed stage' of development.

Nowadays, according to the EU's web pages, 'Typical projects eligible for support might be those with a relatively long development phase often involving new technology.' The EU's statistics are out of date, but by 1996, 23 funds had raised €52 million in capital, supposedly generating 2,876 direct jobs.[25] The EU's most well-known funding effort might well have been the backing of EASDAQ (now NASDAQ Europe since the takeover by NASDAQ).

Operating environment

Summing up, VCs in the US have less regulatory operating framework problems than their counterparts in Europe. In complete contrast with the

US, European VCs face difficulties with cross-border fundraising, tax regimes and pension fund operations (key source of finance). The EU Commission has started to address the problems. But in the meantime, operations remain constrained.

We conclude this section as we have concluded others, with a caveat that many differences in the two blocs may be cyclical, with at least some perceived ‘problems’ being resolved by market forces and acceleration in European activity. To provide one example among many, in Spain the total value of private equity deals in 1996 was around €186 million. In 1999 that rose to over €2.24 billion, or more than ten times higher. Some 932 million of this was in management buy-outs. So Europeans even away from the largest capital centres of Europe are ‘catching on’.[26]

Major US strategic advantages on SME funding: summary

- US financiers are quicker to make an investment decision. This benefits SMEs seeking funding. If this is the case, the policy-makers will need to understand why investments are faster and incorporate the lessons.
- The process for companies seeking equity stakes is simpler in the US with its more fluid institutions (especially the angel investors and VCs) than with more traditional banks.
- US financiers have a clearer grasp of commercial and technical risk through specialisation (sector), better market and technical information, and US focus (thereby making use of their comparative advantage). Europe may have to encourage the growth of similar (especially sector-specific) VC funds through programmes lowering the cost or risk of capital.
- US financiers have a higher risk threshold.
- US financiers are more involved in operations of their client/SMEs than in the EU. This is an advantage to the US SMEs and the VC firms that invest in them. Active investor involvement may also be responsive to policy.
- US financiers offer a greater range of support measures to SMEs than their counterparts in the EU. There could be a need for a reorientation of operations here.
- Firms in the US have access to more long-term credit and equity deals, thereby enabling them to focus on longer-term investments and strategic questions of importance to more rapid growth.
- US firms are better at exiting their investments than their European counterparts.
- Innovations centres are concentrated in the US, as opposed to Europe, where they are more dispersed.
- The US regulatory framework is far more harmonised than its equivalent in Europe, enabling more long-distance private equity.

Notes

1 Venture Economics Information Services, NVCA. *National Venture Capital Association Yearbook 1999*, p. 69.
2 Press release, 'UK Pension Funds Lag US in Venture Capital Investment', *Financial News* (12 July 1999), Aberdeen Asset Management/Murray Johnstone.
3 Lucinda Kemeny, 'Analysis: Government Venture Capital Funds: Laying the Ground for a Nation of Entrepreneurs', *Accountancy Age* (15 July 1999).
4 Venture Economics Information Services, NVCA. *National Venture Capital Association Yearbook 1999*, p. 60.
5 Ibid., p. 70.
6 See glossary.
7 As defined under a stricter definition that used in Europe. Excludes leveraged buy-out and MBO/MBI funds – which make up the bulk of US private equity. European figures tend to include these types of funds.
8 *National Venture Capital Association Yearbook 2000*, Thomson Financial Securities Data/Venture Economics, p. 9, Figure 1.0.
9 *National Venture Capital Association Yearbook 1999*, Venture Economics Information Services, Newark, p. 2.
10 See glossary.
11 *National Venture Capital Association Yearbook 2000*, Thomson Financial Securities Data/Venture Economics, p. 28, Figure 3.10.
12 Venture Economics and National Venture Capital Association (NVCA), as quoted in the web site of the Venture Economics group of Thomson Financial Securities Data – www.ventureeconomics.com
13 Monica McGlinchey, Venture Economics Information Services. 'US Venture-Backed IPOs Escalate to 270 in 1999', news release (7 January 2000).
14 Quote taken from 'Anorexia – New Economy Shares', *The Economist* (11 March 2000).
15 Venture Economics Information Services, NVCA. *National Venture Capital Association Yearbook 1999.*
16 Venture Economics maintains a database of 1,200 venture capital funds in the US and 500 in Europe. The Private Equity Performance Index (PEPI) represents an analysis of internal rates of return (IRRs) for investors based on flows of cash paid in and dividends received expressed as annual returns for given periods – 1, 3, 5, 10 and 20 years. Thus, for example, since the 1980s, average venture funds have returned 18.8%.
17 National Venture Capital Association – www.nvca.org
18 *EVCA Yearbook 2000*, European Private Equity and Venture Capital Association, Luxembourg, p. 8.
19 Ibid., p. 27.
20 See glossary.
21 'Europe: Work in Progress: The New Economy', *Business Week International Edition* (31 January 2000). Cover story.
22 John Wall and Julian Smith, *Better Exits*. Price Waterhouse Corporate Finance, London, p. 6.
23 *National Venture Capital Association Yearbook 2000*, Thomson Financial Securities Data/Venture Economics, p. 24.
24 The European Commission. What is Seed Capital? – www.europa.eu.int
25 Katharine Campbell, *Financial Times*. 'Best Climate in Industry's History' (2 December 1999).

3 Markets for SME publicly quoted stocks in Europe and the USA

'Small-cap' markets – including both SMEs and larger companies – continue to form and grow in the world's financial centres, and some IPOs of smaller companies are now generating returns that people only a few years ago would have considered unimaginable. Yet generally, small-cap stocks and markets have been laggard since 1995 on both sides of the Atlantic.

Reasons not to create special small-cap exchanges for smaller companies include:

- Fears of volatility in the main markets
- Fears that the value and exclusivity of main market listings will erode
- Fears that rules will be altered to suit the special needs of SMEs
- Legal and regulatory constraints. Fears that SMEs will find the 'compliance burden' too much.

Reasons for companies themselves not to list on markets even if they exist include:

- Owners' fears of loss of control
- Unwillingness to disclose financial statements or strategy
- Tax system favouring debt over equity financing
- Underdeveloped accounting systems that would be expensive to permanently upgrade
- Insufficient reporting structure necessary to keep investors regularly informed.

The cost of listing also is prohibitively expensive for the smallest companies on most markets, and can include all of the following:

- One-time introduction fees, ranging in most markets under €100,000 with an average of €8,000 towards the end of the 1990s.
- Subsequent or annual charges, also below €100,000 and frequently scaled to the size of the company.
- Associated costs per listing for other purveyors of services (lawyers,

accountants, bankers, notaries) usually between 5 to 8 per cent of the issued capital at IPO.[1]

These problems of small-cap markets, very briefly summarised, have convinced many important institutions to exit them, while many companies either never consider listing or are de-listing.

Yet the *benefits of small business markets* are believed to outweigh the risks in most developed economies and in most countries with bourses. Further, these markets have attracted hundreds of SMEs to list. *Advantages of building small-cap exchanges* include

- Providing a nursing ground for small companies to expand until they are large enough for the main market
- Maintaining the commercial viability of the companies through economic cycles by providing them with access to capital
- Stimulating regional economies and new paths for capital intermediation.

Finally, *reasons very small companies might seek a listing* include questions of future development, management succession, family inheritance taxes, diversification of funding, and greater commercial visibility.[2]

Countries with securities markets have weighed the risks and benefits, and despite the risks, most are setting up 'small and medium sized business markets' (SMB Markets) if they have not already done so. The figure below shows the results of a survey conducted by FIBV,[3] which covered.

Some countries also meet the demand for small-cap markets by accommodating smaller companies within their main market. For example, NASDAQ started life as a market designed to serve small companies, but now it has outgrown the narrow confines of one of its original key missions. Still, rather than creating another market for small-caps to replace NASDAQ, a small-cap market within NASDAQ has been formed, with less steep listing and reporting requirements than exist on the main market. AMEX, which has merged with NASDAQ, also tends to serve smaller companies as well as trading options. The Tel Aviv stock market provides another example of a market that ably serves both small and large companies. Also, whilst few markets serving a country as the main market would wish to be listed as 'small-cap', in many countries the majority of listed companies are not particularly big by the standards of New York, London, Frankfurt or Tokyo.

Indeed, the biggest problem with the analysis of 'small-cap' markets and especially 'small-cap' firms is that a proper definition of such markets and their companies does not exist. 'A US$ 300 million small-cap company in the United States would be considered large-cap if it were listed in Teheran or mid-cap in New Zealand. Australia's Emerging Markets is suitable for companies seeking as little as €62,000, whereas

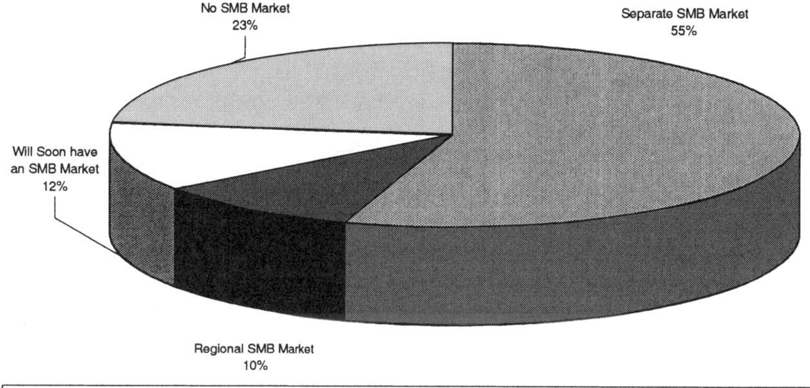

Figure 3.1 Percentage of exchanges with a separate SMB market (1999).

Source: Michael Ashley Schulman, *Medium Size Business Markets* (FIBV Working Committee Focus Group Study on SMB Markets), August 1999, p. 9.

Note

In August 1999, at the request of its membership, FIBV established a working party to create a position paper on SMB markets and the membership' preparedness in relation to them. The working party surveyed all 52 members and obtained 50 responses. Analysis of these responses forms the basis of their report.

NASDAQ's small-cap market requires at least US$ 5 million of free floating shares.'[4]

Definitional problems focus not only on what is a 'small-cap company' but also on what is a 'small-cap exchange.' Arenas of competition for small-caps besides private equity and debt markets include:

- Over the counter (OTC) markets; the border between these and electronic markets such as EASDAQ (now NASDAQ Europe since the takeover by NASDAQ) has become more opaque
- Electronic crossing networks (ECNs), which may be winning market share off exchange trading
- Internet IPOs – a new kind of OTC listing
- Stronger global investment houses that may compete with exchanges, especially if they continue to buy up ECNs.[5]

Some alternative investment platforms, such as OTC markets and Internet IPOs, are more popular in the US than elsewhere; nevertheless, the popularity of OTC boards appears to have decreased with more choices available on the main markets and weaker protection of investors outside the main markets.

Perhaps the central question for countries or trading blocs deciding how to manage markets for small-cap securities then becomes the following: How relaxed should access to listings be? More relaxed requirements are cheaper and easier for companies, and may stimulate listings. On the other hand, the protection of investors against fraud, poor information and illiquidity is likely to be compromised without some conservatism in the rule and enforcement structure – an example being the collapse and eventual closure of the parallel market precursor to the Amsterdam Nieuwe Markt. Comparative discussions suggest that protections against insider trading, as one example of fraud, tend to raise the values of markets.

The balance is particularly important when considering insider trading. A recent study[6] into the cost of insider trading concluded that there were considerable cost of equity savings through the creation and enforcement of effective insider trading regulations. The authors estimated effective regulation and enforcement had the effect of reducing the cost of equity by 5 per cent. Although this might not sound like much – it would be the equivalent to an annual saving of US$ 170 billion for investors in the London Stock Exchange alone. Further, those protections are more pronounced in the US than in Europe, although more pronounced in Europe than in many other places. The US introduced such a regime as early as 1934. However, in the UK such practices did not become illegal until 1984 and in Germany not until the mid-1990s.

Generally, there are similarities in the rules, styles and growth rates of the exchanges for small-caps on both sides of the Atlantic. But the greatest differences between US and European markets emerge with respect to markets for public securities. While small-cap stocks are not growing in line with markets generally on either side of the Atlantic, they are more centrally located, healthier, more aggressively regulated by a uniform regulatory authority, and have a larger market capitalisation in the US. They also attract a more diverse investment community. Negative trends on the rate of growth of IPOs and the valuations of small-caps generally are contrasted by positive trends on the volumes of trades per day, which, with the birth of Internet-based trading and the increasingly commoditised nature of broker services, have risen considerably in the US. It is questionable whether the new phenomenon of 'day trading' is profitable or of any economic significance, but generally greater liquidity tends to imply lower risk for investors.

Overview of small-cap growing pains in Europe and the USA

US small-caps generally profit from an investment climate that is comparatively friendlier towards risk than in Europe. As a result, although the GDP of the US and the EU are roughly equal, the US hosts far larger markets for equity. On the other hand, while US markets are comparatively large and healthy, they are experiencing significant growing pains.

As of 31 December 1998, excluding multiple listings, closed-end investment vehicles, limited partnerships, and non-classifiable companies, there were 2,898 common stocks listed on the NYSE and 5,068 listed on the NASDAQ/AMEX for a total of 7,966 issues. These nearly 8,000 common stocks[7] had an aggregate market capitalisation of approximately US$12.8 trillion.[8] In all, the US has the largest pool of investment capital in the world. Another source, apparently including either more investment platforms (smaller exchanges, OTC stocks and VC investments in private listings) or more up-to-date sources, estimates that US$14 trillion worth of investment capital currently fuels US firms.[9] Clearly, this giant pool of capital benefits both large- and small-cap listings.

Risk negatively correlates with the size of companies; the larger the company, the lower the risk, measured by price volatility and chance of default. Basic financial theory then suggests that investors would only focus on SME capital markets if they are convinced that returns on investment would be higher than in the comparatively stable blue-chip investments. Returns were indeed higher for smaller firms in the US from the 1920s through the mid-1990s.

Yet as larger firms increased productivity and profitability in the early 1990s, in both the EU and the US, small-cap stocks have yielded significantly worse returns on investment than large-cap ones over the short term. The Russell 2000 index – composed of the 2,000 stocks that rank below the

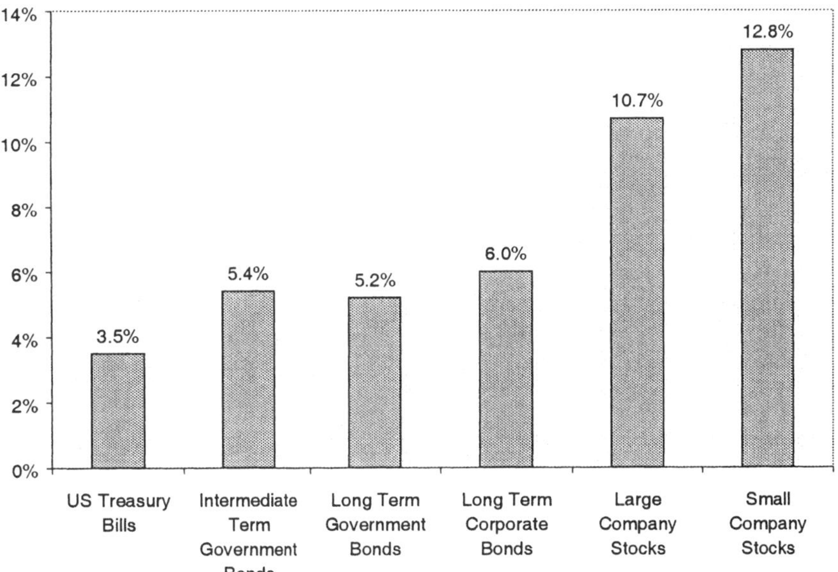

Figure 3.2 Gross annual return by asset (1926–95).

Source: 'Risk Capital: A Key to Job Creation in the European Union,' Communication of the European Commission, SEC (1998) 552 final, April, p. 6.

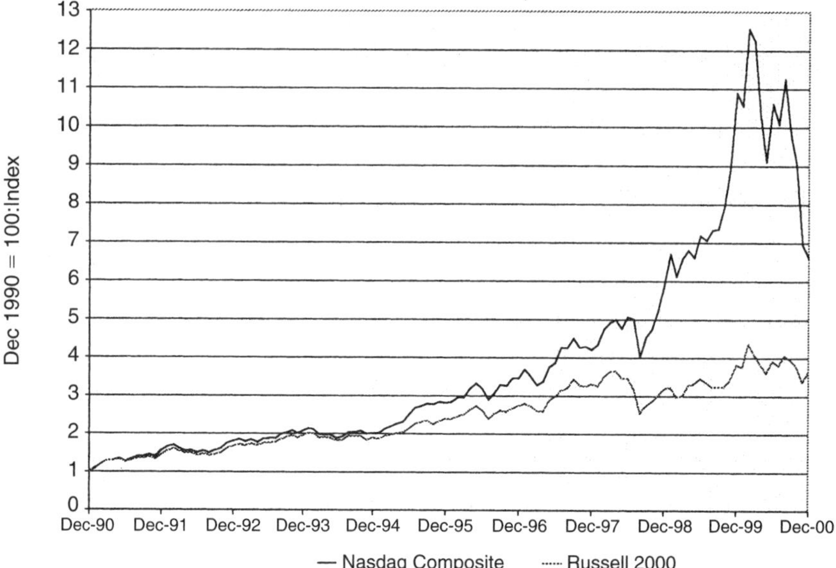

Figure 3.3 NASDAQ Composite and Russell 2000 indices (1990–2000).

Source: NASD Economic Research Department – www.marketdata.nasdaq.com

1,000 stocks with the highest capitalisation in the United States – is the best measure of small stock performance. From the figure below we see that, despite the bursting of the Internet bubble in 2000, the NASDAQ composite index during the 1990s has significantly outperformed the Russell 2000 – by a factor of 50 per cent. By December 2000, the Russell 2000 index had grown four fold, but NASDAQ had grown over six fold.

Furthermore, we see from a comparison of annual growth rates for the two indices in Figure 3.4 that, since the early 1990s, NASDAQ has consistently outperformed the Russell 2000. In 1998, the NASDAQ composite rose 40 per cent, while the Russell 2000 fell 5 per cent. This phenomenon reflects the pull of the Internet bubble. Prior to the rise of the Internet, the Russell tracked closely the NASDAQ Composite, particularly up until 1994.

One should note some unusual characteristics of the current US expansion, the longest bull run in US history. Much of it is not fuelled by high-tech start-ups at all, as people believe, but rather by a handful of incredible, now giant and somewhat more-established performers, especially in computer-related industries. According to recent research and shown in Figure 3.5,[10] a 21 per cent rise in the S&P 500 last year was driven by a mere 31 shares – compared with 216 shares in 1996 leading to a similar rise.

IT companies comprise only 16 per cent of the listed companies on NASDAQ by number, but now account for half of NASDAQ's value; and

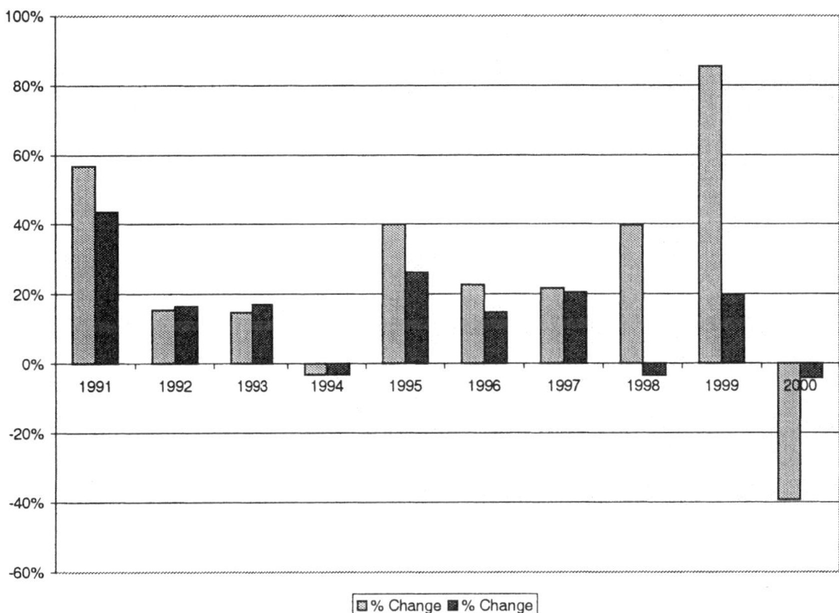

Figure 3.4 NASDAQ Composite and Russell 2000 indices (1990–2000).
Source: NASD Economic Research Department – www.marketdata.nasdaq.com

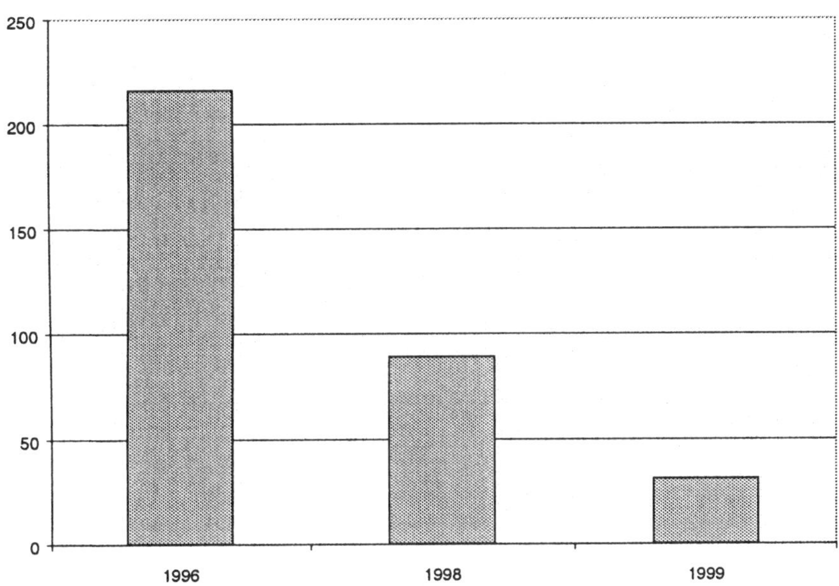

Figure 3.5 S&P 500 core growth shares (1996–9).
Source: Morgan Stanley Dean Witter, *The Economist*.

many of these companies (e.g. Microsoft, Intel) are giants. The confidence this has generated has had a global 'trickle-down' effect, with IT stocks on the Neuer Markt and NASDAQ Europe (formerly EASDAQ) having a similar impact. This was good whilst it lasted. But the impact of a loss of confidence in IT stocks has had a significant impact on all exchanges – but particularly on the newer European technology exchanges, which had started from a lower and narrower base than NASDAQ.

It must be admitted that IPO activity in the US, as in Europe especially between 1997 and 1998, is also down. After a peak of almost 800 IPOs in 1996, raising US$ 37 billion. The situation since then has changed. Although the number of companies coming to market has fallen (with the exception of a brief rally in 1999), the initial offering value in total has continued to increase – from US$ 37 billion in 1996 to US$ 112 billion in 2000. Average offering receipts rose dramatically in 1998, doubling from US$ 64 million in 1997 to US$ 128 million – and almost doubling again to US$ 249 million in 2000.

Problems for small-caps on both sides of the Atlantic are as follows:

- Lower liquidity for smaller companies makes them less attractive to investors.
- Weaker communication channels between smaller companies and investors.

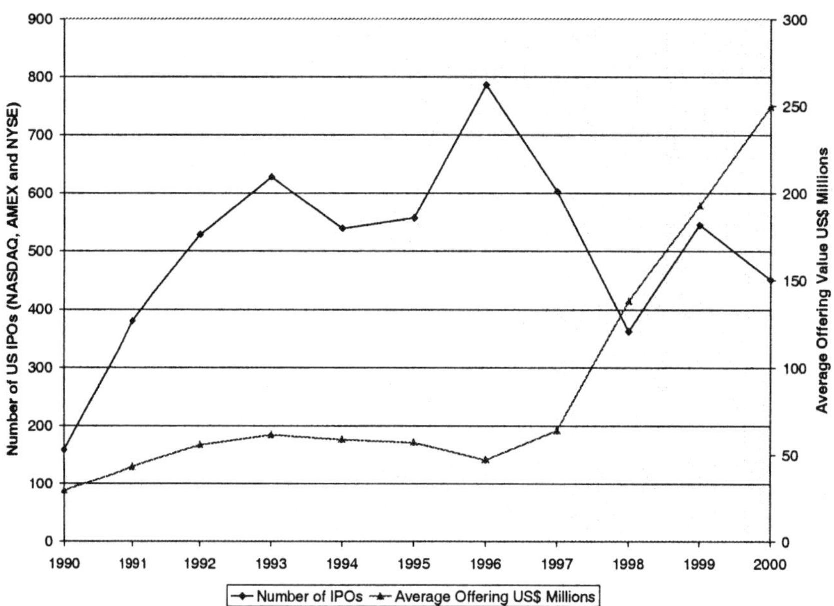

Figure 3.6 US exchange IPO activity (1990–2000).

Source: NASD Economic Research Department – www.marketdata.nasdaq.com

- Information costs are higher for small-company investors, who may require almost the same amount of time analysing a small-cap stock as a large one.
- Indices that frequently cover only the very largest firms in any economy are becoming more and more popular.
- Entering the market has high fixed costs that are disproportionately expensive for smaller firms. These include fees paid to stockbrokers, registrars, lawyers, merchant bankers and financial PR companies, as well as the exchange fee and auditing, printing and distribution of accounts.
- Lack of analyst coverage.

Small-cap stocks may be more subject to fraud and violations of securities laws than larger cap stocks, because, while the stakes are lower, fewer people are watching the activities of these stocks. Further, those issuing and trading them may be less experienced than issuers and traders of larger-caps.[11,12]

Admittedly, for European firms, there may be some advantages to listing in Europe (rather than in the US or not at all) despite the problems described. Advantages are as follows:

- For companies with markets and management based in Europe, initial listings in Europe may make more sense; European investors will be more familiar with the company and its products.
- European exchanges will permit listings in home currencies, or, in the case of NASDAQ Europe (formerly EASDAQ), for example, there is the choice of quotations in Euros or dollars.
- Regulatory burdens on European exchanges are frequently less severe than those of NASDAQ (or NASDAQ Europe).

Despite the caveats on the problems of truly ‘small-cap’ firms in the US described above, temporary problems with small-caps appear to be more pronounced in Europe than in America. To illustrate what may be a growing problem, statistics on the number of firms pulling out of the London Stock Exchange in recent years, as an example, are provided below.

Generally, in the words of *The Economist*:

> Europe still lacks many of the ingredients that have made American high-tech industry so successful. The ‘ecology’ of specialist backers, entrepreneurs, lawyers, and analysts is barely developed. Its capital markets are illiquid, its product markets fragmented – and its citizens afraid to take risks.[13]

The EU and national governments (e.g. the Labour government in Britain) have promoted solutions to these problems. While policies are

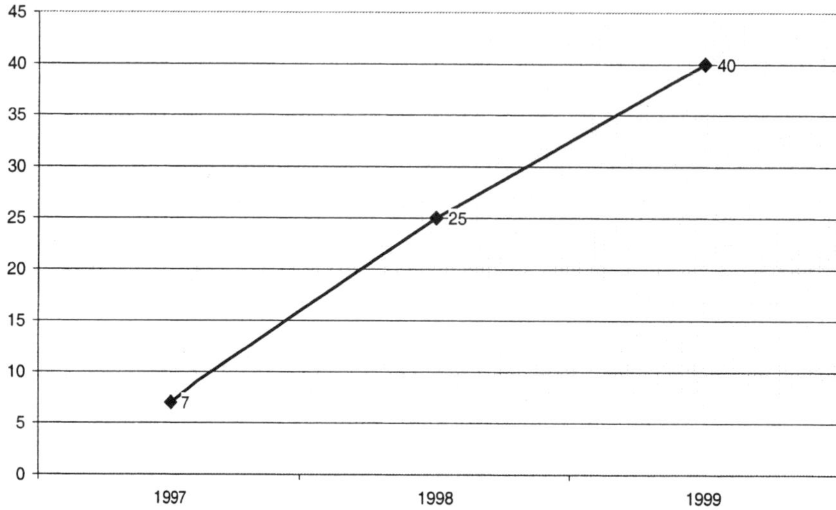

Figure 3.7 London Stock Exchange delistings (1997–9).
Source: London Stock Exchange – www.londonstockex.co.uk

discussed elsewhere in this document, some that can be quickly highlighted include

- Allowing small-caps to be traded only at certain times of the day, so that there is a better two-way flow and small investors are encouraged into the sector; this would help to address the liquidity problem.
- Encouraging private firms, possibly with public backing, that help provide information and marketing of small firms to investors. One such firm is Equity Development, founded by a City publicist named Brian Basham.[14] These help to correct the information problem experienced by investors in small firms.
- Encouraging more ownership of small and private firms through employee share schemes that expand the number of people and broaden the social groups that 'invest' in securities. For example, a proposed All-Employee Share Scheme in Britain will allow owners to award shares based on performance and will allow employees to purchase shares from their pre-tax income.[15]

SME equity markets in the US and Europe compared

US small-cap exchanges

The world's largest exchange that works to attract small-cap stocks is NASDAQ. It has an advantage over other small-cap exchanges in that it is

Table 3.1 NASDAQ key statistics (1995–2000)

Statistic	*1995*	*1996*	*1997*	*1998*	*1999*	*2000*
Share volume (bn)	101	138	164	202	273	443
Market value (US$ bn)	1,160	1,517	1,835	2,589	5,205	3,597
Trading volume (US$ bn)	2,398	3,302	4,482	5,759	11,013	20,395
No. companies	5,122	5,556	5,487	5,068	4,829	4,734
No. issues	5,955	6,384	6,208	5,583	5,210	5,053
Active market makers	512	541	530	479	443	398
Market maker positions[a]	60,590	60,897	60,751	57,404	61,092	65,500

Source: NASDAQ – http://www.marketdata.nasdaq.com/asp/Sec1FiveYrs.asp

Note

a Market maker positions. Sum total of issues in which markets are made. This number, divided by active market makers gives the average number of issue per market maker.

no longer considered important for companies that grow large to transfer, or 'graduate', to another exchange. Unlike the London Stock Exchange's AIM or the European NM markets, it is autonomous, and it now has enough internal momentum to keep some of the world's largest companies (e.g. Microsoft, the largest) from leaving to list elsewhere.

By the end of 2000, NASDAQ had a market cap of over US$ 3.5 trillion. Of course, most of this comprised large-cap securities – and is significantly down on the market cap of US$ 11 trillion at the end of 1999.

Although many small-caps are not SMEs and many IPOs are not small-cap stocks (they include, for example, divested units of large companies), the NASDAQ small-cap index and also IPO activity are better proxies for small-cap dynamism.

At the end of December 2000, there were 907 stocks listed on the NASDAQ small-cap market with a market capitalisation of US$ 18 billion. These stocks benefited greatly from having on average between 5.5 and 8.0 market makers (see figure above). Given the high value attributed to Internet-related stocks, many IPOs are listing directly on the national market (official name for main NASDAQ market). Looking at the market as a whole, in 1999 the number of IPOs increased again following a fall from the peak in 1996. However, the number of IPOs fell back again in 2000.

In 1998, NASDAQ raised $13.8 billion in initial public offerings. In 1999, this amount rose to US$ 50.4 billion and in 2000 to US$ 52.6 billion. Despite the swings in the number of issues, the average offering value has continued in increase. This is seen as a reflection of the combination of diminished market appetite following the burst of the Internet bubble for IPOs – coupled with only 'clear certainties' daring to IPO, given this market sentiment – and hence clear demand.

Admittedly, there are more exchanges than just NASDAQ for secondary markets, as is shown by the complete listing of all US exchanges, below.

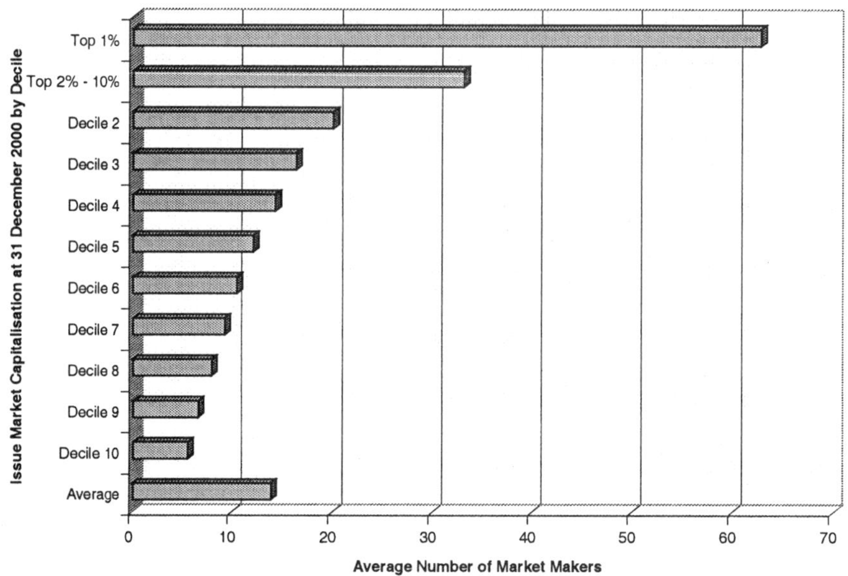

Figure 3.8 NASDAQ market makers (2000).

Source: NASDAQ – http://www.marketdata.nasdaq.com/asp/MpMarketMakers.asp

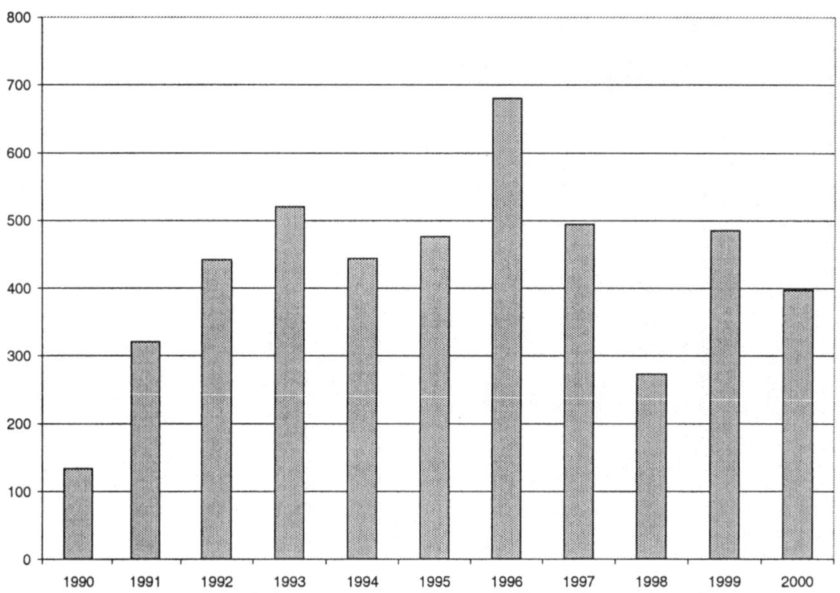

Figure 3.9 NASDAQ IPOs (1990–2000).

Source: NASDAQ.

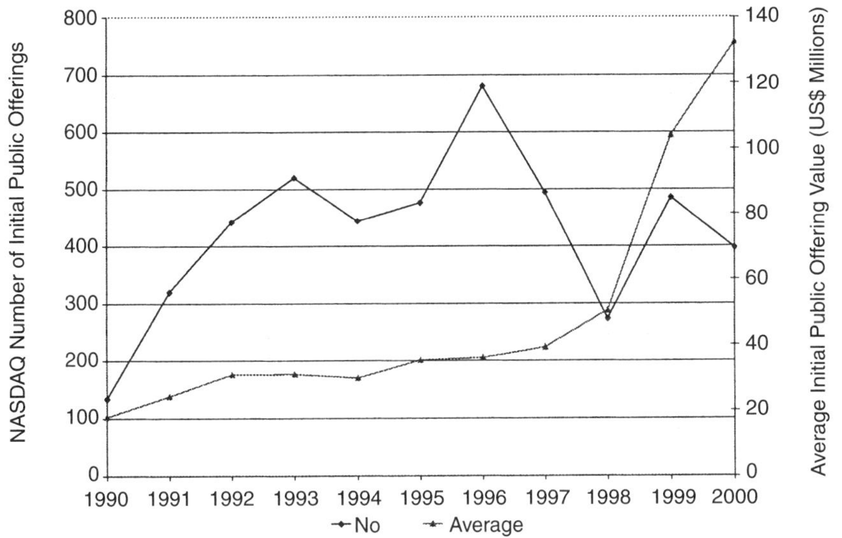

Figure 3.10 NASDAQ IPOs – number and average offering value (1990–2000).
Source: NASDAQ.

The US has twelve stock exchanges that trade under two separate systems. The main system is the Intermarket Trading System (ITS) that enables all the regulated exchanges to trade under one platform. The second are two exchanges for unlisted securities – the OTC Bulletin Board (OTCBB) and National Quotation Bureau (NQB).

Yet the US has a dramatically centralised small-cap market, revolving almost entirely around NASDAQ and its regulatory structure, particularly since its absorption of the American Exchange (AMEX) in the mid-1990s. The process of graduating from the small-cap market to the main market is reasonably seamless, and does not impose significant additional burdens upon the listed companies. The small-cap market alone currently has more stocks listed than all of the parallel markets in Europe combined. However, this has been blurred through the small-cap market also being the repository for listings of international stocks and specialised instruments such as warrants and convertible preference shares. Secondly, particularly with recent Internet issues, there has been a trend to list directly on the National Market.

The New York Stock Exchange (NYSE), meanwhile, has made little effort to go after the smallest stocks. Since its listing requirements are more strict and expensive, smaller-cap stocks similarly see few reasons to woo the NYSE. Other smaller markets are nearly insignificant compared to the momentum of NASDAQ, or are at least insignificant for the listing of smaller-cap securities (they may be focused on commodities or other

Table 3.2 US intermarket trading system exchanges (2000)

NASDAQ
NYSE
American Stock Exchange (AMEX)
Arizona Stock Exchange
Boston Stock Exchange
Chicago Stock Exchange
Cincinnati Stock Exchange
Pacific Exchange
Philadelphia Stock Exchange
San Diego Stock Exchange

Source: Stock exchanges.

products). For example, the Pacific Exchange, based in San Francisco and Los Angeles, trades almost entirely companies listed on the NYSE and NASDAQ and focuses on options – trading over 300,000 daily in comparison to NASDAQ's 4,000 by the end of 1999, and rising to 500,000 and 50,000 daily trades respectively by March 2000.[16] On the other hand, it is worth mentioning that it has 49 exclusively listed companies.

And many of the other markets, although they have listings of their own, primarily trade NASDAQ stocks.

The US OTC bulletin board (OTCBB) is a regulated quotation service that displays real-time quotes, last-sale prices, and volume information in over-the-counter equity securities. It began operations in June 1990, and quoted thousands of securities by the end of that decade.

Some of the features of the OTCBB are:

- By the end of the 1990s, it provided access to more than 6,500 securities
- It included more than 400 participating market makers
- It electronically transmitted real-time quote, price, and volume information in domestic securities, foreign securities, and ADRs,[17] and
- It displayed indications of interest and prior-day trading activity in DPPs.[18]

OTC boards are different from electronic exchanges as shown in Table 3.3.

In bull markets, little heed is given to investor protection and regulatory oversight. However, the establishment of investor protection frameworks are critical to the long-term well-being and reputation of exchanges. When things go wrong, such as happened with the recent insider trading scandals in Germany, the whole exchange is tainted. Here, this reinforces the lesson that not only does a framework need to be in place (as is the case in Germany), it also needs to be enforced. The results of such frameworks are clear for all to see – in perceived risk reduction leading to

Table 3.3 Feature comparison of OTC board and electronic exchange (2000)

Feature or requirement	*OTCBB*	*NASDAQ*
Minimum quantitative listing requirements	No	Yes
Listing and maintenance fees to issuers	No	Yes
Requirements to maintain quotation or listing	Yes[a]	Yes
Real-time electronic quotes for domestic issues	Yes	Yes
Minimum listing processing time	3 days	6–8 weeks[b]
Regulatory oversight and investor protection	Little	Full

Source: 'About OTCBB' – www.otcbb.com, 1999.

Notes

a Issuers of securities that began on the OTCBB after 4 January 1999 are required to file periodic financial information with the SEC or other regulatory authorities.

b A form is not required for listing on NASDAQ, but this is the average time of approval.

widening investor bases, the maintenance of confidence and thus liquidity – the lifeblood of any exchange.

In closing the section on the US exchanges, it is worthwhile saying something about the momentum that NASDAQ now has, even for European firms listing in the US. NASDAQ listed more than 500 corporations based outside the US at the end of 2000. Many of these might more naturally be attracted to US markets than European ones. For example, the largest number of foreign listings comes from Canada, at over 150. These are followed by Israel, at over 90.

Several Caribbean and Latin American firms might also find the US a more logical source of capital than Europe. But there are in addition over 150 firms from western Europe listed on NASDAQ, 50 from the UK alone. Why would these firms seek capital and liquidity in the US rather than in Europe? Many may be pushing to expand into US markets with subsidiary operations, or they may be in the process of moving their primary base of operations to the US, for closer proximity to US markets or capital. Of these European firms, some were also dual listings, and the giant European companies that sought NASDAQ listings (e.g. Ericsson, Volvo) as well as listings in their home markets raised the average, measurable market cap[19] of the European firms on NASDAQ to over US$ 6 billion.

Having said that, some firms clearly regard the US as the most dynamic place to seek capital, and list there rather than in Europe the first time that they list. Either way, it should be noted that the internationalisation of NASDAQ, reflected through the number and proportion of non-US companies listed, is clearly one of its strong points. And many of the firms listing on NASDAQ from Europe are smaller-cap firms, although not necessarily SMEs.

While just over half of the European firms with easily measured market caps had caps of more than US$ 1 billion, many of those that were the smallest had market caps that were unknown; and market caps of less than US$ 1 billion, in fact, probably comprise a majority of the European listings on NASDAQ. So this exchange is attracting both large-cap and small-cap European companies. Further, while the market caps of many firms are not available, the total market cap of more than 150 western European firms listed on NASDAQ may be approaching two-thirds of a trillion dollars. These European resources contribute greatly to the diversity and quality of NASDAQ as a worldwide phenomenon – but a phenomenon based in the US.

European small-cap exchanges

Chapter 7 provides a more detailed discussion of small-cap markets in Europe. Here we provide an analysis of European trends to enable comparisons with the US.

Most countries in Europe have developed a parallel small and medium business (SMB) market. Although the nature and function of the markets differ from country to country, there are two broad types of markets:

- SMB markets for high-growth stocks to capitalise on investor interest in 'new economy' companies. Examples include Neuer Markt and NASDAQ Europe (formerly EASDAQ). These markets are started from scratch and encourage previously unlisted companies to join them.
- Technology market segments. Examples include London's TechMARK and the Nuevo Mercado in Madrid. These markets tend to be established by reclassifying existing quoted entities, although new companies are also encouraged to join.

The sheer number and diversity of the European exchanges, with their myriad of different trading and settlement systems, rules and regulations, operating times and listing requirements puts European capital markets at a severe disadvantage in comparison with the USA, which has only one trading system, the ITS, for trading listed securities.

There were 17 regulated SME equity markets in Europe by the end of 2000. As can be seen from the table below, these markets are significantly difference in terms of size, market capitalisation and liquidity.

Analysis of average market capitalisation by market shows a clear difference between the high-growth markets and the technology market segments. With average market capitalisation in the billions of Euros, technology segment stocks cannot be regarded as SMEs. Looking at individual members of these segments reinforces this. Neither Terra Networks (one of the largest Internet service providers in the world), part of the Nuevo Mercado in Madrid nor Vodafone (the world's largest mobile phone company), part of the TechMARK segment in London can be

Table 3.4 European SMB market key statistics (2000) (€ million)

High-growth exchanges				
Country	*Market*	*Companies listed*	*Market-cap 31/12/00*	*Turnover 2000*
Germany	Neuer Markt	338	120,992	171,062
Italy	Nuovo Mercado	40	25,317	29,485
Europe	NASDAQ Europe	62	24,437	21,338
Greece	Parallel Market	104	10,696	16,862
France	Nouveau Marché	158	24,275	14,652
UK	Alternative Investment Market	524	23,665	21,558
Switzerland	SWX New Market	17	7,989	8,034
Norway	SMB List	77	3,135	4,532
Denmark	KVX Growth Market	12	2,447	4,194
Netherlands	Nieuwe Market	14	894	2,295
Sweden	OM New Market	23	332	2,247
Finland	NM List	18	965	1,123
Belgium	Euro NM Belgium	11	446	305
Austria	Austrian Growth Market	2	65	19
Ireland	Developing Companies Market	4	95	13
	Total	1,404	245,750	297,719
Technology market segments				
Spain	Nuevo Mercado	14	20,478	31,672[a]
UK	TechMARK	246	921,498	1,139,070

Source: Stock exchanges.

Note

a Turnover represents 9 months' activity between 10 April and 31 December 2000.

regarded as SMEs. Both markets have been established more to create an 'instant NASDAQ', and thus attract liquidity, with the hope that there will be a 'trickle-down' effect for high growth SMEs seeking listings. Although the theory is sound, the two examples in Europe do not provide sufficient basis to establish whether it works.

In London, companies first obtain a listing and then apply to join TechMARK. Thus, it is the Alternative Investment Market (AIM) that helps the SMEs to initially list, with the TechMARK there to try and provide some instant respectability for the new joiners through linking them in an index that includes stars such as Vodafone. In Madrid, the Nuevo Mercado was created in April 2000 – just in time to experience the collapse of the Internet bubble. Thus, although the Nuevo Mercado is in theory a hybrid high-growth market and technology segment, market conditions have not yet enabled it to prove its worth.

From Figure 3.12, the wide variation in market liquidity is also

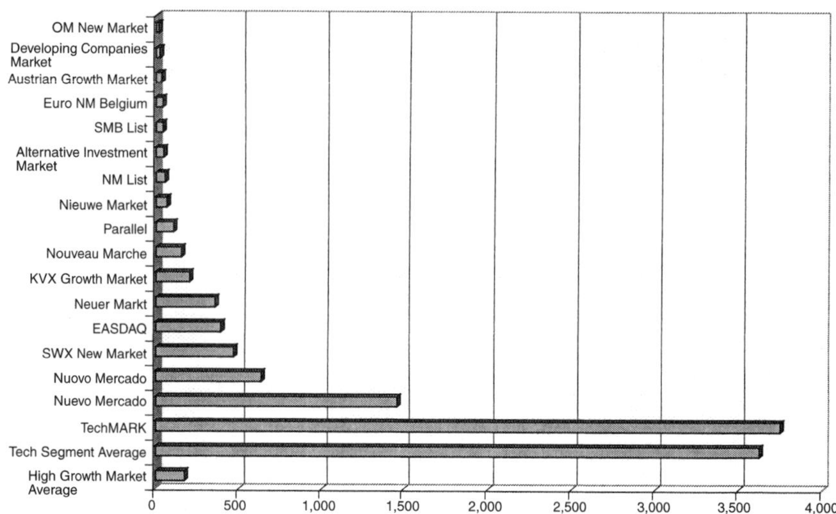

Figure 3.11 Average company market capitalisation (December 2000) (€ million).

Source: Stock exchanges.

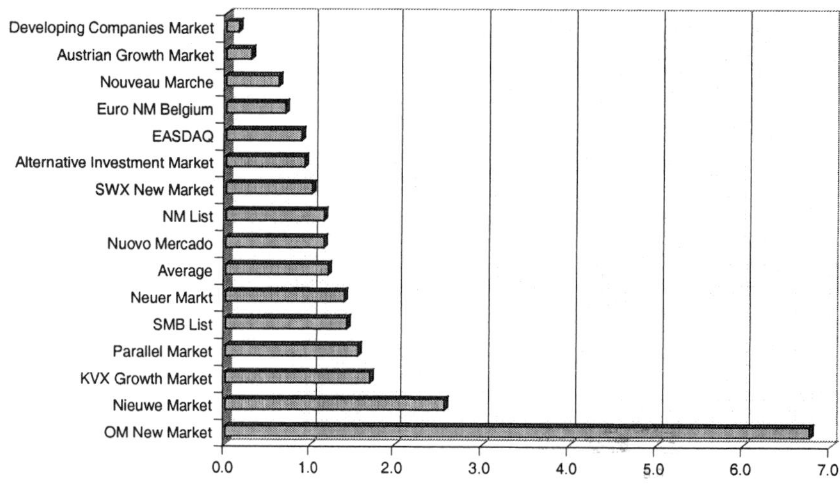

Figure 3.12 Turnover ratio (2000).

Source: Stock exchanges.

Note

Turnover ratio is equal to market turnover for the year 2000 divided by the market capitalisation at 31 December 2000.

Table 3.5 SME capital markets (February 2001)

Country	*SME capital market*	*Alliance*
Austria	Austrian Growth Market	
Belgium	Euro NM Belgium	Euronext
Denmark	New Market	NOREX
Ireland	Developing Companies Market	
N/A	NASDAQ Europe	NASDAQ
Finland	NM List	
France	Nouveau Marché	Euronext
Germany	Neuer Markt	
Netherlands	Nieuwe Markt	Euronext
Italy	Nuovo Mercato	
Norway	SMB List	NOREX
Spain	Nuevo Mercado	
Sweden	OM New Market	NOREX
Switzerland	SWX New Market	
UK	Alternative Investment Market	
USA	NASDAQ Small-cap	NASDAQ

Sources: Stock Exchange websites, Morgan Stanley Dean Witter.

demonstrated. Over half of the markets have a turnover ratio of greater than one, with the Neuer Markt and OM New Market having ratios greater than two. Although encouraging, this does not compare with the US markets. The NASDAQ small-cap market had a turnover of 6.88 over the same period whilst NASDAQ as a whole had turnover of 5.67.

To try and broaden the investor base and improve liquidity – and not just for their SMB markets – many European exchanges have been seeking alliances. Table 3.5 lists the SME capital markets that are part of, or are actively seeking to be part of, alliances. However, alliances that have focused only on growth markets – such as the Euro NM Alliance, have not been successful. The Euro NM Alliance foundered and was officially called off at the end of 2000, having failed to achieve certain core objectives – such as a uniform trading system. This is understandable. Trading, clearing and settlement systems tend to be common across markets within an exchange. It was optimistic to expect the 'tail to wag the dog' in the drive to create small-cap market harmonisation. Only initiatives such as Euronext that involve the entire exchange have managed to achieve this. On this basis, it was perhaps inevitable that the Euro NM Alliance would fail.

Stock exchange alliances

While Europe's decentralised activity is viewed here as an obstacle to greater momentum, Europe does participate in four important alliances that are yielding positive results as follows.

NASDAQ alliances

To springboard off the outstanding success of the NASDAQ market in the US, the National Association of Securities Dealers (NASD) has signed joint venture agreements with partners in Asia and in Europe to develop SME capital markets in both continents that will be linked with the US market. All markets will have the same listing and membership requirements, settlement system, rules and regulations and pricing structure. The aim will be to create the first truly global market for young high-growth stocks. Through an Intermarket system similar to ITS, stocks listed on the individual markets will be able to trade in all markets. This will broaden the investor base to cover the three main capital centres in the world and also offer investors continuous 24-hour trading in stocks. The European shareholders will be Softbank, the large Japanese Internet investment company, Vivendi Ventures, the venture capital arm of Vivendi and Epartners, itself the venture capital arm of News Corporation. Originally planned to commence operations during the fourth quarter of 2000, the bursting of the Internet bubble halted the implementation and made NASDAQ look for other partners to expand into Europe. In May 2000, it announced that it would form part of the ill fated iX alliance between the London Stock Exchange and the Deutsche Börse Group. When this fell through NASDAQ was left without a European partner. Instead, NASDAQ has focused on Canada and Japan, where it launched new markets during 2000. Most recently, NASDAQ changed its strategy to acquire a majority stake in EASDAQ, the troubled Belgian-based electronic exchange. NASDAQ aims to have the exchange linked to its systems by June 2001 and intends to integrate it within the NASDAQ trading platform by 2003.

NASDAQ Europe (formerly EASDAQ)

Since its inception in November 1996, EASDAQ has grown to become a market with 62 companies listed. At the end of December 2000, the market capitalisation was €24 billion. However, the largest four stocks have a market capitalisation of €16 billion. These stocks are largely held by institutions and are hardly traded (free float turnover rate of less than 1 per cent). The remaining 48 stocks represent the bulk of the trading activity in the market but only have a market capitalisation of €8 billion. Turnover during October topped €380 million. EASDAQ failed to capitalise on the Internet boom, recently listing only a handful of new stocks. Sparse trading discouraged IPO candidates and investor confidence was shaken by the Lernout & Hauspie affair. The two created a vicious circle that resulted in an agreed sale in March 2001 to NASDAQ, with the exchange being renamed as NASDAQ Europe.

This market was created by the European Venture Capital Association

(EVCA) in collaboration with NASDAQ to try to emulate the success of NASDAQ in the United States. NASDAQ had only a small participation, which it later sold as part of its strategy to create a new exchange within Europe. The market started trading in November 1996 – only a few months before the Neuer Markt. The market is based in Belgium, but operates across 14 countries in Europe with a single regulatory structure, rulebook, trading and settlement system.

The platform, which draws upon the framework of the various European Directives as well as that of the US Securities and Exchange Commission, is designed to satisfy the needs of companies that are incorporated in a wide range of countries.

The exchange was specifically established to meet the demand for capital of high-growth companies by providing a broad spread of investors within a highly regulated market. The market's pan-European reach and ease of dual listing with NASDAQ gives these companies access to a wide range of capital sources.

The exchange's admission requirements reflect its commitment to supporting the development of high-growth companies and to providing a well-regulated, transparent equity market.

Admission to the exchange is not dependent upon a long profit history, which traditionally has proved an impediment to access public capital for high-growth companies. It offers access public capital for those high-growth companies that can demonstrate a clear market niche and an ability to conform to its entry and reporting requirements.

Nordic Exchanges (NOREX)

NOREX was established in 1998 as an alliance between the Copenhagen Stock Exchange (CSE) and the OM Stockholm Exchange. The alliance provides a common trading platform for equities, futures, derivatives and bonds for both countries. The alliance is for total market activity, not just the SME capital markets.

In June 2000, the Icelandic Exchange became the third member and the Oslo Stock Exchange (OSE) formally joined in October of the same year. The Baltic exchanges of Latvia, Lithuania and Estonia have signed letters of intent to become members. With the entry of the OSE and the Baltic Exchanges, NOREX cover 73 per cent of Nordic equities by market capitalisation and 82 per cent by turnover. The remaining Nordic exchange, the Helsinki Stock Exchange (HSE), decided to enter into an alliance with the Deutsche Börse in Frankfurt and the EUREX derivatives exchange. The intention is for the extended market to begin fully integrated trading by the first half of 2001.

Euronext

Euronext was created in September 2000 from the merger of the Amsterdam, Paris and Brussels stock exchanges. The merger includes the adoption of common trading, clearing and settlement systems. This is an important step forward in the consolidation and streamlining of European capital markets. In particular, it has significant impact for SME capital markets, as all three former exchanges were members of the Euro NM alliance (see below).

Euro NM alliance

Euro NM was the result of an EU initiative to provide young growth companies with access to capital from a broad range of investors. It was an alliance of 'New Markets' in Belgium, France, Germany, Italy and the Netherlands. The five markets that formed part of the Euro NM alliance are shown in Table 3.6.

The objective of Euro NM was to develop an integrated pan-European network of high-growth stock markets, providing single points of access for market information and trading across the entire network. In order to achieve this objective, the key areas in which the alliance co-operates encompassed:

- Market harmonisation
- Market linkage
- Cross-membership
- Information
- Joint marketing.

However the alliance was unable to achieve certain crucial objectives in the areas of market harmonisation. Exchanges were not prepared to adopt different trading systems solely for growth market segments. The realisation by the some of the members that their brand name was what attracted investors and companies alike – rather than the Euro NM trademark, marked the beginning of the end for the alliance, with it officially being terminated on 31 December 2001.

Table 3.6 Euro NM alliance members (December 2000)

Market	*Manager*	*Location*
Nouveau Marché	Euronext	France
Neuer Markt	Deutsche Börse Group	Germany
Nieuwe Markt	Euronext	Netherlands
Euro NM Belgium	Euronext	Belgium
Nuovo Mercato	Italian Exchange	Italy

Source: Euro NM.

Trends

The birth of a NASDAQ Europe, part of a plan to create the first truly global capital market for SMEs, has acted as a wake-up call to the existing SME capital markets. Exchanges are considering their options. Indeed, NOREX, the cross-border alliance between Nordic countries considered becoming part of the Euro NM alliance (when it was still functioning).

By the end of December 2000, there were a total of 561 companies listed on the Euro NM exchanges. The market capitalisation was over €170 billion and average monthly trading volume €18 billion.

Other markets

Smaller capital markets are briefly profiled below with statistics as at the end of 2000.

- *Austrian Growth Market*: This is the Wiener Börse SME capital market. Since its inception in 1997 with two stocks, there have been no new listings. The market had a capitalisation of €65 million and a turnover of €19 million.
- *Alternative Investment Market*: This is the London Stock Exchange SME capital market. AIM at the end of December had a market capitalisation of €23.7 billion and a monthly turnover of €1.8 billion. A total of 524 companies are listed on the exchange.
- *KVX Growth Market*: Market began trading mid 2000. By the end of the year, 12 companies were listed with a combined market capitalisation of €2.5 billion. Monthly trading average €350 million.
- *Developing Companies Market*: This is the SME capital market for the Irish Stock Exchange. In December 2000, it had a market capitalisation of €95 million and a turnover of €13 million. Four companies are listed.
- *NM List*: This is the SME capital market for the Helsinki Exchanges. The market is only recently established and has 18 stocks with a market capitalisation of €965 million and an annual turnover of €1.1 billion.
- *SMB List*: This is the SME capital market for the Oslo Stock Exchange. Since its establishment, the market has grown rapidly. By the end of December, it had 77 listed companies. The market capitalisation is €3.3 billion and annual turnover was €4.5 billion.
- *OM New Market*: This is the SME capital market for the Stockholm Stock Exchange. Like the Oslo exchange it has been recently established and grown rapidly. By the end of December, it had 23 companies listed and actively traded. The market capitalisation is €0.3 billion and monthly turnover averaged €190 million during 2000.

Table 3.7 European small-cap alliance developments (February 2001)

Country	*SME capital market*	*Plans*
Austria	Austrian Growth Market	Unknown
Denmark	New Market	NOREX
Ireland	Developing Companies Market	Unknown
Belgium	EASDAQ/NASDAQ Europe	NASDAQ
Finland	NM List	NOREX
Norway	SMB List	NOREX
Sweden	OTC List	NOREX
Switzerland	SWX New Market	Unknown
UK	Alternative Investment Market	Unknown

Source: Euro NM, stock markets.

- *SWX New Market*: This is the SME capital market for the Swiss Stock Exchanges. It also has been recently established and has 17 stocks listed with a capitalisation of €8 billion and an annual turnover of just over €8 billion.

Small-cap regulatory requirements

The main difference between the listing requirements of NASDAQ the Neuer Markt is in coverage and float requirements. NASDAQ requires at least three market makers and a minimum public float of US$ 5 million. Neuer Markt has similar public float requirements but weaker coverage thresholds. As touched upon previously, this market maker requirement helps complete the virtuous circle that leads to increased investor confidence, information flow and liquidity. The figures indicate the research analyst coverage of NASDAQ quoted stocks by market capitalisation. The small-cap stocks have at least four research analysts covering each stock. This is far in excess of what is achieved in Europe.

A second key difference between US and European (especially continental) markets relates to disclosure. The openness of American markets reinforces investor confidence in the markets. And the effect may be more pronounced on small-caps because of the dearth of information that normally exists about them.

In terms of the publishing of quarterly results and of timely news pertinent to valuations, the US also has particularly strict regulations even on the NASDAQ small-cap markets, with regulations relatively strictly enforced by the New Deal-era SEC. By contrast, to take another European example, even the largest firms on the French markets are not required to release detailed quarterly results. In the 1999 merger and hostile takeover efforts of prominent French banks, all three banks involved in the struggles (BNP, Paribas, SocGen) only started publishing quarterly results as an appeal to shareholders in life and death struggles.

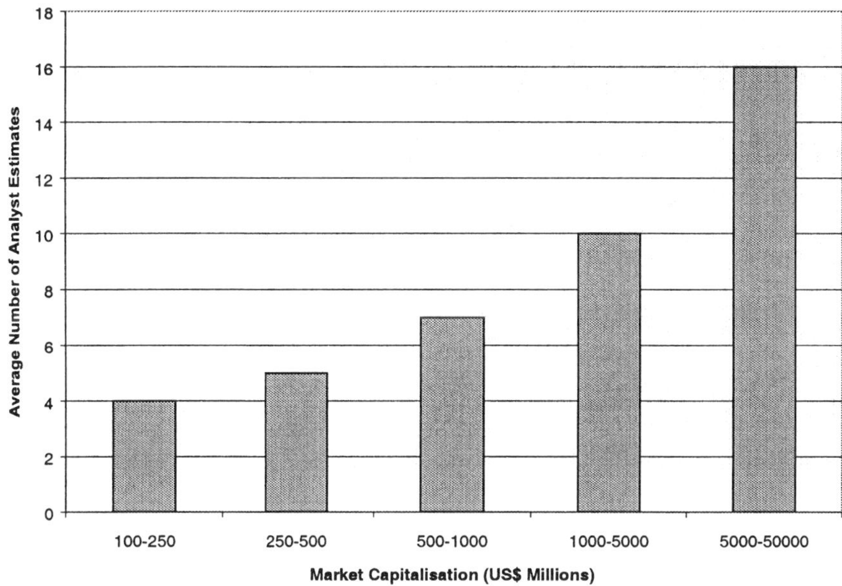

Figure 3.13 NASDAQ research analyst coverage (April 1999).
Source: NASDAQ, IBES Inc (April 1999).

The smaller firms on the Nouveau Marché may publish far more sketchy information about quarterly or timely events of importance to their firms.[20]

The assumption of those who would push for less-rigorous disclosure is not just that disclosure costs money and time, but also that constant disclosure pushes management towards shorter-term priorities. But disclosure laws in the US do not correlate clearly with short-term viewpoints by management or investors. Indeed, in the US investors are far *more* likely to buy companies, especially new companies, with high burn rates, low revenues, and low profits, but presumably strong long-term prospects.

NASDAQ small-cap

The listing requirements for the NASDAQ small-cap market are as follows:

- Net tangible assets of at least US$ 4 million or market capitalisation of at least US$ 50 million or net income, in the latest fiscal year or from two of the last three years, of US$ 750,000 million
- A public float of at least 10 per cent of the shareholder capital and a minimum of 1 million shares
- The market value of the public float to be at least US$ 5 million

- The minimum bid price to be US$ 4 million
- At least three market makers
- At least 300 shareholders holding at least 100 shares each
- An operating history of at least one year. If no operating history, then a market capitalisation of at least US$ 50 million.

Neuer Markt

Although there are some differences between markets, the European markets have similar entry requirements and admission procedures for listing companies and members. These are modelled on, or similar to, the Neuer Markt requirements. Where there are differences, these are indicated.

- Capital increase is a mandatory 50 per cent of issue volume or greater
- Minimum issue volume of €5 million
- Minimum 100,000 publicly traded shares
- At least 20 per cent of equity publicly offered (at least 25 per cent for AIM)
- Minimum shareholder equity of €1.5 million prior to listing (€2.0 million for NASDAQ Europe (formerly EASDAQ)). €1.1 million for AIM
- No minimum track record in terms of total assets, revenues or profitability (€3.5 million total assets for EASDAQ). AIM requires a track record of at least two years
- NASDAQ Europe requires each company to have at least 100 shareholders.

In addition to these entry requirements, listed companies are required to

- Produce accounts to IAS or US-GAAP standards with reconciliation to national standards
- Publish an advance corporate action calendar
- Produce quarterly unaudited interim reports
- Produce a prospectus in English, which is to EU standards and includes a statement of risk factors
- Report in English
- Undertake a 100 per cent shareholder lock-in for a minimum of six months or 80 per cent for a minimum of one year – the decision to be made by the market. NASDAQ Europe only has the former option. If a new entrant has less than a two-year track record then AIM enforces a 100 per cent shareholder lock-in for one year
- List in Euros
- Have a minimum of one sponsor and market maker
- Ensure that the maximum market maker spread is 5 per cent.

The admission process is through a formal market admission committee. A company wishing to be listed must be sponsored by an exchange member.

Membership requirements

Market members are required to be:

- Regulated investment firms
- ISD qualified (regulatory authority for dealers).

The Neuer Markt: the next NASDAQ?

This section provides details on the Neuer Markt to show how the market is turning into an impressive listing site that may soon gain more of a 'buzz' as the European answer to NASDAQ. In terms of regulations and disclosure, it offers many of the same attractions as NASDAQ. Yet it is a very different market, heading in unique and some ways opposite directions to NASDAQ, despite its successes.

The Neuer Markt became the most successful small-cap exchange in Europe in a matter of only three years. Although it is still dwarfed by NASDAQ, the latter has been in existence ten times longer. More interestingly, NASDAQ increasingly is moving to becoming a mid- to large-cap exchange with new issues going straight to the national market. This is in stark contrast to the Neuer Markt – which started out as mid-cap market and has moved to capture the small-cap high growth segment of new issues.

Background and development

The Neuer Markt came into existence on 10 March 1997 as a member of the Euro NM alliance of exchanges. It is operated under the auspices of Deutsche Börse Group. The exchange has grown rapidly over the few years it has been operating and now is the largest member of the Euro NM alliance. Together with the Nouveau Marché in Paris, the Neuer Markt represents most of the capitalisation and activity currently on the Euro NM exchanges.

The Euro NM alliance was established in response to a European Community initiative to increase the availability of risk capital for young high-growth companies in Europe. Although the NASDAQ Europe market had already been established, the limited success of this market encouraged policy-makers to recommend an alliance of markets providing pan European access with a physical presence in each country rather than a single physical market providing a similar service. As the Euro NM alliance has demonstrated, this formula has been highly successful to date.

The cornerstones of this success are as follows.

- *Crafting a market suited to the needs of young high-growth companies*: Companies with ideas and plans for new products, new services or new markets make a significant contribution to the development of European economies. These corporations require sufficient equity capital in order to finance their future growth.

  Outside capital in the form of debt is not the most suitable form of financing for an innovative fast-growth company seeking capital. On the one hand, it may not be able to fulfil the traditional criteria for creditworthiness. On the other, outside capital is expensive for a young company and the interest on loans places a strain on cash flow.
- *Creating new opportunities for European private and institutional investors to invest in high risk/high reward companies*: In Germany alone monetary assets are estimated to be some US$ 2.7 trillion.[21] The demographics of wealth are changing with a greater share held by a younger generation who are more favourably disposed towards investing in equities and also in higher risk/reward opportunities offered by young high-growth technology companies. The ageing population also means that the institutions that manage pension funds have an increasing need for investment opportunities which serve to cover pension requirements. In particular, owing to demographic patterns in the coming decades, the statutory pension insurance will need to be substantially backed up by private pension and equity plans. Investment funds and private investors are showing a growing interest in strong-yield investments.
- *Enabling transparency through private ownership*: The Neuer Markt was established as an entity under private law and thus the first of its kind in Germany. This has enabled Deutsche Börse to set groundbreaking and detailed rules. Neuer Markt sets far higher standards than the traditional first and second segment markets of the Frankfurt Stock Exchange, which operate under public law. The exchange operates fully in line with international standards.

  Transparency and comprehensive information are the key criteria influencing investment decisions. Specifically in the case of companies listed in Neuer Markt – which as a rule offers greater opportunities but entail greater risk. The disclosure requirements set by Neuer Markt are in line with international standards and therefore afford a real opportunity for communication. They include quarterly and annual reports in German and English drawn up according to IAS or US-GAAP as well as regular events for analysts and investors. The key conditions that have to be met in order to go public in Neuer Markt are as follows.

A company must:

- guarantee an issue volume of at least Euro 5 million
- assure a free float of at least 20 per cent (25 per cent is recommended). In order to ensure a strong spread of the shares and thus sufficient liquidity, issuers undertake to place at least 20 per cent of the ordinary share capital on the exchange
- issue exclusively ordinary shares
- appoint two designated sponsors for trading. The designated sponsors nurture sufficient liquidity in trading and support the issuer after the IPO on all aspects of internal regulations, disclosure requirements, and sales
- publish a sales prospectus in line with international standards
- forbid sale of shares by old shareholders for at least six months after the IPO
- sign the takeover code
- compile publications in German and English
- base more than 50 per cent of the issue on an increase in capital, if possible.

The key subsequent duties of companies listed in Neuer Markt include:

- publishing quarterly reports at the latest two months after the end of the respective business quarter
- publishing an annual report at the latest three months after the end of the business year
- preparing accounts in line with international standards based on IAS, US-GAAP or German Commercial Code and including a transitional statement
- disclosure of the shares held by the supervisory and management boards
- ensuring a broad mix of innovative and high-growth potential companies.

Companies typically listed in Neuer Markt are based in industries with a strong future and above-average long-term sales and earnings prospects, such as telecoms, biotechnology, multimedia or environmental technology. However, corporations from traditional sectors are also listing on the Neuer Markt.

Market trading

All shares listed on Neuer Markt can be traded between the hours of 8.30 a.m. and 5 p.m. on the electronic Xetra platform and on the floor of FWB, the Frankfurt Stock Exchange. Xetra is an order-based system and features automatic matching of investors' desired trades in a central order ledger. Xetra offers substantial advantages over floor trading

- market transparency during exchange price formation is enhanced
- market participants have equal, decentralised access to trading
- additional service functions are available

An additional trading dimension has been added through the creation of *designated sponsors*. A designated sponsor acts as a financial intermediary providing liquidity in specific equities; either voluntarily or on request, he posts binding bid and offer limits for the equities sponsored, in this way stimulating trading, with the result that the bid/offer spreads contract, as therefore does the time spent waiting to find a matching order on the other side of the order ledger. In this way, investors are reassured that it is easier to buy or sell sponsored shares. The goal is to avoid price discounts resulting from illiquidity.[22]

By virtue of the fact that they constantly monitor the market, designated sponsors acquire an expert knowledge on the equities in which they foster liquidity – and on the industries the companies in question are based in. Depending on what the designated sponsor offers and what the issuer requires, this knowledge can be used for further services such as in research, investor relations, publications, sales and market reports.

The small-cap market of choice for VCs

When it was first established, the Neuer Markt was seized upon by established Mittelstand companies as a means to raise additional capital and, to a lesser extent, realise gains. However, as can be seen from the table below, this picture had changed by the end of 2000 with the market being primarily an exit for VC backed SMEs. Average placement value has risen

Table 3.8 Key statistics for the Neuer Markt (to December 2000) (€ million)

Year	*No. IPOs*	*Avg. value*[a]	*Avg. sales*[b]	*Avg. staff*	*Main backer*			*Dec. 00 Avg. mkt-cap*
					VC	*Firm*	*Owner*	
1997	16	43	200	949	4	4	8	1,245
1998	45	36	66	470	13	9	23	249
1999	140	54	120	239	60	37	43	293
2000	140	99	43	206	n/a	n/a	n/a	366

Source: Own research, Neuer Markt.

Notes

a Average IPO funds raised in € million.

b Average of either annualised sales for IPO year or full year results for period prior to IPO. Converted using average rates for period of results. In € million.

from €43 million to €99 million. The size of companies, measured by sales at the time of listing, has declined from €200 million to €43 million and employees from 949 to 206. As interesting, the average market capitalisation, excluding the truly large companies that listed in 1997, has not declined. Rather, it has risen from €294 million for companies listing in 1998 to €366 million for companies listing in 2000. As previously mentioned, the proportion of VC backed IPOs has increased from 25 per cent in 1997 to almost half by 1999 (the latest year for which figures are available).

Further analysis and prospects for small-cap exchanges

One document from the European Union sums up some of the positive developments that are driving capital markets towards growth in Europe:

1 Pension funds and insurance funds are now growing steadily, although from a lower base than in the US, and public funds such as the EIB[23] are small but nonetheless have a positive role to play.
2 The Internet and web-based e-commerce is not growing as rapidly as in the States, but nonetheless Europe is the second largest Internet and e-commerce market.
3 A final very positive development, the launching of the Euro in 1999, is a big help, although the large-capital market of the UK is not yet a part of it. The removal of exchange risks between participating countries frees up money from larger institutions such as pension and insurance funds which, in the past, had to worry about currency matching requirements between assets and liabilities. Monetary union also is acting to reduce public deficits, thereby diminishing their 'crowding out' effect and lowering interest rates.[24]

However, in January 1999, the European Commission produced a report[25] that concluded despite successes and sources of strength, the EU markets are still hampered by

- fragmentation,
- institutional and regulatory barriers,
- taxation differences and burdens,
- the paucity of high-tech SMEs in the EU,
- human resources, and
- cultural barriers.

The Commission concludes 'culture is the main barrier to the development of risk capital markets'. It is argued that European investors are simply more conservative than American ones. Investments in deposits, the most risk-free investment available to most citizens, are emphasised more in

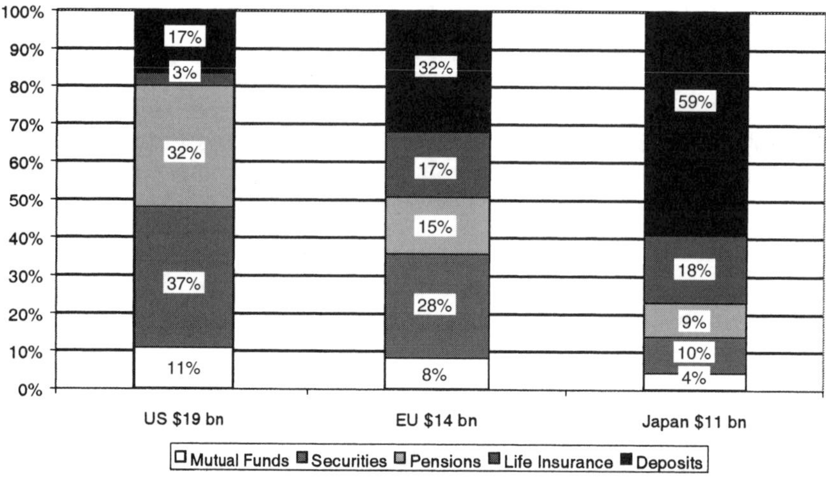

Figure 3.14 How people save in the largest economies (1996).

Source: European Commission: 'Risk and Capital Markets, A Key to Job Creation in Europe: From Fragmentation to Integration', *Euro Papers* (No. 32), January 1999, p. 10.

Note
Statistics are from 1996.

Europe than in the US, while investment in securities is lower. Differences are even more striking if one focuses only on the continent, but the figures below which include the UK, originally from Goldman Sachs and other sources, still demonstrate the point that while Europe is less conservative than Japan, it is far more conservative than the US in its investments.

Recent announcements from some of Europe's smaller national stock exchanges indicate that they are at last responding to the many competitive threats to their existence and, in the words of the Economist, 'Not a moment too soon'.[26] The members of the London Stock Exchange decided on 15 March 2000 to demutualise, giving the exchange a mandate to pursue mergers across Europe. On the same day, the Belgian Finance Minister, Didier Reynders, announced that the Brussels Stock Exchange was in the advanced stages of talks with its competitors in Amsterdam and Euronext amazingly represents the first cross-border merger amongst Europe's stock exchanges. Both London and Frankfurt have been looking for ways to safeguard their futures without too much success. The ill-fated proposed merger, announced in 2000, to form iX, that also was to involve NASDAQ Europe, was shortlived. Should it have gone ahead, Europe's two largest SME capital markets (Neuer Markt and AIM) would have been linked with TechMARK (London's high-technology segment) and the expertise of NASDAQ to form Europe's largest SME capital market.

The successful merger of Paris, Brussels and Amsterdam to form

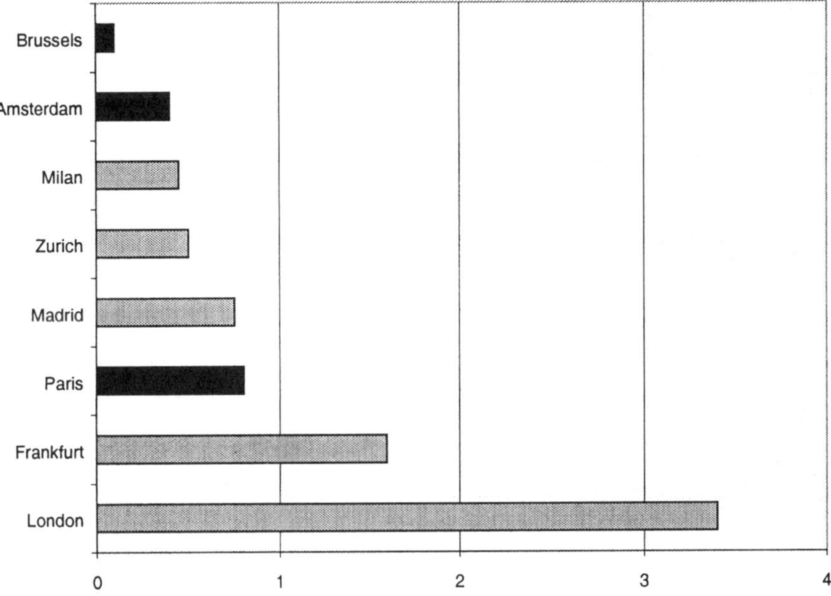

Figure 3.15 European stock exchange turnover (1999) (US$ trillion).

Source: FIBV, *The Economist.*

Note

Brussels, Amsterdam and Paris have merged to form Euronext, which would represent Europe's second largest exchange after London based on these figures.

Euronext shook up the sector and led to a number of bold proposals which to date have come to nought. For example, the OM group, owner of the Stockholm Exchange, made an audacious bid for the London Stock Exchange, following their successful takeover of the London Metal Exchange.

Conclusion: on culture, taxes and cycles

A very small portion of our ECMI-sponsored study is focused on the market for corporate bonds, but the European Commission provides statistics that reinforce its conclusion that culture is a significant factor, with the culture of bond investment in the US and Europe demonstrating fundamental differences. The US and European markets for corporate bonds are of almost the same size, with the US issuing US$ 510 billion of corporate bonds to Europe's US$ 598 billion (17 per cent more) in a sample 18 month period, 1997 through the middle of 1998. But the US investors are far more willing to invest in much higher-risk bonds than the Europeans. This could be due to sophisticated hedging tools for high-yield debt,

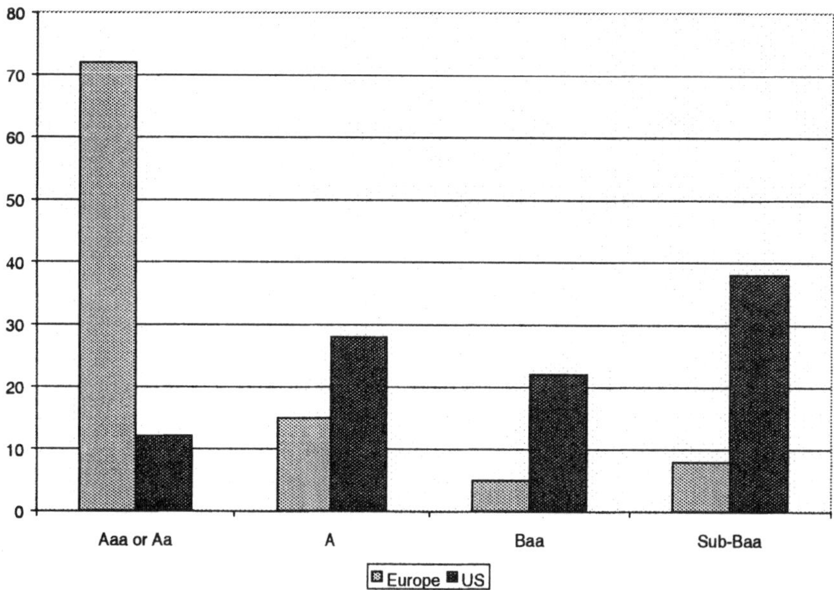

Figure 3.16 US/European corporate bond issues by classification (1998).

Source: European Commission: 'Risk and Capital Markets, A Key to Job Creation in Europe: From Fragmentation to Integration', *Euro Papers* (No. 32), January 1999, p. 9.

differences in bankruptcy law and, one would expect, cultural differences on each side of the Atlantic in willingness to tolerate bond risk. It may also be the result of the ever-increasing equity valuations, driving the more confident firms towards equity rather than debt issues in their hunt for capital.

As part of their analysis of different cultural views, the Commission also focuses on differing views about bankruptcy and the negative stigma attached to it in the EU. 'In the US the "right to fail" is considered a part of the learning process of a business.'[27]

It should also be noted that 51 per cent of small businesses held short-term loans in Europe, compared to 26 per cent in the US.[28]

So is culture at the heart of the matter when studying differences with respect to SMEs and public equity? We would concur with the EU findings and agree that culture matters. But we would emphasise the first three factors that the EU lists (fragmentation, barriers across markets and taxation) as at least as significant or more significant than culture. On the paucity of high-tech SMEs, for example, Europe is a leader in aspects of the communications revolution (wireless mobile telecommunications), the electronics revolution, machinery and manufacturing, etc., but not a leader in small-cap markets for these industries despite this.

As stated in our introduction, culture is a difficult variable to quantify, and methodologically testing its importance is difficult in any case, because it is frequently both a cause and an effect of any societal framework. But we would treat culture more than the European Commission is willing to as a 'residual variable'. Cultures are never fixed in stone, and apparent 'cultural barriers' in highly fluid capital markets might change dramatically with regulatory changes. This is suggested by rapid increases in the size of capital markets in the late 1990s on both sides of the Atlantic, and also by the dozens of successful high-tech, high-growth, 'high-flying' corporations with European owners and CEOs, perhaps still located in Europe, yet listing every year in the US. Another EU document on a similar theme discusses a 'rapidly increasing number of Europeans working in Silicon Valley'.[29] These people are born of the same culture as those who manage the European capital markets, but what attracted them to Silicon Valley's high-risk environment if not the potential for very significant returns and the freedom to go after them? These emigrants are risking more than many investors by uprooting families. Something more than culture must explain why they begin their careers or corporations in Europe, but then work and list elsewhere.

We would provide taxation systems as a variable that is certainly recognised as important by the Commission, but might receive more emphasis. The Commission acknowledges, for example, that equities are frequently penalised with higher taxation than low-risk investments, even though equities are more risky. It further posits that fiscal incentives such as the 401K in the US, individual retirement accounts (IRAs), employee stock ownership plans (ESOP), and other common features of the US equity market 'would not only develop risk capital markets but also help to develop an equity culture in Europe.'[30]

Similarly, we would argue that taxes on inheritance may dampen the market more than European politicians have so far realised. Since the European Commission's reports cited here frequently focus on capital markets as a means of job creation,[31] inheritance tax reform is discussed only as a means to get entrepreneurs to list: taxes on their heirs increase dramatically if the value of their firms are known to publicly increase. Hence, lower inheritance taxes could be a means to get high net-worth investors and ordinary individuals into public equity – a very public form of investment – and out of conservative deposit accounts in offshore tax havens and low-profile banks. Of course, some countries both have acknowledged and alleviated problems with inheritance tax burdens (e.g. Spain), but they are still very high, running well over 50 per cent of the value of the inheritance in many countries.

A discussion on stock options at the end of the same EU report contains a very useful, concrete proposal that might also change culture rapidly while changing the structure of the market. *Many tax regimes in*

Europe suppress the use of stock options. This should be changed as recommended in this excerpt of the commission report:

> For many high growth companies, issuing stock options is the best way to attract and keep the highly qualified personnel they need, without paying salaries they cannot afford. By contributing to increasing employees' involvement in the company, it can have a positive effect on productivity and profitability.[32]

Depending on taxation regimes, taxes on stock options can be payable on the grant of the option, on the exercise of the option and/or on the sale of the underlying shares. The beneficiary can be liable to income tax or to capital gains tax. Taxation before the sale of the underlying share will mean that the beneficiary becomes liable to tax before he receives any disposable proceed, while taxation as an income is often higher than as a capital gain. The most attractive taxation regime is when beneficiaries are only liable to capital gains tax at the sale of the underlying shares.

But in many European countries, taxation on stock options is too high to make them attractive for employees.[33]

As a note for further research, it would be useful to test whether US and European groups invest differently because of different wealth differentials at the highest incomes. Wealth differences in the US are higher than in Europe, although they are also growing in Europe. This may mean that US investors at the highest level of wealth simply have more money to invest at an earlier period, and hence they take a more long-term view towards risk and return. Further research on the demographics of high-risk investors is needed to judge correlations between very high net-worth and higher-risk investments. These correlations would be complex to carry out, because categories of investment such as 'pension funds' would need to be further broken down to examine the demographics of the pension fund owners; the demographics of 'private individuals' would only tell part of the picture.

Finally, it should be re-emphasised that all comparisons of trading blocs are affected by the cycles in different economies. The US just surpassed all records in early 2000 to enjoy the longest bull run in its history. Some (including Alan Greenspan) would argue that much of the capital markets activity is a chase for overvalued assets in an overheating market. Europe, by contrast, is only now picking up similar steam. To provide an illustration: in the first three quarters of 1999 alone, the average capitalisation of market flotations in the UK multiplied almost five times to over 350 million GBP. This would almost certainly guarantee that while in the past, most IPO money went to genuine SMEs, nowadays this is not the case at least in the UK: the capital markets are growing massively, as are the firms attracted to them. Paradoxically, as in the US, this may be bad for smaller-cap listings. On both sides of the Atlantic, the valuation explosion is for the privileged, large-cap issues, which are crowding out the smaller caps and perhaps even extending times to market: if so much capital is needed to attract attention, then firms have to wait until they can raise it.[34] At the same time, many of the trends witnessed in the US are also being demonstrated in Europe, and one should not be too decisive in any conclusions about greatly fluctuating, recent developments.

Notes

1 Michael Ashley Schulman, FIBV Working Committee Focus Group Study on SMB Markets. *Medium Size Business Markets*, August 1999, pp. 27–8.
2 Ibid., pp. 6–17.
3 Ibid., p. 9.
4 Ibid., p. 7.
5 Ibid., p. 11.
6 Utpal Bhattacharya, Hazem Daouk, Kelly School of Business, Indiana University Working Paper. *The World Price of Insider Trading*. Summarised in *The Economist*. 'Insider Trading: The Cost of Inequity', 22 January 2000.
7 The phrase 'common stocks' also includes American Depository Receipts and American Depository Shares – mechanisms by which non-US companies list on US exchanges.
8 Michael C. Carty, *Financial Planning*. 'Measure for Measure: The Dow is Outdated', May 1999.
9 'Raising Money: Let's List', *Computer Reseller News*, 8 July 1999, VNU Business Publications Ltd.
10 *The Economist*, Morgan Stanley Dean Witter. 'Fairy Tale', 26 February 2000.
11 James Dow, *The Scotsman*. 'When the Only Way is Up – Or Out Altogether', 20 October 1999, p. 11.
12 Bertrand Benoit, *Financial Times*. 'Professional Expenses Prove a Deterrent to Maintaining Stock Market Exposure', 31 August 1999.
13 *The Economist*. 'European Venture Capital – The Best Laid Plans', 25 September 1999.
14 John Jay, *Sunday Times*. 'Small-cap is Beautiful', 26 September 1999.
15 Initial feedback from Focus Groups organised by a share-ownership – lobbying group called ProShare on behalf of Inland Revenue indicates that companies are pleased with the scheme. Yet it is regarded as complex and potentially costly for sponsoring companies, which will need to appoint a third party to handle all the administration. Further, the programme is limited to 3,000 GBP worth of shares granted, and another 1,500 purchased (with matching grants by corporations) per employee per tax year. 'Tax on New Employee Scheme Too Complex ProShare', press release, 21 July 1999 – www.proshare.org.uk
16 'To Infinity and Beyond: Technology Shares', *The Economist*, 18 March 2000.
17 See glossary.
18 See glossary.
19 A firm has a 'measurable market cap' when NASDAQ itself has been able to measure it. Many of the smaller firms, and many firms with listings that are not common stocks, do not have market cap information provided by or to NASDAQ.
20 'Euro Impact on Business Practices', *Financial Times*, 21 May 1999.
21 Neuer Markt – www.neuermarkt.com, www.exchange.de
22 Designated sponsors are solely active in Xetra, and they must be available

throughout trading hours. Quotes posted by designated sponsors must fulfil specific quality standards set by Deutsche Börse. The strictness of the standards depends on the characteristics of the share, e.g. its volatility. If a designated sponsor does not duly discharge his duties in trading, Deutsche Börse can withdraw its admission to trading.

23 European Investment Bank
24 'Risk Capital: A Key to Job Creation in the European Union', Communication of the European Commission, SEC (1998) 552 final, April 1998, p. 10.
25 European Commission: 'Risk and Capital Markets, A Key to Job Creation in Europe: From Fragmentation to Integration,' Euro Papers (No. 32), January 1999, p. 10.
26 'European Stock Exchanges: Yes, There's Life!', *The Economist*, 18 March 2000.
27 European Commission: 'Risk and Capital Markets, A Key to Job Creation in Europe: From Fragmentation to Integration', *Euro Papers* (No. 32), January 1999, p. 13.
28 European Commission, 'Action Plan to Promote Entrepreneurship and Competitiveness', Luxembourg: EC, 1999, p. 10.
29 European Commission, 'Risk Capital: A Key to Job Creation in the European Union', Communication of the European Commission, SEC (1998) 552 final, April 1998, p. 11.
30 European Commission: 'Risk and Capital Markets, A Key to Job Creation in Europe: From Fragmentation to Integration', *Euro Papers* (No. 32), January 1999, p. 13.
31 European Commission, Ibid.
32 Ibid.
33 Ibid., p. 12.
34 Christopher Swann, 'Appetite for tiddlers on the wane', *Financial Times,* 2 December 1999.

4 Institutional policy towards SMEs in Europe and the USA

This study has grouped proposals to improve the business environment for SMEs around two basic themes: (1) industrial and educational policy, and (2) taxes and savings. The second theme seems more important than the first in terms of building stronger links between SMEs and capital markets, and in making both dynamic and successful.

With respect to tax and savings policies, the first section of this chapter provides some details on where they are most and least punitive to capital markets.

With respect to industrial and educational policy, this is often a focus of EU policy, and a later section of this chapter provides some detailed information on an important example, relating to EU structural fund donations. Yet it is argued here that planning or investing for industry – including policies to channel government investments into new sectors and to 'promote entrepreneurship' through government-funded university and corporate programmes focused on particular industries or management structures – are not likely to be as successful.

Industrial policies used to focus on heavy industries with massive economies of scale, where barriers to entry were high and governments may have been somewhat efficient investors. This is because governments themselves were knowledgeable owners, producers or contractors of infrastructure (railroads, canals), transportation (war or merchant ships and planes), energy (colonial or nationalised mines, refineries and distribution companies) and other heavy industries.

Now, services are more important than industrial goods to advanced economies, and even industrial companies, as we have seen, have become smaller and more specialised. It then becomes more and more difficult to pick winners in the highest value-added, 'high-tech' sectors or even to understand how to define the NACE[1] boundaries of those sectors or their companies. For example, in the USA, is Monsanto Corporation, a primary producer of genetically modified crops and seeds, in a traditional, low-growth industry (agriculture) or is it a biotech firm in a high-tech, high-value added, new industrial sector? Is AOL after the purchase of Time Warner primarily an Internet company or a publisher providing entertainment? Is its competition, Disney (entertainment/publisher/broadcasting network), Yahoo (ISP[2]), or AT&T (telecommunications/cable/ISP)? While companies become more specialised in the new economies of Europe and the US, the classification of their niche markets becomes more overlapping, dispersed and difficult to define.

Similarly, defining 'entrepreneurship' and who is an 'entrepreneur' is increasingly difficult, or at least an overly focused definition may be decreasingly correlated with the diverse sources of success in a given economy. For example, this study suggests that rates of start-up activity (comparatively low in Germany) may not be tied to VC investments in start-ups (reasonably high and growing in Germany), to successes of broader capital markets for SMEs (starting from a low base in Germany but growing very rapidly), or to successes of SMEs overall (impressive in Germany). Sweden, to provide another illustration, would profit from more 'entrepreneurial' start-up activity, but one reason start-up rates are low there may be that qualified 'entrepreneurs' (broadly defined) choose to create significant, new value for themselves and for industry by heading new business units of Sweden's disproportionately successful large firms. And from the perspective of capital markets, even VC markets, large-firm success is probably more important than small-firm success.

With increased international investment and decreased tariff and non-tariff barriers, defining national or even regional investment priorities is also more difficult than previously. This is especially true with respect to 'national' companies issuing securities, which are more likely than ever before to have significant international ownership even if they are small.

Hence, this study emphasises government tax and savings policies as a more important key to understanding capital market strengths and weaknesses for large or small-cap stocks. Favourable tax and savings policies are linked to dynamic capital markets as a whole and also correlate with stronger ties between capital markets and the SMEs that they sometimes overlook.

Tax and savings policies: EU and US

Focusing on taxation policy first, Figure 4.1, with OECD figures from 1996, demonstrates that the US has lower tax rates as a percentage of GDP than seventeen European economies.

The average tax burden in the EU (42 per cent) is much higher than that in the US (28.5 per cent), and while the average US tax burden remains more or less unchanged since 1970, the average has increased from 30 per cent to the current 42 per cent in Europe over the same period.

As important as the total tax burden are the origins of tax revenues. As can be seen from Figure 4.2, there are wide variations in these between countries within Europe.

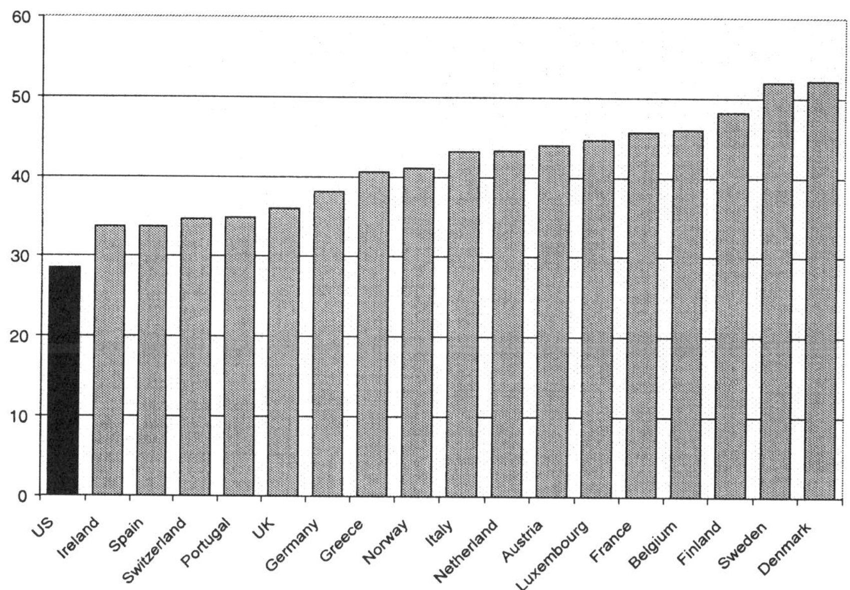

Figure 4.1 Total tax receipts as a proportion of GDP (1996) (percentage).
Source: OECD.

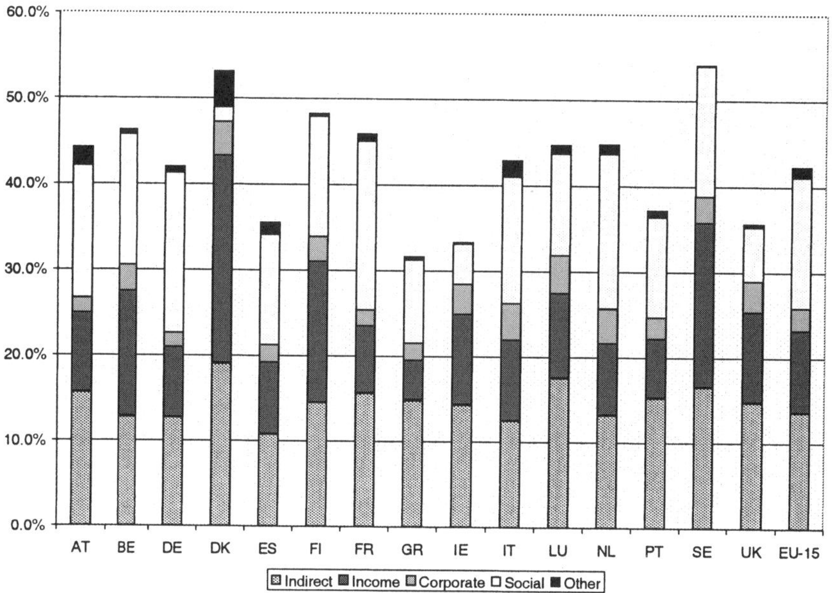

Figure 4.2 Origins of the tax burden (1990–6) (EU).
Source: *The Spectre of Tax Harmonisation*, Kitty Ussher, 1998, Centre for European Reform, p. 28, Table 6.

Further, higher employer social security contributions in Europe account for much of the differences on either side of the Atlantic.[3] The EU is even now considering a 20 per cent minimum tax on savings, to limit tax breaks and level differences in tax rates between states. This might directly impact on the nexus between individuals and capital market risk investments and make differences with the US system that much greater.

Taxes are employed by European welfare states in part to protect against higher trade risk (most countries have a larger percentage of their economies exposed to international trade than the US) and in part as mechanisms of equality and redistribution (again, reducing risks such as the threat of poverty from unemployment).[4] Direct or indirect taxes on corporations may also shield corporations from trade risk and other economic risks, but presumably it is the most successful corporations – those high-tech, high-growth companies profiting from equity market sales – that are least in need of this support.

It should be emphasised that there is no necessary correlation between the size of a welfare state and its level of efficiency, and there is no attempt to suggest correlation here.[5] Improvements in nutrition, health, housing and education can all raise productivity and efficiency while also increasing welfare, and larger economies appear to require larger governments to manage them. As a result, the dynamic liberal economies that are the most open to trade are also the economies with the largest government expenditure as a percentage of GDP.[6]

Yet the argument here is that punitive tax regimes may be particularly punitive to the highest-growth companies and the financial markets that serve them. Programmes emphasising equality and redistribution will necessarily impact on the greater success stories, which are comparatively taxed, the wealthier entrepreneurs, who will be looking for tax havens elsewhere, and the financial markets, which have as almost their sole goal the creation of large net capital gains. The comparatively low tax burdens in the UK and particularly the US help to fuel comparatively dynamic VC and public equity activity. Japan is also a country with low tax burdens compared to Europe, and even in the current, protracted downturn, it has the third largest capital market in the world, well ahead of Germany.

It should be noted that many of the largest states in Europe are also halting their growth or allowing their share as a percentage of the GDP to decline. Specifically with respect to Germany, although taxes as a percentage of GDP were higher in Germany than in the UK or the US, they did not advance in Germany through the 1990s. Countries where taxes actually declined as a percentage of GDP include Belgium, Ireland, Luxembourg, the Netherlands, Mexico, Norway and the United Kingdom. Many of the arguments above suggest a logical prediction: if the German regime can continue to hold tax rates down compared to, say, France, German VC activity is likely to pass French VC activity in the coming years. There are of course many other factors involved, but empirically, German VC

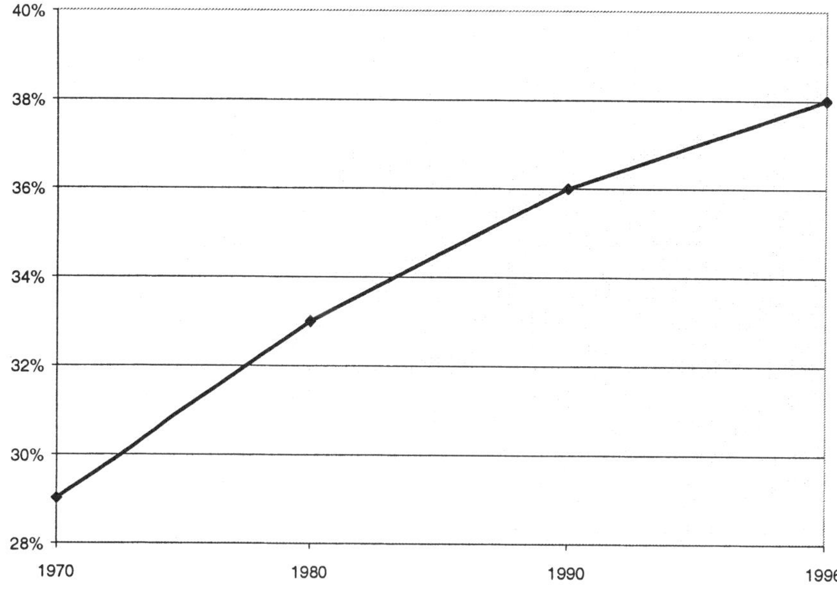

Figure 4.3 Tax rates in OECD (1970–96).
Source: OECD, 1998.

activity does appear to be growing at a faster rate. Stable rates in the US and declining rates in some European countries help to show why OECD tax rates generally, although still growing as a percentage of GDP, are growing at a slower pace than in previous decades.

The political focus on taxes in the US may be an issue of declining importance after two decades of public posturing by both parties, but this is in part a result of two decades in which the state's activity did not advance. A broad comparative perspective on many decades of capitalist activity would suggest that the correlation between the checking of state influence and the *general* economic boom is simply correlation and not causation; but the same comparative analysis would suggest stronger *causation* between comparatively low tax rates and the *specific* explosion in financial activity on both coasts that accompanied the good times. Indeed, with an anticipated budget surplus of over one trillion US dollars, US politicians are already talking anew about additional tax cuts.

Aside from the broadest taxation comparisons, in the US it can also be said that policy-making elites and their supporters are more ready to embrace risk than European authorities. The negative result may be greater inequalities, greater threats to be denied health care considered standard in much of the industrialised world, and other problems. But one positive result is of course greater spending power and, particularly for the wealthy, far greater resources to channel towards profitable investments, and lower tax punishment for successful investments.

Tax rates of direct interest to corporations and their stocks are difficult to measure, and the overall tax burden probably serves as the easiest proxy. This is because even taxes entirely levelled on individuals (e.g. income taxes) affect the free resources of individuals to buy stocks, and hence the price of domestic stocks in an economy. Taxes on goods and services also suppress consumption of products from corporations operating in that market, and hence revenues; and while taxes on corporations alone are not high in Europe, taxes on labour and other factors of production are rising dramatically. Much of this is also paid by corporations. Hence, if we discuss the size of the 'private' economy, per capita, it is much higher in the US than in Europe. This can benefit securities markets – both large and small-cap. Furthermore, while governments obviously re-invest most of the tax burden of a country back into the country in one way or another, the lower tax burden may particularly benefit the most successful firms that wish to sell public or private equity with the promise of particularly high after-tax profits.

Although we would again emphasise the 'big picture' – that is, the entire tax base – it is worthwhile to point out that taxes on corporate profits within the EU tend to be lower in the UK than in its largest EU competitor states. This may complement the UK's capital markets. Taxes on corporations also tend to be a bit lower than one might expect in Sweden and Finland (but not Denmark), and this may help to show why capital markets in Sweden and Finland (but not Denmark) are comparatively dynamic. Meanwhile, comparable tax rates in southern Europe are low, but again, southern Europe makes up for this with other taxes, for example, indirect taxes on labour and employment. Finally, Germany stood out at the end of the 1990s as the country that was, in theory, most ready to penalise corporate profits, and this may be harming German capital markets. This information is illustrated in the figures. However, when focusing on the effective tax rates, we see that Germany does not fare so badly – having rates that are less than for most of Scandinavia and only slightly higher than the UK. More importantly, when considering the contribution of corporate taxes as a proportion of GDP (see Figure 4.2), Germany with 1.7 per cent of 1996 GDP was the lowest of any EU country.

In terms of taxes on capital gains, they are also comparatively low in the US. This is true not only for the richest Americans, but also for the average employed worker. Tax discussions can get complex, but Table 4.1 generally demonstrates that tax rates on capital gains in the US now tend to be as low or lower than both overall tax rates (taxes as a percentage of all private production) and overall private income tax rates.

The low taxes on capital gains, combined with encouragement of directly funded pension schemes, 401K[7] plans and IRAs,[8] helps to show

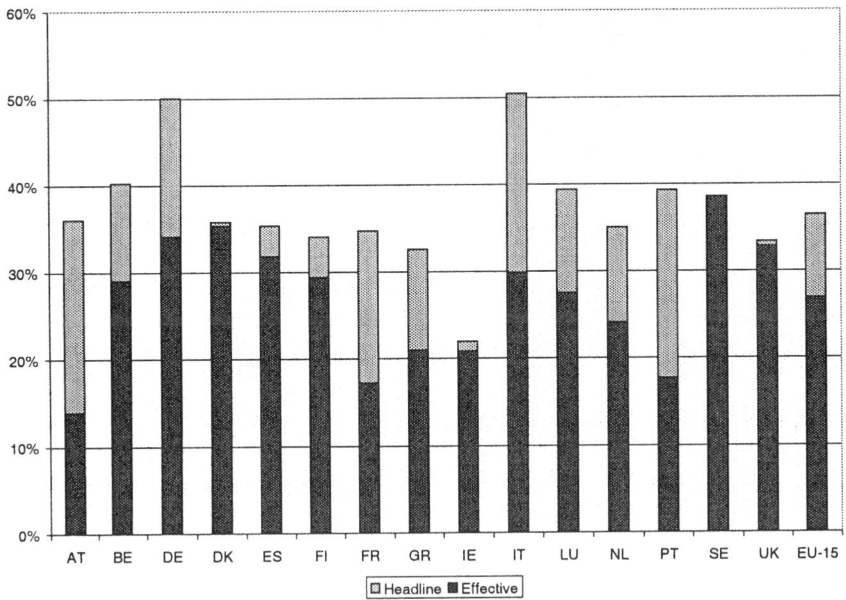

Figure 4.4 Effective vs. headline tax rates (1990–6) (EU).

Source: *The Spectre of Tax Harmonisation*, Kitty Ussher, 1998, Centre for European Reform, p. 14, Table 3.

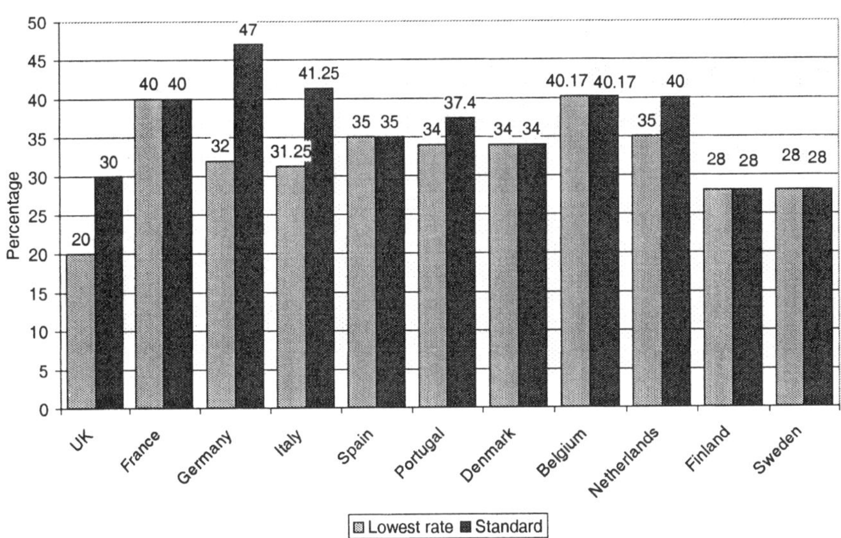

Figure 4.5 EU corporate tax rates (1999).

Source: *Taxation of Corporate Profits, Dividends, and Capital Gains in Europe*, Luxembourg: European Venture Capital Association, 1 February 1999, pp. 4–5.

Table 4.1 US capital gains tax rates (1999)

Source of net capital gain	*Tax rate (%)*
Net sales receipts	28[a]
Special rate for gains from certain SME activities	28[a]
Special rate for certain gains that are not reinvested	25[a]
Other gain (and regular tax rate is 28%+)	20
Other gain (and regular tax rate is 15%)	10[b]

Source: IRS. Data from 1999 – www.irs.gov.

Notes

a 15 per cent, if regular tax rate is 15%.

b 10 per cent rate applies only to the part of net capital gain that could be taxed at 15% if there are no capital gains rates.

how public policy may lead to diversified, dynamic markets for investment capital that fuel both financial institutions and capital markets. So while culture matters, government policy towards profits, unearned income and financial markets can be seen more as a force shaping investment cultures than as one shaped by them.

By contrast, shareholder capital gains taxes in Europe tend to be far higher. The highest rates tend to be lower in Britain and Italy than in

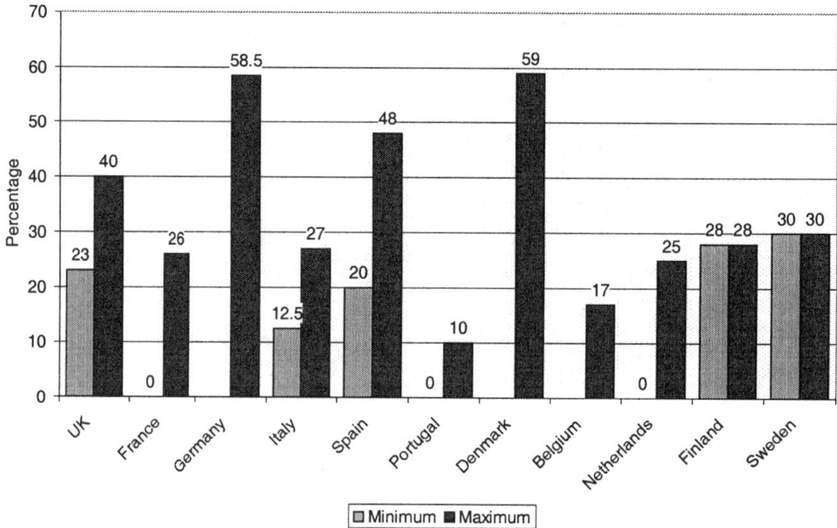

Figure 4.6 Shareholder capital gains taxes in Europe (1999).

Source: *Taxation of Corporate Profits, Dividends, and Capital Gains in Europe*, Luxembourg: EVCA, 1 February 1999, pp. 16–17.

Note

Minimum tax not listed if complex or not easily framed in percentage terms. Minimum taxes in France, Portugal and the Netherlands are zero on small-capital gains or when the individual either owns a low percentage of the company or small holdings of all companies.

France, Germany and Spain, but generally, rates tend to be higher in Europe than in the US.

The discussion below provides further background summaries of US and European policies, including less numerical discussions on taxes and savings. It then homes in on the European Commission's Structural Fund donations to illustrate some of the themes above with respect to other policies unrelated to savings. These donations are described as examples of government planning that might be less effective than encouraging a more favourable tax and savings environment through more private management of a larger savings pool. Finally, the conclusion discusses a World Bank survey of company executives worldwide and their attitudes towards government. Much of this study suggests reasons why the business environment in the US is *more favourable* than that in Europe for a secure and growing link between SMEs and capital markets. The World Bank survey does not focus directly on this issue, but in a discussion of policy, it seems worthwhile to note that US executives are actually more ready to *attack* their government as burdensome than European executives. This is particularly true with a focus on SMEs.

The United States

It is clear that the most important and powerful institutions of the US government have a more dramatic effect on the business environment for all businesses, including small businesses, then any activities of small business bureaux on a national or state level. The most important activities of the US government towards the general business environment, for example, are those that focus on macro-economic stability (e.g. the activities of the Federal Reserve); the rule of law (e.g. the efforts of the SEC and justice department to monitor fair trade, insider trading, monopoly activities, etc.); and other regulatory and tax burdens (Department of the Interior, Justice Department, Internal Revenue).

Nevertheless, the discussion here focuses on the US Small Business Administration (SBA). SME policy and support measures are defined and channelled by the SBA, which has an Office of the Business Advocacy that acts primarily as a One-Stop Assistance point. There is no similar institution catering for SME interests in Europe. Our qualitative research on US is largely based on the information and policy papers produced by this organisation.

SBA has proposed the following measures to ensure greater SME say in government:

- *Governor's Advisory Council*: SBA has proposed an active involvement at this level of decision-making. The council, formed by an executive order, handles issues such as legislation, regulations, programmes and other initiatives to boost businesses.

- *Legislative Committee on Small Businesses*: These cover commerce and economic development businesses. Past agendas have often left out SMEs. In order to correct this, SBA has proposed SME committees to spearhead new legislation in their favour.
- *Office of Advocacy/Ombudsman*: The proposal calls for the appointment of a person to speak within government on behalf of SMEs.

Other relevant recommendations with respect to regulatory environments are as follows:

- *One-stop assistance*: Each state is to set up an Office of Advocacy to act as one-stop centre for SMEs.
- *Compliance guidance*: These are publications summarising information on compliance and new regulations. The issues can cover environmental matters, financial reporting, etc.
- *Training regulators*: This component is required in order to improve efficiency in the definition and communication of legislation to SMEs.
- *Rule development and review*: The essence here is to put together small-business outreach and participation programmes, mainly through leadership forums.
- *Equal access to justice*: SMEs have greater problems than other businesses in fighting court actions and administrative decisions. These actions are expensive. States are required to alleviate this burden by enacting an equal access to justice act in favour of SMEs.

Small business development

To promote small business development, the SBA has proposed three programmes, each with a number of components:

- *Networking existing resources*: One of the main requirements seen by SBA is to undertake an inventory of all the SME assistance programmes already in existence within each of the states. It is interesting to note that a similar effort has also been suggested for the EU by associations and observers.
- *Access to capital*: With respect to access to capital, the SBA further promotes the following policies:
- *Micro-lending*: SBA proposes the establishment of a state-wide programme capable of extending loans of up to US$ 35,000 to SMEs employing less than 10 people and generate less than US$ 500,000 in revenues. Several states are on already on board.
- *Incubator*: Small business incubators are being put together across several states. These provide shared services and equipment to new businesses at affordable rents. The facilities include telephones with voice mail, fax, computers, business libraries, copy machines and con-

ference rooms. Sponsors can include both government and larger companies.

- *Seed and patient capital*: Through public-private partnerships, states are quickly developing venture funds making investments in SMEs, especially start-ups. An example of such facilities includes the Illinois Development Finance Authority, a fund with US$ 5 million making equity investments in early and seed-stage technology companies.
- *Small business loan guarantees*: There are several such guarantee facilities operational across states in the US. One of the most important and successful is the California Loan Guarantee Program. This includes loans, lines of credit and farm debt finance. SBA loan programmes provide mainly guarantees to banks making loans to SMEs. The facilities are structured mainly through a trust fund (supported by the various states).
- *Venture capital*: SBA actively promotes the concept of states setting up venture capital facilities to complement the work of private entities and other financial instruments covering debt and equity finance. The specific proposal of the agency is to set up 'capital access companies' with new federal regulatory exemptions. In addition to this proposal, SBA also canvasses greater state involvement in other facilities such as ACE-Net, an Internet-based securities listing service for investors seeking equity financing in the range typically falling below that of venture capitalists (i.e. US$ 25,000 to US$ 3 million).

Government procurement opportunities

SMEs are often barred from government procurement contracts. SBA, in common with the European Commission, has been promoting greater access by SMEs to these contracts. Government also benefits from greater competition. In addition to access, the agency has also been promoting the concept of prompt payment.

Summing up the US case

It cannot be said that the US is extremely coherent in its policy, or far more coherent than Europe. The SBA alone hosts a hodgepodge of programmes, ranging from managerial advisory work (e.g. the Service Corps of Retired Executives, or SCORE, which helps over 12,000 people provide advice in almost 400 chapters around the country) to VC-style support. But the majority of the work described above, besides guaranteeing or providing small commercial loans and buying some tiny equity investments, focuses on open administration and open access to information. In terms of real VC work, during the election year 2000, President Clinton proposed only $2.5 billion in venture capital assistance under the Small Business Investment Company (SBIC) programmes, plus $150 million for

Table 4.2 SBA loans and loan guarantees (1999)

Programme	*Number of investments*	*Value of investments (US$ billion)*
Certified Development Company Loan Programme	5,280	2
General Business Loan Guarantee Programme	43,639	10
Small Business Investment Company Programme[a]	3,100	4.2

Source: US SBA[b].

Note

a Both equity and debt.

b 'SBA Sets New Records In FY 1999 for Small Business Lending; Boosts Small Business Capital by More than $16 Billion', SBA Press Release, 20 October 1999. See www.sba.gov

new market venture capital companies, and $30 million in technical assistance.[9] Equity and debt investments for 1999 were similar, with the majority of the direct financial assistance granted to businesses in the form of loans or loan guarantees.

And it should be noted again that a focus on the SBA highlights financial support efforts that are not central to most of what the US government does for small businesses. The work of more powerful organisations than the SBA, such as the SEC or Justice Department, is de-emphasised here. At a macro-level (looking at the government's annual budget of more than $1 trillion), financial support is very low, the SBA budget is very small (less than $1 billion in operating expenses), and 'strategic planning' generally is not a particularly prominent aspect of what the US government does.

Closing this section, a chronology of US SME policy is provided below.[10]

1890	Sherman Anti-Trust Act, first anti-trust legislation
1911	Dissolved the Standard Oil Company
1914	Federal Trade Commission Act and Clayton Act, again anti-trust legislation to prevent price discrimination and thereby make US business more competitive
1933–42	390 anti-chain store bills considered as a reaction against US merger boom preceding the great depression.
1942	Small Business Act, to ensure small business participation in Second World War contracts
1953	Small Business Administration established through Small Business Act, originally as a temporary agency; made permanent in 1958

1958	Small Business Investment Act, creating small business investment division aimed at increasing the flow of long-term debt and equity investments to small businesses
1964	Civil Rights Act has a provision to provide aid to small businesses founded by socially disadvantaged groups
1968	Amendment to Equal Opportunity Act of 1964 requires the SBA to invest in urban, low-income, and unemployment-prone areas of the US
1976	Office of Advocacy, SBA is designed to reduce bureaucracy faced by small businesses
1976–82	The smallest businesses are made exempt from many regulations related to affirmative action, occupational health and safety restrictions, legal burdens in financial suits against the government, and paperwork burdens; also permitted to charge interest in late payments by federal agencies
1982	Small Business Innovation Research Act – provides assistance to small businesses with strong technological spin-off and research potential
1985	Export Administration Act, provides provisions to make obtaining export licenses easier for SMEs
1986	Patent and Trademark Office authorisation – programme to subsidise patent fees for small businesses
1988	Minority Business Opportunity Development Reform Program, establishes a Commission on Minority Business Development giving more aid to the establishment of minority-run small businesses
1991	Women's Business Development Act – creates 26 centres designed to provide long-term business education and counselling to women
1990s	SBA remains the most important policy instrument for SMEs under the Clinton administration: Its portfolio of business loans, disaster loans and loan guarantees rises to $45 billion US, and it claims to provide management and technical services to over one million small business owners by year 2000.

SME policy in Europe

The European Union is placing increasing emphasis on SMEs as engines for growth and stability. Although a topic covered under the Treaty of Rome, enterprise policy had not actually been accorded institutional form until recently. In the past few years the Commission, and certain member states, had tried to remove bottlenecks on the growth and development of SMEs. But most initiatives were far too disparate and ad hoc. As a result, most failed to reach the intended beneficiaries.

The situation has been partly corrected since 1995 with the publication of the *Madrid SME Policy Paper*.[11] This recognised SMEs as important job creators and thus a vehicle for tackling one of the priority social problems in the Union. The paper focused on basic market/policy imperfections and failings and suggested a set of measures to exploit opportunities. While there were pronouncements of policy towards SMEs before this Madrid paper, and there have been several since, this clearly established a framework for SME policy that has not changed substantially. We therefore discuss this paper in some detail.

The priority recommendations (later converted into Council Decisions) were as follows:

- Reduction of red tape
- Involvement of SME organisations in policy- and decision-making
- Finance
- Reduction of market distortions and inefficiencies
- Actions to promote research, innovation and training
- Encouragement of competition and internationalisation.

The EU is also actively encouraging the standardisation of operating rules for VCs and capital markets operators. The idea is to free up markets, make them more efficient and permit greater investment in VCs, which in turn will pull a greater deal flow among SMEs.

Simplification of the business environment

The main concerns of the European Union in this context are to cut back on administrative and regulatory red tape. Specific measures suggested to alleviate bureaucratic burdens are as follows:

- *Involvement in policy formulation*: This measure will integrate SMEs in the definition of Union policies.
- *Simplification of legislation*: Unnecessary administrative burdens and high compliance costs resulting from Community legislation affect SMEs. The Council has endorsed the concept of promoting appropriate measures aimed at eliminating these constraints. The same intentions appear in the context of VCs and capital market operators.
- *Transparency and administrative/regulatory framework*: The intention here is to set up programmes to disseminate best practices, especially in the area of administration (the aim being to achieve greater simplification and efficiency). The EU is also keen in promoting actions relating to the transfer of businesses and the retention of title clauses.
- *Framework for transnational operations*: The concept here is to promote the development of alternative methods of settling transnational disputes between enterprises. This is a major constraint to both SMEs and many of their financiers. The Union is trying to

address part of the problem through the European Economic Interest Grouping Programme (REGIE).

Financial environment improvement

This is one of the key areas identified for support by the EU. It affects SMEs and their fund providers. The specific measures suggested are as follows:

- *Access to loan and risk capital*
- *Reduction of late payment periods*
- *Development of improved financial instruments*: SMEs by definition have a comparatively narrow capital base, high dependence on internally generated funds and considerable working capital needs to support investment and sales. The EU is conscious of the need to come up with new and more innovative financial products capable of easing cash flow pressures. *Factoring and credit insurance* are two products that may well meet the bill in this context. Quasi-equity instruments will also be important contributors to the well-being of companies. The US is much more 'aggressive' with the use of financial instruments. It makes greater use, for instance, of specialised equipment and vehicle finance, export credits, leasing, mortgages and longer-term credit instruments. These facilities complement and make more efficient the use of capital contributed by all the SME sponsors, including the VCs.
- *Taxation regime*: In addition to the taxation problems mentioned above, the EU has argued that the VAT system is also unfriendly to SMEs, especially its cumbersome administrative arrangements. This aspect affects young businesses much more than those already well established. A significant improvement measure would be the introduction of a system based on the *principle of origin*.[12] Besides the work of the Commission, the member states themselves could carry out basic fiscal reform to aid the sector. Specific measures could include tax relief on the establishment of new SMEs, tax incentives to *business angels* fostering MBOs, and breaks on investments by private equity and venture capital companies.
- *Development/improvement of framework conditions for capital markets*: The EU is very keen to develop new markets to house and trade SME stocks. The Commission and the venture capital industry have been instrumental, for instance, in the setting up of EASDAQ (now NASDAQ Europe following its takeover by NASDAQ in March 2001) and subsequently Euro NM. There is no doubt whatsoever that establishment of *liquid and successful markets* are a key factor to unlocking the potential of SMEs in Europe. The lack of liquidity, uncommon rules and high costs are negative aspects of most of

the junior markets set up in recent years. Some enjoy tax breaks on trades (e.g. Germany), while others actually face stamp duties (AIM). Lack of consistent benchmarking and information are other obstacles to the growth of SMEs, VCs and markets. An improvement in market conditions will lead to an increase in fundraising at the level of VC and hence to an increase in the value and volume of placements in markets across all sectors.

Europeanisation and internationalisation of SMEs

Specific actions that are required and expected in this area include the following:

- *Information services*: The proposal calls for a Community-wide information service for SME enterprises. The EU has suggested a Euro info-centre network as a possible 'first-stop shop' capable of directing requests to the most appropriate service providers, including EU member country national services. Some of the information 'items' might be the subsidy programmes available from the EU, the list of venture capital companies and their track record/investment criteria and the banks with an interest and expertise in SME financing.
- *SME policy actions and networks*: There is a need (and the EU has agreed in principle to start) SME promotion campaigns and European business weeks. The effort should also include the establishment of business partner-search networks – covering both confidential and non-confidential information.
- *Partnership programmes*: The concept here is to develop instruments capable of fostering direct contact between SMEs themselves. There is a need to cross borders much more easily and cost effectively. A Europartnership and Enterprise Programme is envisaged by the EU for this purpose.
- *Subcontracting partnerships*: The EU proposes a set of actions aimed at promoting subcontracting of SMEs between different countries. This is an interesting idea, although the actual implementation might be difficult to achieve. The service sector (e.g. consultancy) is suitable for this type of programme. High-tech and industrial operators may find the concept somewhat more difficult.
- *Internal market access*: There is a need to facilitate the involvement of SMEs in public sector contracts. Many tenders for the delivery of goods, works and services simply exclude smaller companies. Criteria such as a strong capital base and high turnover are limiting factors. The US is much friendlier to SMEs in this respect. Public sector contracts (if paid on time) can open the way SME take-off. These contracts can often be extended and can thus provide the necessary cash

flow and credibility to expand product coverage, technology and size. A sound and reliable business pipeline will make it easier to attract VC finance and growth.

- *Internationalisation*: SMEs in Europe are highly relevant to businesses in various emerging markets. They have not only expertise but also appropriate technology. Many countries in the new transition economies of Eastern Europe and the CIS, for instance, would benefit greatly from SME involvement in contracts and investments. But the selection criteria and financing instruments of many financial institutions backing beneficiaries in emerging markets act as a deterrent. For example, projects funded by some multilaterals have a clear bias towards larger foreign companies as strategic sponsors. Although this is a sound practice (since it reduces risk), it would also be encouraging to see more SMEs accepted as sponsors. In fact, these banks would be truly 'additional' with their financing. Large multinationals have their sources of finance and political risk coverage points.

SME competitiveness and access to research, innovation and training

SME development in Europe requires greater support in the fields of research, innovation and training. This is recognised by the EU, which envisages the following specific programmes to aid SMEs:

- *Pilot schemes*: The EU plans schemes to introduce best practices and test specific approaches in business through pilot schemes. The key areas of support target new-technology based firms (NTBFs). There is also a recognition of the need to stimulate the use of information technology by SMEs, most likely fostered through exchange programmes and better means of access.
- *Management support*: The EU is planning to identify and test positive approaches in the area of training, mainly through the exchange of good practices and by introducing management improvement programmes. Measures resulting in better business plans, familiarity with corporate governance, strategy development and stronger financial controls, will facilitate VC financing.

Promotion of entrepreneurship and support for target groups

SMEs would also benefit greatly from the development of a business culture and entrepreneurship based on best practices. There is a need to support in particular areas conducive to greater SME involvement – including crafts and micro-enterprise, commerce, distributive trades and IT. Women and young business entrepreneurs are some of the beneficiary support groups earmarked by the EU. Initiatives include SCREEN (electronic networking of enterprises) and BEST (dissemination of best practices through websites, conferences and a network of experts).

Policy instrument improvement

The EU is planning to consult more regularly with all organisations connected with SMEs. This is a welcome and much needed move. The aim is to learn more about the sector and to involve representatives in the definition of policies. Specific plans already include improvement of statistics; European Observatory for SMEs; studies and databases concerning SME policy measures.

Financial instruments

The European Union has put together, or encouraged a number of financial instruments geared to SMEs. These are more numerous than those available in the US. But also more haphazard. Although each of the facilities is welcome, some are more relevant than others. The proliferation of instruments can actually be counterproductive. There is a need for rationalisation, better management and access. There is also a need for the removal of exclusion clauses by which SMEs are sometimes prevented from receiving assistance from two bureaux simultaneously. Below we summarise the most important facilities currently available from the EU. Some support SME development, others are intended to finance exports and trade and several focus on training and research.

EU regional funds

The most important products are the following.

Structural funds

The most important structural funds include the European Regional Fund (ERDF), the European Social Fund (ESF) and the European Agricultural Guidance and Guarantee Fund (EAGGF). These funds are intended to reduce differences between regions in the EU and bring about greater cohesion and economic welfare. SMEs are clear indirect beneficiaries. The products include subsidies covering up to 15–85 per cent of investment plans/budgets. These funds are difficult to access and requests are put forward by national and regional governments rather than companies.

Community initiative for SMEs

The structural fund has an important component directed at SME financing. The most important priorities of this fund are as follows:

- Improvement of SME production and organisational systems
- Environmental protection and rational use of energy
- Co-operation between SMEs, research centres and universities
- Access to markets
- SME network development
- Skill upgrading
- Access to credit and equity finance.

The facility is interesting but quite difficult to access. In common with several other EU financial products, one of the main constraints is the actual bureaucracy associated with accessing them. A further dichotomy is that SMEs are the least prepared of all the potential users to confront this problem. Nonetheless, we are not aware of any plans to modify SME access procedures.

European Investment Bank facilities (EIB)

The EIB finances investments in regional development aimed at protecting the environment and improving industrial competitiveness, including the European telecommunications network. The bank applies two financial instruments for this purpose: (1) global loans for SMEs with fixed assets standing at less than €75 million and less than 500 employees and; (2) EIB low rate loans for SMEs aimed at creating jobs.

SMEs can only benefit indirectly from EIB financing facilities. The latter operates through bank to bank credit lines to financial intermediaries in the operating member countries. These financial intermediaries are then responsible for on lending to the SMEs – based on the submission of business plans and subject to specific criteria on capital, loan amount and a tight guarantee package. The latter can exceed 150 per cent of the loan amount. This is quite restrictive on most SMEs.

European Social and Cohesion Fund

This facility can be used to finance training and job creation. But government rather than the SME sector drive the utilisation. The Fund is applicable in countries such as Ireland, Greece, Portugal and Spain.

Enterprise-specific financial instruments

The most important instruments of this nature available from the EU are as shown in Table 4.3.

Other special financial support programmes

Other programmes are geared towards an incredible variety of goals through a plethora of bureaux. These include programmes to support

Table 4.3 SME loans and loan guarantees (1999)

Fund	*Description*
Eurotech capital	This facility is aimed specifically at SMEs and focuses on developing transnational and high-tech projects. About 14 venture capital companies benefit from this facility within the EU. The latter may invest a minimum of €50 million within the programme. The venture capitalists also undertake to finance up to 20% of a given transaction out of their own resources. This instrument is relevant and useful. It represents one of the first facilities sponsored by the EU targeting capital as opposed to debt finance.
EIF	The EIB and 76 financial institutions operating within the EU have established a major fund with two components: (1) Trans-European Networks (transport, energy and telecommunications) and (2) SMEs, especially for those operating within a specific supported geographic region. The fund provides *guarantees* to banks and financial institutions financing SME-led projects. The facility supports, therefore, debt rather than capital finance.
Seed capital	This fund has 24 contact points. Its objective is to promote the creation of SMEs. The beneficiary firms must meet a set of criteria, of which the most important are: that they must be legally and financially independent; investment in venture capital should not exceed €50,000: annual turnover should be less than €100,000; the number of employees should be less than 10; and the value of capital should not exceed €1.5 million. The fund is useful but its impact on the SME sector is limited because of its size, access difficulty, paperwork and eligibility criteria.

Source: European Union.

trade with Eastern Europe and developing regions, programmes to support SME partnerships and information exchanges and programmes with exotic dot-com type names supporting specific high-tech industries and industrial research.

Table 4.4 Other special financial support programmes

Programme	*Description*
AL-Invest, 1996–2000	Facility supporting industrial co-operation and investment in Latin America through exchanges, technology transfer, etc., between SMEs.
Asia-Invest 1996–2000	Support to SMEs operating in Asia. Provides finance for meetings, business priming and dissemination of information on potential investments
Europartnership	Co-operation programme between SMEs carried out in less advanced countries and in projects involving agricultural and industrial development. Open also to Baltic and Mediterranean countries.
Interprise	An initiative to encourage SME partnerships.
European Group of Economic Interest	Legal instrument to support transnational co-operation. It supports SMEs submitting business proposals under tenders
JEM	Promotion of trade and investments between Asia and EU. Helps with the establishment of links between companies, including SMEs.
Exprom Japan	Promotes export initiatives to Japan – through management training, promotion campaigns and SME-based agreements.
Promotion to Third Countries	Promotion of SME exports to third countries. Finances exhibitions, seminars, missions and market studies. Specific to some sectors and SMEs.
ECIP 1996–2000	Assists with the creation of joint ventures between EU SMEs in Latin America, Asia, North Africa and South Africa. Covers up to 50% of the required investment.
EDF	The European Development Fund is used to reinforce SME companies operating in Africa, Caribbean, Pacific and Ultramarine Territories by helping to develop partnerships with SMEs.
Centre for Industrial Development	Connected to EDF and SMEs operating in ACP states. Provides funding facilities and contacts through joint venture contracts, sub-contracting and licensing.
Stabex	Co-operation programme between the EU and ACP[a] states. The aim of the programme is to fund the effects of

continued

Table 4.4 continued

Programme	*Description*
	declining exports to the EU by ACP countries. In the process it finances programmes, including the provision of insurance against potential recession. EU companies benefit indirectly or directly if located in one of the recipient countries.
Sysmin	The programme focuses on the mining sector in ACP countries. It provides financial support to maintain production levels or support diversification efforts by SME companies.
Meda	Co-operation programme targeting Mediterranean countries. Activities focus on SMEs and can be of a commercial, financial, social, technical, industrial and even political nature.
Phare	Technical assistance programme funding development projects in Eastern Europe. Also provides grant finance to technical assistance mandates financed by EBRD[b] and EIB.[c] Mandates involve only EU advisory firms, most of which are SMEs.
Tacis	Similar programme to Phare but with a focus on the republics of the Former Soviet Union.
Jopp	Integrated within Phare and Tacis. It supports the establishment of joint ventures between EU SMEs and companies in Eastern Europe and the CIS. It funds business plan preparation and initial project development.
The Office of Connections of SMEs	Supports SMEs wishing to contract an SME from another country.
Business Co-operation Networks, BC-Net	Groups 460 consultants to help find partners for SMEs.
Euro-Info-Centres EIC	Dissemination of information through 210 sites.
ECEI	Commercial and technical assistance to SMEs to support specific projects, especially those related to R&D.
IBEX	International buyer's exhibitions aimed at establishing contacts and relationships between firms.

Notes

a African, Caribbean and Pacific.

b European Bank for Reconstruction and Development. Multilateral agency established by international community working with emerging markets of Central and Eastern Europe, Former Soviet Union and Central Asia.

c European Investment Bank. Investment banking arm of the European Union.

Information technology

The most important programmes available under this heading are as shown in Table 4.5.

Table 4.5 Information technology related special financial support programmes

Program	*Description*
Brite-Euram 3	This programme targets the design of eco-compatible products for production systems combining technology and human factors.
Normalisation, Measurement and Climate	Programme aimed at improving competitiveness in Europe, across all sectors and industries. It promotes research and system harmonisation. Focuses on less favoured areas and SMEs
Environment and Climate	Research theme and finance via SMEs
Mast 3	Focus on marine systems, promoting harmonised policies worldwide.
Biotechnology	Focus on living cells in order to make progress in agriculture and industry. Various Community programmes in place, some benefiting directly SMEs.
Biomed	Health industry development support scheme. Focus on disease programmes.
Agriculture and Fisheries	Scientific research on rural and agricultural development.
Non-Nuclear Energy	Finance for programmes targeting optimum energy supply mixes.
Transport	Development of a European transport policy. Funding of research to integrate results of programmes.

Table 4.6 SME-driven financing schemes

Programme	*Description*
Exploratory Subsidy	This finances SMEs, with up to 500 employees but with a turnover below €38 million, wishing to join a European Research programme. Funds can be used to prepare feasibility studies and detailed research proposals.
Technology Stimulation: Co-operative Research Craft	Financial support for SMEs with technical problems requiring research infrastructure and where the SME would benefit from the support of universities, research centres, etc.
Innovation: Diffusion and Valuation	Aimed at Research and Technical Development (RTD) operations. Funds the use by SMEs.
Validation and Transfer of Technology	Funds the dissemination of research results to SMEs.
Innovation Relay Centre	Helps enterprises participate in the results of RTD, irrespective of sector of origin.

Applied research

Several programmes in operation focusing on SMEs: Eureka (co-operation between SMEs and research bodies); Life (environmental project support); SAVE (energy management to contribute to environmental protection by acting on CO_2 and other harmful gases); MLIS (addresses linguistic barriers); Info 2000 (multimedia products and services); and Ten-Telecom (addresses telecommunication networks).

Education and training for SMEs

The European Union runs a number of programmes tackling SME requirements in these areas. The most important of these are Adapt (a transnational initiative helping individuals respond to changing requirements in the labour market) and; Leonardo da Vinci (measures addressing training systems and linguistic skills).

In summary

The European Commission claims that high-growth companies spend over 40 per cent more on process innovations than low growth companies. They also spend almost 40 per cent more on developing new products and services. Still, the problem of paperwork re-emerges in its 'Action Plan to Promote Entrepreneurialism and Competitiveness': The cost of filing and maintaining a patent is six times more expensive in Europe than in the USA, and this is why two-thirds of the 170,000 SMEs in Europe that invent new products or processes do not apply for patents.[13]

Case study: the EU Commission's structural fund donations

In this section, we provide some details on the programmes of the EU that most resemble the loan guarantees, loans and equity purchases of the US Small Business Administration. Then we highlighted some possible problems with the EU programmes, which are larger and more prominently emphasised than those of the SBA. Finally, we present some comparisons between the two sets of programmes. Whilst the EU provides more money to SME investments despite the far smaller size of the EU government, it is argued that the money may be poorly utilised – and the US may be wise to significantly downplay similar programmes in its priorities towards SMEs. Tax and savings policies, and an open regulatory environment, seem far more worthy of emphasis.

The EU outlines six objectives for its structural funds, all of them tied to problems of employment in the EU:

- *Investment in basic infrastructure*, in particular in favour of trans-European networks (TENs).
- *'Improving the productive environment'* and the international competitiveness of small firms, in particular in the service sector (boosting the information revolution and quality management).
- *'R & TD and the information society'*: The guidelines require special attention to be paid to aid measures for technological innovation.
- *'Environment and sustainable development'.*
- *'Human resources and education'*: 'Attention is drawn once again to the need to move from a passive to an active employment policy.'
- *'Equal opportunity for men and women'.*[14]

Countries and regions funded

The largest recipients of structural funds are the southern European states, Germany and France. Much of this money in all cases goes to the poorer regions of these countries: eastern Germany, Spain outside of Madrid, central-southern France and southern Italy.

While most of the money is geared towards poorer areas, some goes to special scientific development zones, with contributions geared more towards the kinds of firms and areas that might interest capital markets. Developmental zones and the types of firms funded there include the following:

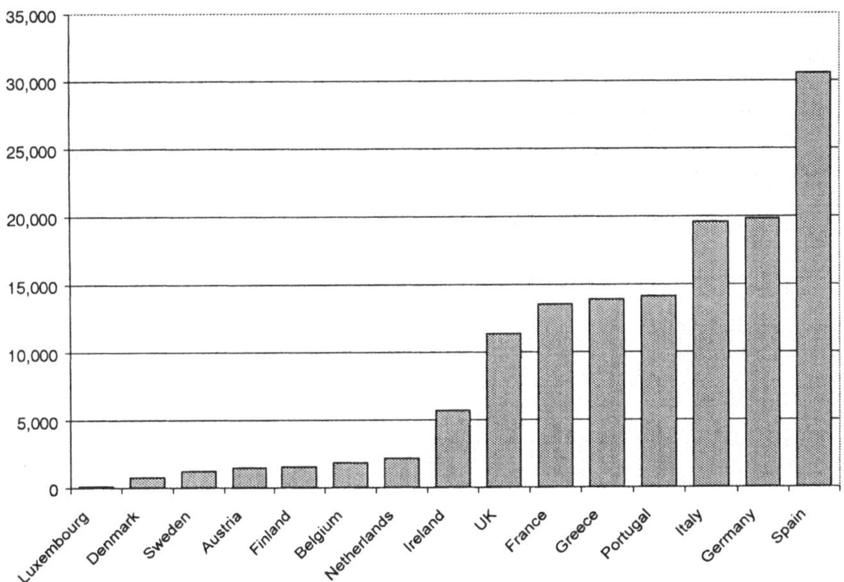

Figure 4.7 EU structural fund assistance (1994–9) (€ million).

Source: European Commission, *The Structural Funds in 1997: Ninth Annual Report*, Luxembourg: 1999, p. 30.

- *Belgium*: Projects funded include a Crachet Science Park and a Eau d'Heure project that supposedly helped promote the stated goal to fund enterprises employing over 20 staff and concentrating on 'frontier technology and high value-added sectors'.
- *Denmark*: A 'Nordjysk Innovation' project has been set up in North Jutland bringing together the Novi science park, the University of Aalborg, and two technological information centres in the region.
- *Germany*: A research and technical development project has been started at the Berlin-Buuch campus designed to qualify scientists and technicians in modern biomedicine and biotechnology with a view towards their future employment in private industry.
- *Greece*: In Crete the ERDF supports a science and technology park set up by one of the best-known Greek research institutes, FORTH, to make the intelligence of the universities and others widely available and diversify the island's agricultural/marine economy.
- *Spain*: In Malaga in Andalucia the ERDF has been helping since 1992 to finance a technology park now home to dozens of firms. Scientific organisations in the park include the Andalucian Institute for Advanced Automation and Robotics, the Andalucian Centre for Documentation on Standards and Manufacturing, the Andalucian Image Processing Institute and the Regional Institute for Millimetric Waves. This centre also hosts the head office of the International Association of Science Parks (IASP), which covers some 200 parks, 4,000 firms and 800 research centres throughout the world.
- *France*: In Nord/Pas-de-Calais, the ERDF has financed a European Business and Innovation Centre at the University of Valenciennes to encourage contacts between universities and the small business sector, groups often seen as distant. The centre is a forum for meeting and sharing between business executives, managers, university research workers and service sector managerial disciplines, including some financial services.
- *Italy*: On Lake Maggiore in Piedmont, the ERDF has part-financed the Piedmont technology park ('Tecnoparco'), the first of its kind in northern Italy, providing research and experimentation laboratories in addition to common services for the handful of enterprises established there.
- *The UK*: In Merseyside the business university project managed by the University of Liverpool is intended to help local firms and assist graduates of the university to find jobs in them.[15]

Yet even these programmes, geared towards firms that are not overly small and regions with a potential for high-tech momentum, may not be ideal. In comparison to the US, for example, funds remain scattered and don't necessarily go to the areas with the greatest dynamism even within disparate countries. They are also run largely through official channels with limited private involvement in selection of 'winners' or in distribution.

The structural funds would profit from far greater concentration of resources towards a few high-tech, high-finance centres, probably in suburban locations or university towns, where street signs, government, financial and educational services are provided in several international languages. This might be politically more difficult than current policies – dispersing funds country by country – but far more effective at achieving some of the EU's objectives. The EU's goal of focusing on a fair distribution among member states' citizens would then concentrate instead on ensuring that a particular development centre for business ideas and financing was international in focus and accessible to member states' citizens. This policy might also, to a limited extent, encourage greater labour mobility, which would aid employment policies. As an example, the suburbs of Munich or Berlin, which already contain the international or domestic headquarters of a vast number of large and small firms in high-tech or biotech sectors, might be appropriate locations for European (as opposed to German) corporate parks, VC stands, conferences and educated labour mobility. Cambridge, England and the Basque region of Spain are similar, regional pockets of SME-entrepreneurial-technologically developed dynamism.

More importantly, they require greater use of financial intermediation, matching funds for private citizens' or VC firms' financing initiatives, or other efforts to diversify governing funding methodologies themselves should be encouraged. Such efforts tied to broader ideas about 'reinventing government' and privatising government services, might spark more private initiative and might go a very long way towards quality control and the achievement of longer-term objectives.

Generally, encouraging people to invest 1 per cent of their savings in a co-operatively run mutual fund (perhaps with government matching funds), rather than collecting and investing the money for them through legislated taxes, might go a lot further towards meeting community objectives promoting more dynamic high-growth sectors and labour markets. If the goal is to promote the welfare of people in the poorest areas of the EU, then the matching funds could go to those areas, encouraging a broader sector of the local populations to manage their money more effectively and to invest collective funds, however small, in local (or preferably nationally or regionally concentrated) private enterprises. Average citizens would then have a significant stake in ensuring that the funds are efficiently distributed, and the skills gained through the financing and management of recipient projects might surpass current achievements on employment, labour markets, SME development and structural adjustment.

Total fund values

> The Community . . . specifically earmarks 15 to 20 per cent of the total resources of the [Structural] Funds (e.g. €23 to €30 billion) for measures to encourage small firms to improve their productive facilities and economic environment.[16]

In the newer member states (Austria, Finland and Sweden), concentration on small firms is substantially higher. Figures provided below are the total value of the EU's structural funds (for large and small firms) from 1994 to 1999:

Table 4.7 uses this data to illustrate that by far the largest fund is the European Redevelopment Fund. This and the European Social Fund focus to some extent on post-industrial structural adjustment, whereas the European Agricultural Guidance and Guarantee Fund and the Financial Instrument for Fisheries Guidance focus on areas dependent on agriculture and fisheries.

A critique of the EU structural funds

It is recognised that one primary function of these funds is to redevelop the poorest regions of Europe. Another is to improve employment, and a

Table 4.7 EU structural fund assistance (1994–9) (€ million)

Country	*Total*	*ERDF*	*ESF*	*EAGGF*	*FIFG*
Belgium	1,850	852	727	245	26
Denmark	755	118	344	151	143
Germany	19,794	8,516	6,803	4,285	189
Greece	13,902	9,367	2,585	1,818	132
Spain	30,544	16,860	8,456	4,089	1,138
France	13,545	5,363	4,725	3,229	228
Ireland	5,708	2,604	2,009	1,048	48
Italy	19,562	10,822	4,982	3,385	373
Luxembourg	85	16	27	42	1
Netherlands	2,173	598	1,379	140	55
Austria	1,482	353	539	588	2
Portugal	14,107	8,763	3,184	1,952	208
Finland	1,550	417	524	582	27
Sweden	1,218	315	652	205	45
UK	11,355	5,431	5,216	584	124
Fund Total	137,630	70,395	42,152	22,343	2,739

Source: European Commission, *The Structural Funds in 1997: Ninth Annual Report*, Luxembourg: 1999, p. 30.

Notes

All numbers are in 1997 € million as of 31 December 1997. ERDF = European Redevelopment Fund; ESF = European Social Fund; EAGGF = European Agricultural Guidance and Guarantee Fund; FIFG = Financial Instrument for Fisheries Guidance.

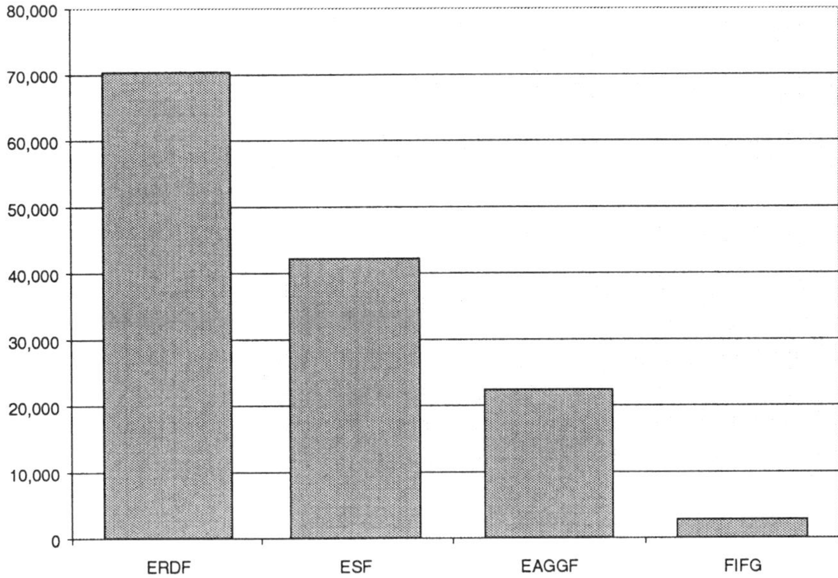

Figure 4.8 European structural fund assistance (1994–9) (€ million).

Source: European Commission, *The Structural Funds in 1997: Ninth Annual Report*, Luxembourg: 1999, p. 30.

Note
All numbers are in 1997 € million as of 31 December 1997. ERDF = European Redevelopment Fund; ESF = European Social Fund; EAGGF = European Agricultural Guidance and Guarantee Fund; FIFG = Financial Instrument for Fisheries Guidance.

third is to improve the fate of SMEs, largely because of the importance of SMEs not to financial markets but to jobs. Further, some of the special technological parks listed above complement some of the themes presented here.

From the perspective of this report, the goals of the *European Investment Bank* are different from those of most structural funds above and worthy of notice. It has supported many firms through billions of Euros of grants, and under the Amsterdam Special Action Program (ASAP), the EIB introduced a variety of financial instruments to help innovative small firms and those with strong growth potential to gain access to bank finance. The European Technological Facility, for example, was established by the EIB and the European Investment Fund to support investment on the part of innovative small businesses by taking shares in intermediary structures such as venture capital funds.

Yet even this bank is in a competition to 'pick winners' with a contribution that will never match the contribution possible through the vast pools of money that might come from public and private pension schemes, or disparate individuals saving more money in the private sector and investing it in private institutions.

In sum, the Commission's Annual Report on Structural Fund donations suggests eclectic policies that might profit from more sorting of priorities and more focus.

Comparing the EU investments with those of the US SBA, the EU investments seem considerably larger, although as usual statistics are not perfectly comparable. The EU invested €138 billion from 1994 to 1999. By contrast, the SBA claimed a portfolio of only $45 billion by the year 2000, primarily comprised of loans and loan guarantees. Meanwhile, much of the US 'investments' were geared towards minority-owned businesses (28 per cent of all loan dollars in FY 1999) or women (16 per cent). These very small loans look to be a lot further from some sort of industrial policy for small businesses.

There are significant sums of money going into the EU programmes, yet the money may be overly dispersed or poorly invested as a result of a lack of policy focus on particular objectives. From the perspective of capital markets, there are four issues worth addressing:

1 *SME funds are intentionally dispersed to regions that are either rural or faced with declining industrial sectors, yet this may not be the best investment for SMEs, their work force, or capital markets.* The EU might profit from an equivalent to Silicon Valley, the Boston Metropolitan area, or New York City in the United States, where the majority of venture fund money is filtered and a vast percentage of the US ventures seeking funding receive it. Some industries naturally cluster around given production centres or retail and distribution districts, and capital markets may be one of them. But even regional policies geared towards high-technology and the information revolution are dispersed across very small and disparate technological parks with questionable growth potential in each member nation of the EU. Some goals of the EU also seem at cross-purposes with others. For example, *the EU wishes to promote 'trans-European networks' of infrastructure, but de facto the opposite approach is taken when it comes to building up already successful places like 'silicon Fen' in Britain, the Munich metropolitan area in Germany, or the Basque country in Northern Spain.* Policies to benefit regions facing problems of post-industrial structural adjustment or declining agricultural prospects may provide a small boost to some locales, but accepting labour mobility towards places with a growing experience with dynamic capital market investments might create more wealth, more jobs, and more positive 'spill-over' effects within a country or European region. Even as an employment strategy or a strategy of structural adjustment, on a national level these channelled but dispersed investments may be of limited use.

2 *Many of the funds provide seed money directly from the Commission to very small firms of 1–10 employees, with no apparent strategic focus and limited use of capitalist intermediaries.* 'Reinventing government' schemes – where funds are distributed through private intermediaries, in this case fund managers specialising in a particular market, investment strategy, or goal set – have apparently not been pursued (except by the EIB). *Programmes are viewed as efficient and properly run if funds are distributed at a certain target date, with no apparent focus on return on investment.* This further disperses skills in the financial sector, side-steps the development of angel and VC organisations, and almost certainly leads to inefficiencies, where an emphasis on bureaucratic spot checks against corruption frequently replaces market-based mechanisms to check progress. If funds are geared towards what people said they would use them for, then this is regarded as satisfactory; perhaps it should not be.[17] Further, the frequent focus on the very smallest firms may also not be particularly helpful to the development of capital markets. And while some high-growth seed money projects admittedly may attract attention from an investment community, the low-tech operations that more frequently receive funding will not.

3 *Many funds are supposed to be distributed to 'high-tech' or 'high-growth' projects, but these appear to be insufficiently defined.* 'High-tech restructuring projects' appear to be at least in part a question of fashion. For example, most funded firms outside of rural areas appear to be involved in manufacturing, but VC funding on both sides of the Atlantic does not focus on manufacturing. Further, the goal sets of many of the businesses funded appear complementary to traditional relationship management banking and commercial loans. By contrast, computer software firms, communications firms, biotech firms, and more recently Internet firms are likely to be considered too well-connected, wealthy and large to interest the administrators managing distribution channels, yet they are prime targets for VC-style financing. It must remembered that the definition of SMEs – the organisations responsible for the majority of the EU's job creation – can include firms of up to 250 employees, but the largest firms are likely to be excluded from the funds. Even 'seed money' for the smallest projects, while useful, could at least focus on those with explosive commercial growth potential. This focus is most likely to be achieved through the use of highly specialised, financial intermediaries (e.g. managers of pension funds) rather than direct government attempts to 'pick winners'.

4 *There is limited effort to link other policies of the EU to the activities of these funds, particularly with respect to financial markets.* For example, welcomed policies on tax reform and paperwork reduction are designed to encourage investment, and other administrative divisions

of the European Commission (e.g. the 'Financial Services Policy Group') focus on some of the goals outlined here. But few of the highlighted examples of fund recipients in the structural funds were businesses promoting tax advice, savings advice, low-level financing of co-operatives, consumer savings, or other 'small business to small business' or 'small business to consumer' investment, financing or intermediary services. This is of particular relevance to northern Europe, which does not have the system of *Gestorias* (independent administration support services – particularly with paperwork, grant applications, bookkeeping and paralegal matters) that abound in Spain and other southern European countries. Admittedly, a full survey has not been carried out on the projects that do and do not receive funding, and some other EU projects, such as the European Technical Facility of the European Investment Bank and Amsterdam Special Action Programme, are complementary to these goals. Yet an impression is gained from the European Commission's *Annual Report* on structural funds that some industries are more popular than others, and that these are not necessarily industries that currently attract VC interest.

Executives' perceptions of government obstacles to success

An interesting study by the World Bank,[18] measuring the opinions of SME executives on government 'obstacles to success', covered dozens of countries. But a focus on the European and US data provides interesting counterfactuals for this study. We often provide information that backs a US approach to policy, but the data from the World Bank suggests that European SME leaders are still more satisfied with their governments' respective policy agendas.

A caveat presented here is that the US data in particular polls a paltry number of business leaders. The data is most interesting for comparisons of the responses of SME executives and larger-enterprise executives within all of Europe. That data is far more complete. Still, overall, with a score of 'one' suggesting low obstacles to business development and a score of 'five' suggesting high ones, only Italy's SME executives provide their government with higher (more unsatisfied) scores than those of the US on all government criteria.

On government obstacles to SMEs: higher scores mean more obstacles

It is interesting that while the US citizens and business leaders frequently moan about 'high taxes' and taxes are always a question on the US policy agenda, US SME leaders give their government far better (lower) comparative scores when it comes to tax and regulatory burdens. Perhaps some of

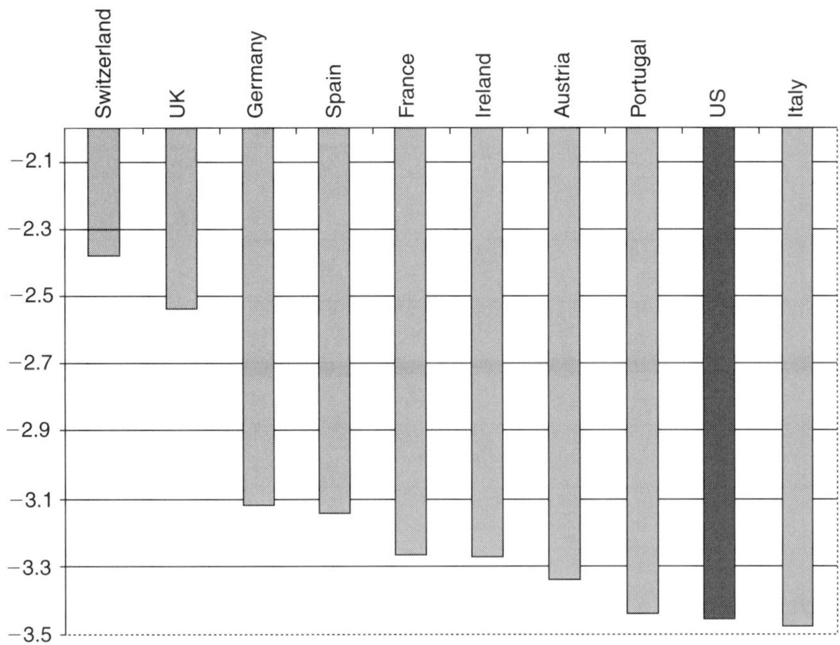

Figure 4.9 Government obstacles to SMEs – quantified (1997).

Source: World Bank.[a]

Note

a Ajay Chhibber, 'The State in a Changing World', *World Bank Report 1997*. Data downloaded from www.unibas.ch/wwz/wifor/survey/

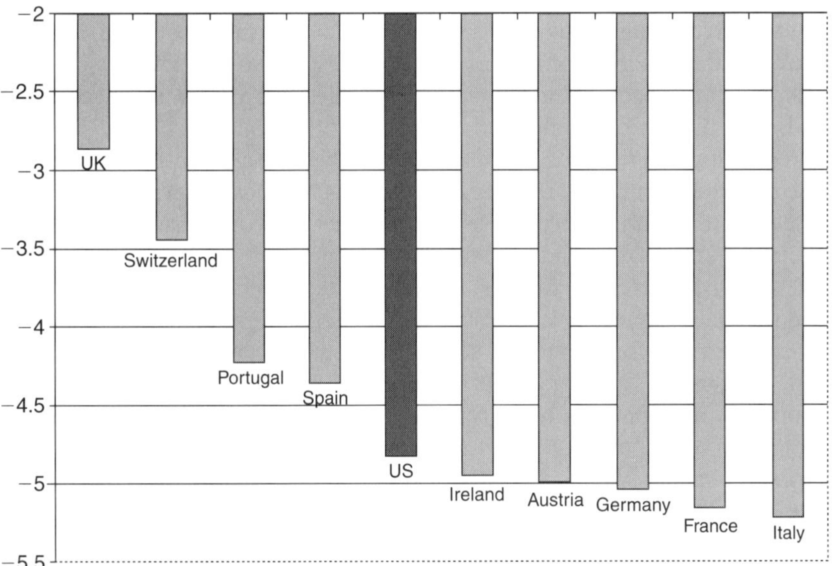

Figure 4.10 SME executives' perceived tax regulatory and payment burdens (1997).

Source: World Bank.

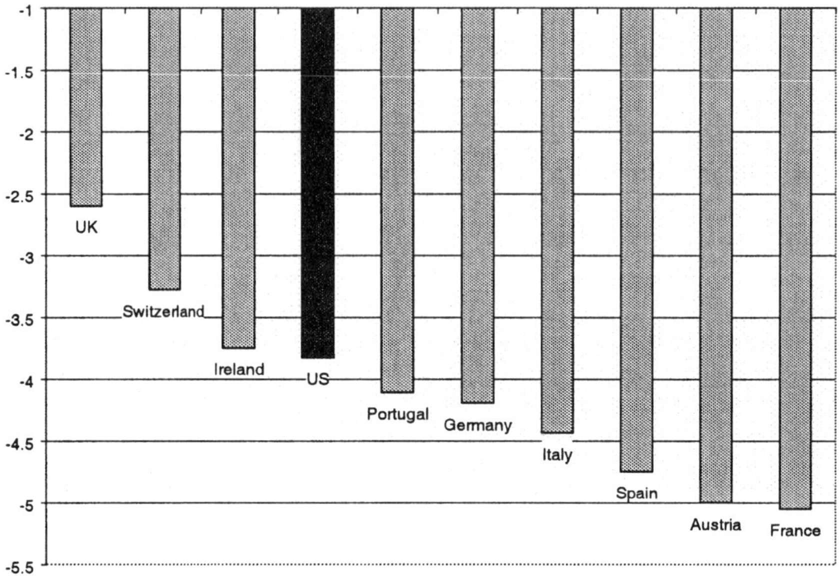

Figure 4.11 SME executives' perceived government burden of labour regulations (1997).

Source: World Bank.[a]

Note

a Ajay Chhibber, 'The State in a Changing World', *World Bank Report 1997*. Data downloaded from www.unibas.ch/wwz/wifor/survey/

the executives realise (like UK citizens, who are most satisfied on this issue) that their taxes, from a comparative perspective, are low.

On regulations governing labour, UK SME leaders are again the most satisfied, with the US ones falling in the middle of the pile, even though again US regulations on firms of less than 50 employees are much less strict than those in Europe on hiring, firing and benefits such as health care provision.

Because the data is very provisional for the US, comparisons of smaller European enterprise leaders and larger ones are more likely to be representative. Here, the smaller firm leaders tend to be (slightly) more satisfied than larger ones on most issues (labour regulations an apparent exception), suggesting more perceived support and smaller perceived burdens.

In conclusion, we see that perceptions of business leaders within Europe, with respect to key areas covering regulatory burden, taxation and labour areas, are comparatively consistent across all areas covered. For example, the UK and Switzerland rank as the most pleased for all three areas, whilst leaders in France and Italy are the least pleased. Although there may indeed be valid reasons for certain of these elements, this is not always the case. Social security contributions in Austria represent 15.4 per cent of GDP in 1996, whilst for Germany amounted to 18.7

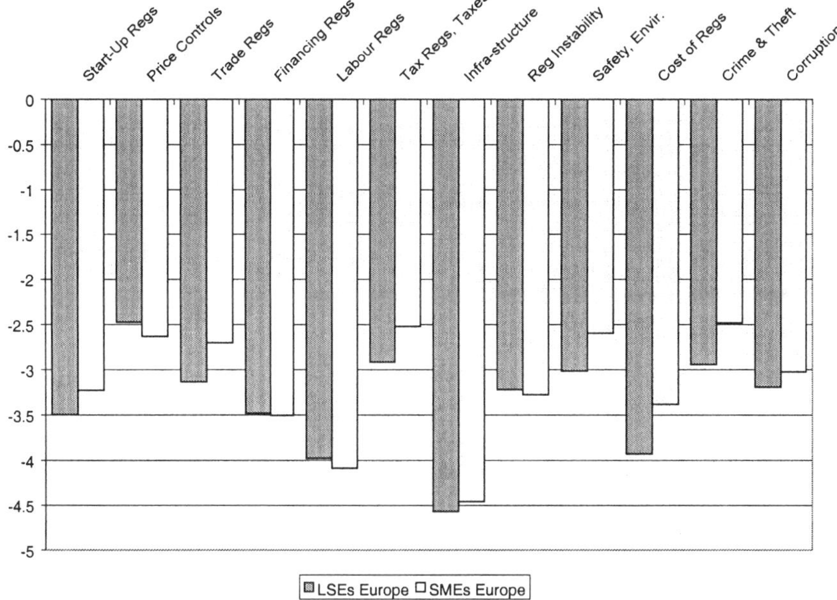

Figure 4.12 Satisfaction levels of European SMEs and LSEs (1997).

Source: World Bank.[a]

Note

Lower numbers imply higher satisfaction levels (fewer burdens).

a Sample size of 198 firms in the following countries: Austria (16), France (19), Germany (22), Ireland (14), Italy (24), Portugal (20), Spain (18), Switzerland (26), the UK (16), the US (23); all countries' results are weighted equally. See Ajay Chhibber, 'The State in a Changing World', *World Bank Report 1997*. Data downloaded from www.unibas.ch/wwz/wifor/survey/

per cent.[19] Yet the Germans only ranked 'mid-table' in perceived government labour burden, whilst Austria ranked as having the worst perceptions, along with France. In the case of France, this is clear, as with social security contributions of 19.7 per cent of GDP in 1996 where the highest in the EU. Thus culture has a significant part to play in relative perceptions.

Conclusions

This chapter makes no effort to provide a complete literature review of critiques of government policies, but it closes with a review of a handful of policy recommendations for SMEs from public and private bodies. As stated in the introduction, entrepreneurship is defined in a European Commission report as 'a dynamic process by which individuals constantly identify economic opportunities and act upon them by developing, producing and selling goods and services. This process requires qualities such as self-reliance, a capacity for risk-taking and a sense of personal commitment'.[20]

We have repeatedly said that 'fostering entrepreneurship' is a difficult and illusive goal. Yet recommendations from the Commission to foster entrepreneurship in some ways reinforce many of the policy themes outlined above. They include many useful suggestions, some of which relate to taxes (including payroll and inheritance taxes):

1 *Simplification of the administrative environment*: Slow, complex procedures when registering businesses hamper and delay business start-ups. The total annual cost of administrative formalities which businesses in Europe face was estimated to be €200 billion in 1995, representing up to 3 per cent of the community's GDP.[21]
2 *Facilitating the transfer of businesses*: It is estimated that about 30 per cent of the businesses that could be transferred disappear because of poor preparation, high inheritance or gift taxes, and because of a lack of interest on the part of young people to take over or buy businesses.
3 *Lowering high taxes*, including payroll taxes, disproportionately high administrative costs for SMEs in collecting and dealing with tax and social security contributions, and tax disincentives for businesses that take out equity capital rather than loan capital.
4 *Limiting state aid*, amounting to some €100 billion annually in the EU in the mid-1990s.[22]
5 *Reducing the cost of filing patents* and other efforts to protect and commercialise intellectual property.

All of these suggestions are logical and important (e.g. reducing paperwork, making patent applications easier) but are less relevant to a discussion on SMEs and capital markets.[23] Generally, the proposals are useful, largely because the definition of entrepreneurship provided is so broad as to encompass all kinds of activities that are important to all industry. It would be difficult to measure levels of 'entrepreneurship' under this fungible definition, or to prove that it has been sparked due to any of the policies above. Yet these policies are generally similar to other recommendations supported here.

We would also reiterate that any effort to encourage entrepreneurship or provide learning at a public level should permit commissions to the private sector that might provide these services more efficiently or even stimulate new services. European funding bodies have tried to educate SMEs on opportunities in foreign markets and administrative time-saving tips. But 40 per cent of SME executives surveyed by the European Commission felt that the EU's external services, for example, were expensive, and another 26 per cent felt they were not geared towards SME needs.[24] We do not have data that accurately compares reactions to national and EU governments, but views towards the European Commission are frequently more negative than they are towards sponsoring national administrations, and the Commission will have to work to correct this.

Other useful suggestions on policy directions can be culled from the *European Venture Capital Association's White Paper* entitled 'Priorities for Private Equity: Realising Europe's Entrepreneurial Potential', which presents policy recommendations in apparently random order. Their listing, later categorised and analysed, is as follows:

1 *Improve education in entrepreneurship*: 'European universities should develop courses and departments in entrepreneurship', teaching students new business ideas, marketing, and how to access technical information.
2 *Gain a better understanding of the importance of MBOs and MBIs* as essential means of exit for high-risk investors.
3 *Clarify intellectual property and licensing ownership.*
4 *Help commercial research.*
5 *Promote a flexible work environment*, with flexible labour laws, portable pension funds, and more flexible hiring and firing laws.
6 *'Engender an entrepreneurial environment in emerging markets'*, particularly Eastern Europe.
7 *'Create incentives for entrepreneurs and managers'*: A low capital gains tax rate, tax deduction of losses, and up-front investment relief are ways to 'offer reward and motivation for the significant personal risks inherent in launching or joining a new business'.
8 *Promote stock options*: In many European countries, gains realised from options are taxed at the same rate as income, even though they involve greater risks. The ECVA recommends 'no tax on the issue or exercise of options to buy shares, provided that their exercise price is not less than the market price was on the date the option was granted'.
9 *'Encourage funded pension systems through Europe'*: Most countries 'rely on pay-as-you-go social security pension systems. But demographics indicate that shortfalls loom for this unfunded type of system'. Exceptions are the UK and the Netherlands.
10 *'Ease Asset Allocation Restrictions'*: Throughout much of Europe, pension fund allocation is handicapped by unfavourable regulations, taxation, and investment restrictions. This is in contrast to the US and the UK, countries with superior pension fund performance measured by return on investment. Specifically, ECVI would encourage 'prudent man rules' and 'safe harbour' regulations.
11 *'Lift geographic restrictions'* requiring a proportion of assets to be invested in a country's own capital markets. Rather, performance within prudential guidelines should determine allocation.
12 *'Make investing in small-cap stocks efficient'* primarily by allowing institutional investors more freedom to make such investments.[25]

It is a belief of the authors of this study that *industrial and educational policies* above – to promote education in entrepreneurship, to aid commercial research, to promote more flexible labour laws – *are important but of declining significance, increasingly difficult, and less important than tax and savings policies*.

Some of the industrial planning in these policy statements may be difficult for political reasons (e.g. more flexible labour laws), but at least the suggestions wisely focus on broader policies beneficial to businesses generally, rather than those that would select particular sectors or corporate sizes (e.g. independent proprietorships) as worthy of focus.

Other policies (e.g. education on entrepreneurship, channelling investment, promoting entrepreneurial activities in central and eastern Europe) come closer to 'picking winners', winning strategies, or important new markets, and this may be increasingly difficult for reasons described above.

By contrast, proposals related to taxes and savings seem easier to implement and particularly important. *A low capital gains tax rate, tax deduction of losses, lowering taxes on stock options, providing tax savings to funded pension systems and permitting them to take on more diverse or aggressive investment strategies* would all have positive effects on business environments and might be particularly useful in building links between SMEs and more dynamic capital markets.

A few interesting studies from academia, specifically the Manchester Business School, are also worthy of mention. For example, a primary conclusion of one study from *the Manchester Business School is that the taxation system in the UK blocks the development of SMEs by weighing them down with a steep tax burden; and yet taxes in the UK are somewhat low for the EU*. Proposals of this Manchester study are more specific than those of the EVCA and include the following:

- Increase the VAT registration threshold to £100,000
- Compensate small firms for administering the collection of payroll and social security taxes.
- Introduce tax relief for profits re-invested in the business.[26]

Of these proposals, the third is the most thoroughly analysed and the most important:

> Present tax rules require re-investment decisions (such as the purchase of new equipment) to be made before the end of each business accounting year, when most firms do not yet know how profitable they have been. In contrast, the decision to extract money from the business (e.g. for pension scheme contributions or director's bonuses) can be made after the end of the accounting year, when the business tax liability has been calculated. If profits re-invested in the firm were treated for taxation in the same way as funds extracted, this could have a positive effect on investment patterns. Many SMEs would be encouraged to re-invest profits.[27]

Were a tax on retained profits introduced, 55 per cent of respondents to a British poll of firm leaders said that they would invest the extra money in new capital equipment while 46 per cent said they would generate more sales. A further 46 per cent would use the money to repay borrowings.[28]

Another study by the same authors at the Manchester Business School focuses more narrowly on high-tech firms. It concludes again that the ability of technology-based small firms to grow is hampered by the UK taxation system, and states:

> In absolute terms, the value of the tax liability of TBSFs ['technology based small firms'] was lower than for the low technology firms because TBSFs were, on average, much smaller. However, TBSFs in both the service and manufacturing industries paid higher taxes, as a proportion of their total assets, than low technology businesses.[29]

The study would again recommend tax relief on these firms for profits reinvested in the business.

Ending on a positive note, it should remembered that both the EU and the US have provided regulatory and fiscal environments that are, by the standards of the day, extremely friendly to business and extremely successful. In each case, small businesses comprise over 99 per cent of all firms, host the majority of job-growth, and fuel-rich economies. Yet this chapter highlights some differences in ideas about public policy and, with EU and US SME funds as an example, demonstrates how different policy deals translate into different outcomes. The discussion is necessarily selective, and in the EU case it glosses over broad differences within the member states. Subsequent chapters provide a clearer picture of these differences by homing in on developments within the EU, state-by-state.

Notes

1 See glossary.

2 See glossary.

3 See also John Hawksworth (Head of Macroeconomics, Price Waterhouse), Business Tax Harmonisation in the New Europe – see www.pwc.com

4 Dani Rodrik, 'Why Do More Open Economies Have Bigger Governments?'. *Journal of Political Economy*, 106:5 (1998), pp. 997–1032.

5 See also Theodore Geiger, *Welfare and Efficiency: Their Interactions in Western Europe and Implications for International Economic Relations*, NPA, London: Macmillan 1979, p. 12.

6 Dani Rodrik, 'Why Do More Open Economies Have Bigger Governments?', *Journal of Political Economy*, 106:5 (1998), pp. 997–1032.

7 Government-backed scheme that encourages additional voluntary contributions through providing matching funds. Created to counterbalance underfunding fears resulting from most pension schemes being defined contribution rather than defined benefit schemes.

8 Independent Retirement Account. State scheme that encourages individuals to save through pension plans by offering tax concessions.
9 'President Clinton's New Opportunity Agenda Proposes Record Level of Investment, Financial Assistance for America's Small Businesses', Press Release of the SBA, 7 February 2000. See www.sba.gov
10 Small Business Administration.
11 Report presented to the 1995 Madrid European Council on the role of SMEs, later enshrined into the Council Resolution of 9 December 1996 – 97/C 18/01 – 'realising the full potential of small and medium-sized enterprises (SMEs), including micro-enterprises and the craft sector, through an integrated approach to improving the business environment and stimulating business support measures'.
12 VAT recognition system whereby (in simplistic terms) tax on value-added is deemed payable in the country where goods have been manufactured or where services have been provided – rather than in the country where the company is based.
13 European Commission, 'Action Plan to Promote Entrepreneurship and Competitiveness', Luxembourg: EC 1999, p. 12.
14 European Commission, *The Structural Funds in 1997: Ninth Annual Report*, Luxembourg: 1999, p. 20.
15 Ibid., pp. 54–104.
16 Ibid.
17 To provide an example: 'The mid-term review ... demonstrated that Portugal is one of the Member States which makes the best use of the Funds: 70 percent of assistance was committed and 56 percent paid by the end of 1997, well above the Community average', ibid., p. 96.
18 Ajay Chhibber, 'The State in a Changing World', *World Bank Report 1997*. Data downloaded from www.unibas.ch/wwz/wifor/survey/
19 *The Spectre of Tax Harmonisation*, Kitty Ussher, 1998, Centre for European Reform, p. 28, Table 6.
20 'Fostering Entrepreneurship in Europe: Communication from the Commission to the Council', Brussels: 7 April 1998: COM (98) 222 final, p. 1.
21 Ibid., p. 4.
22 Ibid., p. 7.
23 European Commission, 'Action Plan to Promote Entrepreneurship and Competitiveness', Luxembourg: EC, 1999, p. 12.
24 Ibid., p. 14.
25 'Priorities for Private Equity,' EVCI White Paper European Venture Capital Associate.
26 Francis Chittenden, Panikkos Poutziouris and Nicos Michaelas, 'Taxing Investment in Small Firms', Business Development Centre, Manchester Business School, 1999, p. 4.
27 Ibid.
28 Ibid.
29 Ibid.

5 SME development and constraints

Comparisons within the EU

While previous chapters are helpful to analyse broad differences between the US and Europe, it must be acknowledged that SME and equity–market differences within Europe are far greater than they are within the US. That is, while California and the northeast Atlantic cities may have more of a 'buzz' associated with their venture capital and SME dynamism than other parts of the US, the US market generally is far more uniform from region to region than Europe's. Also, within the US, some of the regional differences which do exist are exaggerated by the fact that financial centres (e.g. New York) agglomerate the capital of many parts of the country, and then invest the money of diverse citizens from one central location. In other words, the headquarters of a national pension fund may be located on Wall Street, but the money flowing in and out of that fund may be national. This exaggerates the power of financial centres as apparent 'controllers' rather than channels of national capital. In terms of regions that absorb extensive investment, California (especially Silicon Valley), Massachusetts (especially around Boston), New York (especially NYC), and Texas are more dynamic than other locations, but the people who are creating business headquarters in these locations could be from any part of the country, employing workers from any part of the country. It could be argued that California in particular has a more high-risk climate for entrepreneurship than other states, especially in the 1990s, but it could hardly be said to have self-contained cultural or political institutions or a self-contained local, regional, or even national population. The entrepreneurs who settle there – to seek capital, a high-quality workforce, markets, and ideas – are from all over the US and indeed many parts of the world.

By contrast, in much of Europe, language barriers, differing financial institutions, different craft and guild traditions, differing levels of government expenditure, differing views on corporatist political arrangements, more conservative attitudes towards changing jobs and labour mobility, and finally differing tax and legal institutions make investment cultures even at roughly similar economic development levels more distinct. Trade and monetary unions and the European Commission are helping to level differences within the EU, but peculiarities of enterprise size, success and culture are likely to persist for some time.

Hence, this section of the report provides comparative analyses of countries within the EU, and also case studies of particular EU countries or regions.

Looking within the EU for correlations, anomalies, and peculiarities, one can draw the following conclusions:

- *There is no clear statistical correlation between the wealth of an economy and the relative importance of its SMEs in the EU-15.* If we analyse the statistics without the largest and smallest EU economies (Germany's and Luxembourg's), we do find some negative correlation, suggesting that in much of Europe richer countries rely more than poorer countries on large firms. Yet correlations are affected by a host of factors outlined below, and generally weak correlations imply that governments hoping to boost either enterprise success (which creates wealth) or capital markets for enterprise securities (which create wealth) might be most successful if they seek broad, fundamental reforms to benefit all enterprises, large and small, and all capital markets, large- and small-cap. That is to say, for the generation of wealth or capital markets, there is no obvious reason to focus on SMEs or small-cap markets *per se*. Further, it could be argued that developing the markets for securities of larger firms are a greater priority, since these firms form the vast majority of equity markets everywhere, even in the US. The implication for governments might be that a focus on the general business environment (for example, low business taxes, low capital gains taxes) might be more likely to generate wealth than a focus on microeconomic SME legislation (e.g. tax breaks for start-ups). *Generally, there is no reason to believe that 'small is beautiful' or more beautiful than large.*
- *Numbers of SMEs correlate closely with population size regardless of government policy, culture, wealth levels or structural economic factors, and this has implications for policy-makers.* For example, policies to stimulate agglomeration or decentralisation at the SME level, to stimulate 'buy-out' activity below the level of larger firms, or to stimulate 'entrepreneurship,' may be of weaker effect, or particularly inefficient, if there is a 'natural' number of firms in existence that closely correlates with population. Hence, countries like Sweden or to some extent France, which historically favoured the development of larger, national firms (or, in a sense, discriminated against smaller firms), may have paid a price for this not only in lower SME density (Sweden has among the lowest in Europe) but also in other externalities. In the EU in the mid-1990s, countries saw an average of one SME for every 50 residents (not 50 employees per SME, but rather 50 residents per SME). Urban or industrial areas saw a higher density, and rural, agricultural areas a

lower density. Densities are also dependent on the kind of industry (heavy or service sector) dominant in a region. But if 50 residents per SME, adjusted slightly to account for the extent of urbanisation and industrialisation, is even to a limited extent close to a kind of 'natural' level of density in a given historical period, then this extra-governmental, extra-cultural structural correlation reinforces the idea that policies to benefit all enterprises may be more useful to create wealth than policies to benefit any particular size of enterprise.

- *In Europe, those hoping to boost capital markets in particular, especially markets for small-cap securities, should not study all SMEs but rather the larger SMEs most likely to attract angel investors, VCs, and stock markets.* Regionally within Europe, the countries with the larger capital markets have also hosted larger than average SMEs with much higher than average turnover, and hence a more important pool of firms eligible and attractive for more liquid capital market investments. By contrast, while a great deal has been said about the importance of craft trades in Italy and the somewhat impressive numbers of SMEs in Portugal, Italy and southern Europe generally, the vast majority of SMEs in much of southern Europe are too small to boost capital markets significantly, with the exception of the markets for small-business loans from local commercial banks and traditional relationship bankers. This study discusses important EU reforms to aid start-ups, but to study VC and angel avenues to success, we need to focus primarily on the SMEs that are *not* micro-enterprises.
- *Germany emerges from a detailed look at the statistics as the country with the largest pool of larger SMEs (10 or more employees) by far, and in part for this reason as the country with the most untapped potential for dynamic VC and angel investment activity.* This is not to say that Germany is a failure in attracting angel and VC investments, but simply that the disproportionate quantity and power of its larger SMEs has not yet resulted in a market for high-risk investment that is anywhere near its apparently full potential. Since Germany is the largest economy in Europe, and several VC firms might use a knowledge of the German market to launch investments in other German-speaking markets, Germany could serve a bit more as a rising tide to lift many boats – but instead, at least until a very recent burst of new activity, it has drifted along at a somewhat unimpressive pace with respect to high-risk SME investments.

On SMEs and wealth levels in the EU

An analysis of statistics on SME numbers and many others, such as SME turnover, GDP data, and demographics, suggest that in Europe and indeed in advanced, industrialised nations, *there is no correlation between the wealth of a country and the importance of SMEs in that country.*

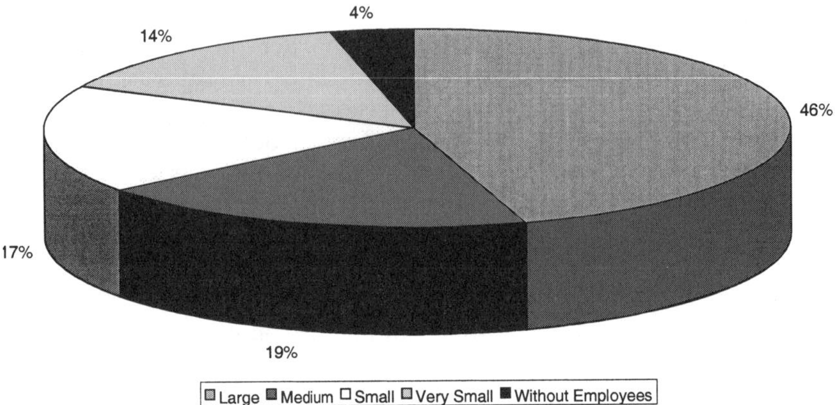

Figure 5.1 €17.1 trillion EU enterprise turnover by size of enterprise (1995).

Source: European Commission, *Enterprises in Europe: Data 1994–1995*, Luxembourg: Eurostat, p. 30.

First, it should be acknowledged that although large enterprises are only a fraction of the total number of enterprises in the EU, they account for more than one-third of total employment and almost half of total turnover.

Figure 5.2 continues to break down the statistics on SMEs by size of SME, and outlines the average turnover per EU enterprise in 1995 using a logarithmic scale.

Firms of 1–9 employees, that is, very small firms, demonstrate a turnover of less than €0.5 million on average in 1995. Many of these small firms are clearly selling much more than this and are big enough to interest angel investors and some VCs. Further, it should be pointed out that in some industries revenues frequently come later and employee numbers are lower, but angel investors may still be very interested in a high-growth story. So, for example, Internet businesses often have low staffing and focus on issues other than revenues, including 'market presence' or 'number of hits'. But we can assume for the purposes of this discussion that the vast majority of the firms with fewer than 10 employees are of little interest to the more organised high-risk investors and especially institutional investors.

By contrast, it is the firms in the 10–49 employee range, with turnover approaching €3 million annually on average, that are most likely to interest the more organised small players in the financial markets, including VCs, some investment banks, and even small-cap exchanges. Many of these firms are earning much more than the average; some may even be seeking second-round funding or trading over-the-counter.

With the average larger enterprise generating turnover almost ten times

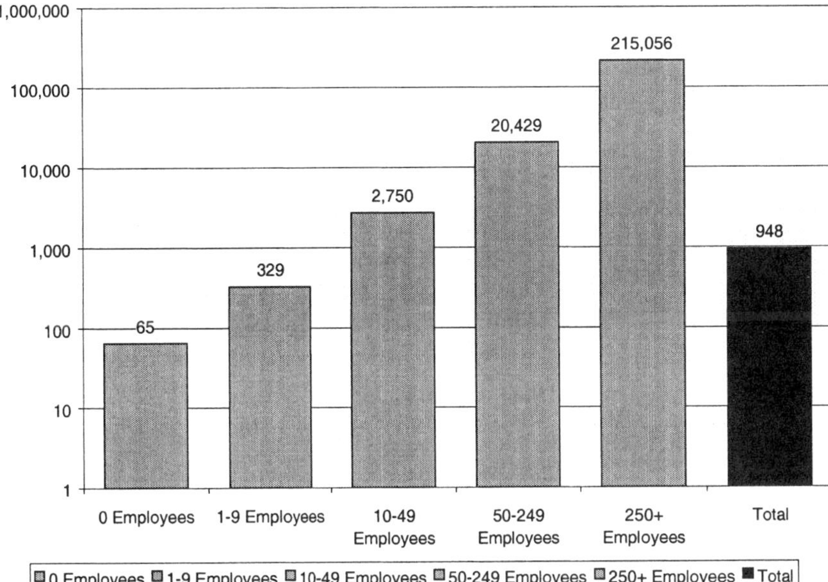

Figure 5.2 EU-15 average turnover by enterprise size (1995) (€ '000s).

Source: European Commission, *Enterprises in Europe, Fifth Report: Data 1994–1995*, p. 31.

higher than the average medium-sized enterprise, it is easy to understand why far more institutional investors are willing to 'make markets' in these larger firms and turn them into valuable, liquid investments. While this study focuses on SMEs, the leading importance of LSEs to capital markets cannot be ignored.

At the same time, the importance of firms of any size should not be exaggerated or romanticised. With GDP per capita serving as a wealth proxy and the percentage of a country's GDP that is comprised of SME sales revenues serving as a proxy for the relative importance of SMEs, statistics on 15 EU countries from 1995 demonstrate an insignificant correlation that is surprisingly close to zero (−0.02) between wealth and SME importance. Alternatively, we can drop SME turnover (affected by levels of trade) and use SME Gross Value Added (GVA) per unit of GDP as a more accurate proxy for the importance of SMEs in an economy. But even then, again using 1995 statistics as a sample year, the correlation between 'SME importance' and wealth is very weak in the EU-15 (0.17). Even if the public sector's expenditures (usually higher in richer countries) are factored out of the equation, there still is almost no correlation between 'private GDP per capita' (public expenditures excluded) and SME turnover as a percentage of public or private GDP. This means that, within Europe at least, a higher reliance on SMEs for production does not imply greater, or lesser, wealth.

In the US, meanwhile, since the end of the Second World War, there has been a greater reliance on SMEs as agents of economic expansion and job creation as the US has grown richer. Yet generally, it has been noted that SMEs are much less important to the US economy than to economies in Europe. Since US and European wealth levels (GDP/capita) are roughly similar despite different levels of reliance on SMEs on both sides of the Atlantic, this only adds to reinforce the conclusion that there is no clear correlation between SME importance and wealth.

If we exclude the largest and smallest (Germany and Luxembourg) EU economies from analysis, there is a statistically interesting negative correlation (−0.53) between wealth and the relative importance of SMEs measured by SME turnover as a percentage of GDP, meaning wealthier countries tend to rely more on larger enterprises than do poorer countries. However, dropping turnover and using SME gross value added as a percentage of GDP as our proxy again suggests almost no correlation between SME importance and wealth (−0.16).

Several intervening variables in the world economy make one question the extent to which wealth and SME correlations can be meaningful. For example, while all EU countries have grown steadily richer in the post-war period, reliance on both large and small firms has grown at uneven rates.

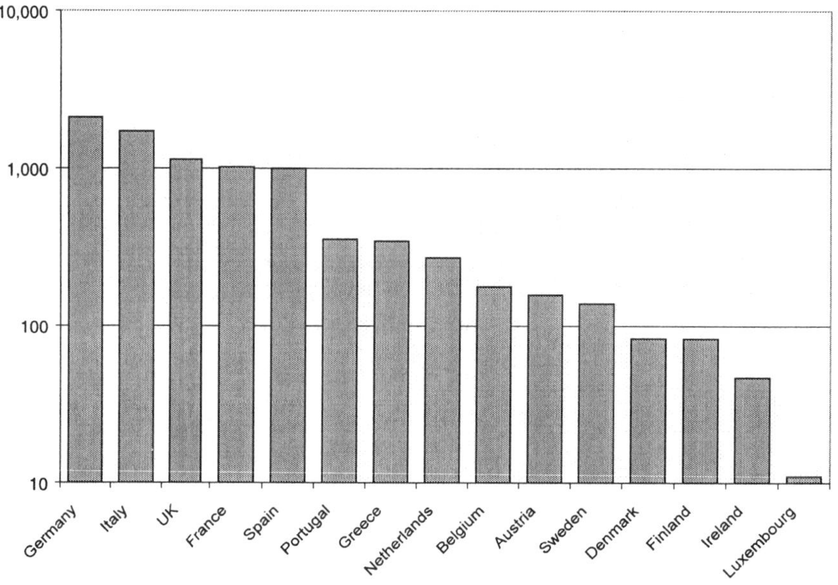

Figure 5.3 Number of SMEs in EU (1995) ('000s).

Source: European Commission, *Enterprises in Europe: Data 1994–1995*, Luxembourg: Eurostat, pp. 220–38.

Note
Logarithmic scale.

Larger firms lost ground to smaller firms throughout the post-war period, but partly as a result of productivity gains in absolute terms and relative to smaller firms, LSEs began to bounce back in the 1990s.

Capitalism appears to favour larger firms at some times and smaller firms at other times. Since governments are unlikely to 'beat the market' in predicting which organisational form will be more critical at a given period, European countries should not act to favour one organisational structure (independent proprietor, partnership, SME, large firm) over another.

Statistics on the number of SMEs in select EU countries in 1995 are again provided. Is there any country that stands out in producing SMEs?

Because of the very high numbers of very small firms in Italy, statistics on the number of SMEs in that country outpace what one might expect from the size of its economy. Italy was the fourth largest EU economy in 1995, just behind the UK, but it hosted the second-largest number of SMEs, outpacing the UK by over 50 per cent and France by over 65 per cent in SME numbers. The rest of southern Europe (Greece, Portugal and Spain) demonstrates relatively high SME numbers.

Yet SME gross value-added correlates almost entirely with the size of economies in the EU, and here southern Europe does not stand out. The correlation between SME GVA and GDP is a surprising 0.99, meaning almost perfect correlation in statistics dating from 1995. Hence, on the

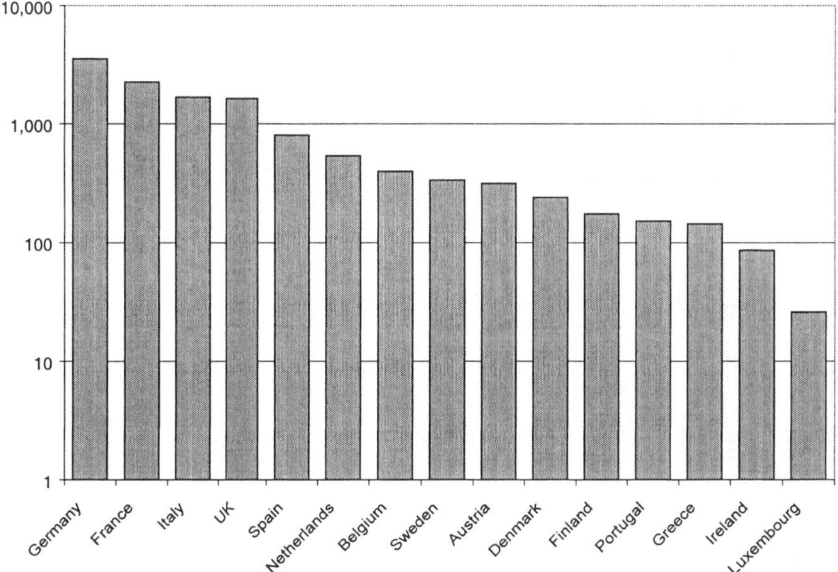

Figure 5.4 All SME gross value added (€ billion).

Source: European Commission, *Enterprises in Europe: Data 1994–1995*, Luxembourg: Eurostat, pp. 220–38.

chart below, the largest economies also host the most SME GVA, with the four largest European economies in 1995 proceeding more or less in order as the four greatest SME successes measured by SME GVA.

Again, Greece relies comparatively more on SME turnover as a percentage of GDP, and Scandinavian economies comparatively less. Finally, it is worth noting that Italy, despite its high number of craft tradesmen and micro-firms, is not a striking success in terms of SME turnover.

Considering labour productivity, measured as value added per occupied person and expressed as a percentage of country average, we see marked differences in productivity by country. As can be seen from the figure below, only two countries have relative labour productivity greater than 100 per cent (which signifies that SMEs are more productive than the average). These are Iceland, which is an SME dominant country and therefore you would expect this result and Germany. Germany, which is a LSE dominant country (i.e. majority of workers employed by large-scale enterprises), has SMEs that are more efficient, that average is down to the preponderance of medium sized enterprises in the economy. It is the existence of the German Mittelstand that underline this statistic. At the other extremes, we have Spain and Ireland with the lowest relative labour productivity. Spain is explained by the dominance of small enterprises, which are relatively inefficient – and Ireland by the dominance of a few LSEs.

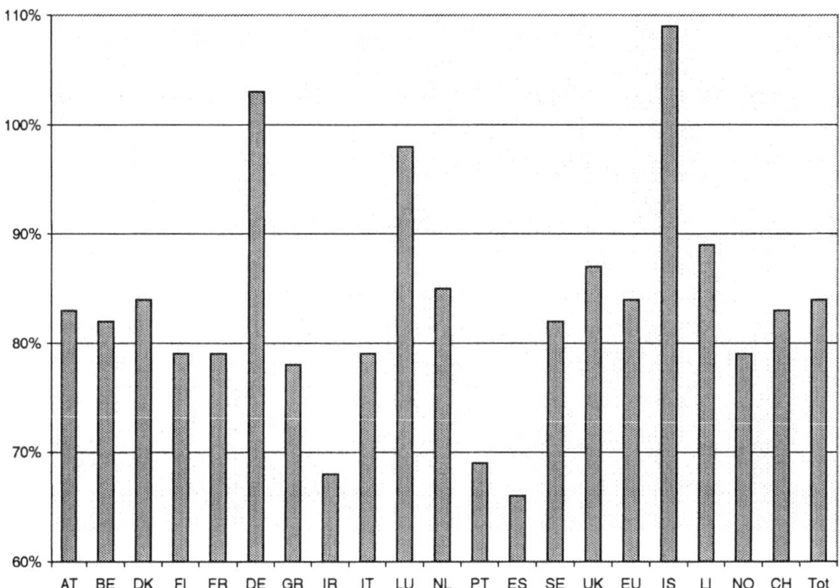

Figure 5.5 Relative labour productivity (1996) (percentage).

Source: *The European Observatory for SMEs Fifth Annual Report 1997*, European Network for SME Research, p. 49, Table 1.2.

On SMEs and the size of EU states

Statistical measures of success for European SMEs correlate best *not* with wealth measures, but rather with more mundane, structurally fixed, and predictable information such as the size of the country's GDP and the size of its population. It is not surprising that bigger countries almost always have more SMEs, more SME turnover, and higher SME gross value added than smaller countries. This is demonstrated with statistics on GDP, SME numbers, SME turnover, and SME GVA in 15 EU countries for a sample year, 1995. Still, there are a few facts worth noting.

In 15 EU countries, there are nearly perfect, positive correlations (all above 0.97) between the size of a country's population on the one hand and both SME gross value added and SME numbers on the other. While one might expect a close correlation between population and both SME GVA and numbers, these correlations are so close to perfect that it is worthwhile to ponder possible implications for policy-makers.

Before beginning the analysis, it is important to point out that while the correlation is very close to perfect, it is not perfect. The average number of residents per SME in Europe was around 50 in 1995, but the smaller EU states created anomalies: Portugal had the best record of business formation per resident (one SME for every 28 people) and Ireland the worst (one SME for every 77 people). Even in the ten largest EU states, one can find differences in SME numbers vs. population, with Italy supporting far more SMEs per person than Sweden. This same data is provided as SMEs per capita, with more countries listed.

Further, some regions within countries are real pockets of SME (and commercial) activity, whereas other regions may sport far less activity. According to the European Commission's statistical office, urban and industrialised centres attract the most SME activity within countries.[1]

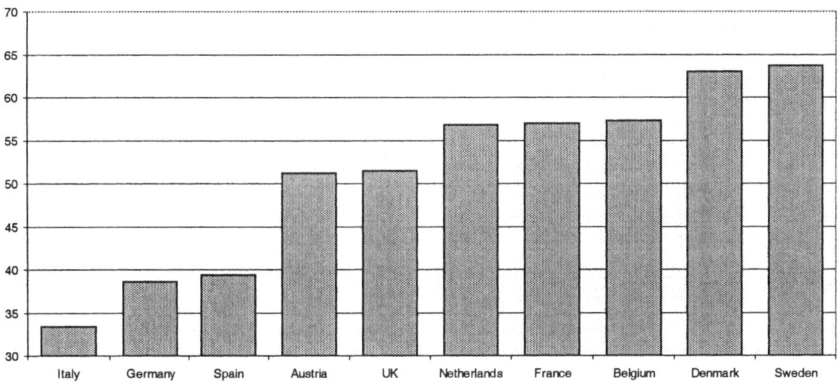

Figure 5.6 Residents per NASE and SME – 10 largest EU countries (1995).

Source: World Bank, Eurostat.

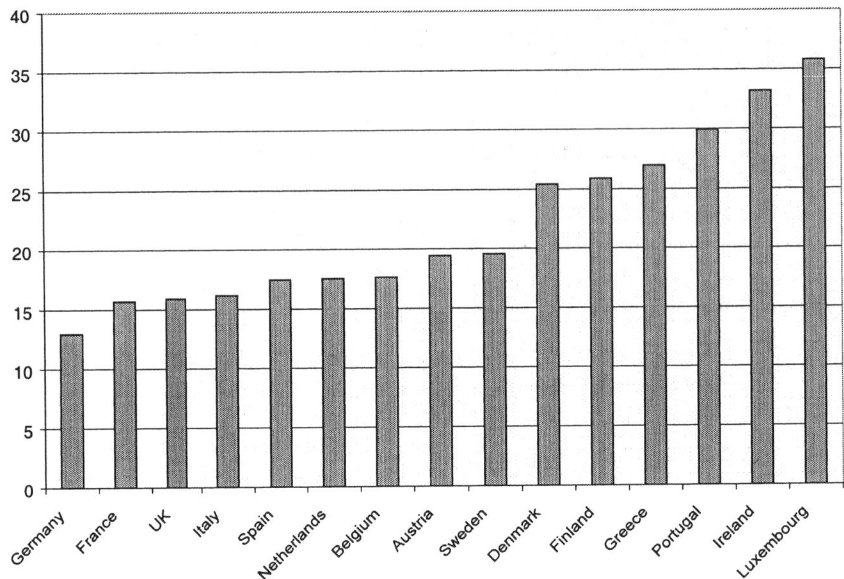

Figure 5.7 SMEs (excluding NASE) per '000 capita (1995).

Source: World Bank, Eurostat.

On the other hand, SMEs are of far greater importance to the local economies in poorer places: 'Less favoured rural areas generally have a relatively high share of employees in SMEs.'[2]

Yet if a general, broad correlation between population and SME numbers is one of the closest correlations available in SME statistics (closer than GDP size to SME numbers, for example), then this suggests policy-makers face at least limited structural barriers to changing the relative importance of SMEs or emphasising success for one type of firm over another for reasons of national pride, tradition, or for economic considerations.

To provide an example, policies to encourage or discourage agglomeration or decentralisation of firm leadership may be greatly inhibited in most industries if there is a natural SME density level for economies that are very broadly similar (all wealthy, capitalist OECD nations in the same turn-of-century world economy, in the same free-trading bloc, working to achieve a single currency). Coupled with this, Western Europe exhibits a clear political and policy dichotomy between, on the one hand, the urge to 'back winners' and thus help create the next Silicon Valley through investing in areas that already exhibit clear tendencies this way, and on the other hand to distribute structural and social funds to poorer regions. The former, though economically laudable, is often politically unacceptable whilst the latter (with a few highly expensive but similarly successful exceptions such as Ireland) often has little impact – merely bringing everybody to an average level. From an economic standpoint, the 'us and them' subsidiarity of Europe's member states is juxtaposed with the US 'one nation' approach.

Many countries from the US to Italy, Greece, and Germany to some limited extent are said to have a traditional 'soft-spot' in their culture for independent proprietors, 'yeoman' rural capitalists, start-up entrepreneurs, or small businesses generally. By contrast, some countries are thought to support larger firms as an element of the social contract (Sweden) or of national pride (France). Yet this romance with small (or large) business is difficult to justify empirically as correlating with economic success.

A possible, roughly natural rate of SME density also has limited implications for policies designed to promote 'entrepreneurship'. The logic is as follows: Let's assume that heading a small firm is an important mark of entrepreneurship, since the founder of a firm that quickly disappears may be less entrepreneurial than the leader of an SME that exists and survives, whether or not the leader was the original founder. In this analysis, the number of SMEs then becomes a proxy for the number of 'entrepreneurs': Entrepreneurs are the independent leaders of SMEs. Once we accept that this assumption is one logical proxy of entrepreneurial activity (although by no means the only one), we can then say that a roughly natural rate of SME density implies there is little that can help, or hinder, entrepreneurship at the national level in a broadly liberal trading environment. Ratios of 'entrepreneurs' (leaders of SMEs) are somewhat constant across European national populations. If one measures entrepreneurial activity by the rates of start-ups, then the analysis would change; but it is not clear that high start-up rates on a national scale really correlate with economic success either. The lowest start-up rates in Europe are in rich Sweden, the highest are in southern Europe, where unemployment is high and GDP per capita is lower. Definitions of entrepreneurship should encompass success measured by economic production and profits, and not just frenetic activities, primarily in the low-tech service sector. If this is accepted as one aspect of entrepreneurship, then countries like Sweden and Germany demonstrate less embarrassing 'entrepreneurship' than is sometimes claimed in academic studies focused exclusively on the founders of firms.

This is not to say that approximately one SME for every 50 residents *per se* is a number cast in stone. Rather, the conclusion is that the number is sufficiently similar across countries that it must be closely tied to structural developments in demographics and turn-of-the-century capitalist production which policy, wealth, and cultural differences affect only slightly. To phrase this another way: while this section of the study highlights many differences within Europe, with respect to SME density, Europe is already a partly (but by no means completely) unified market.

Table 5.1 Correlations in the EU (1995)

Population and SME gross value added	0.99
Population and SME numbers	0.97
Population and SME turnover	0.92
GDP and SME numbers	0.92
GDP and SME turnover	0.87

Sources: The World Bank for population and GDP statistical comparisons, Eurostat, Dun & Bradstreet for SME numbers and turnover.

There is a somewhat weaker but still very powerful correlation between the size of a country's population and SME turnover. Because population and GDP are also closely related, there is again a very powerful correlation between GDP and the number of SMEs that any country hosts. Similarly, there is powerful correlation between an economy's GDP and the turnover of SMEs.

The flow of the lines below demonstrates some of these very strong correlations, with (1) a few very small 'camel humps' (southern Europe on

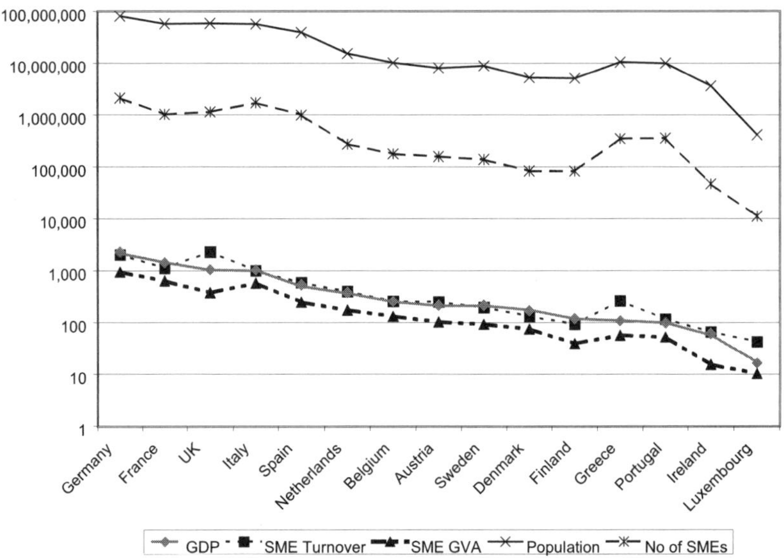

Figure 5.8 Inter-relationship of key SME indicators by country (1995).

Source: The World Bank for Population and GDP statistics, Eurostat, Dun & Bradstreet for enterprise statistics.

Note
SME turnover is measured by total value of production of all SMEs, not total value added. Therefore, turnover is close to GDP and in fact exceeds GDP in several states.

Units: GDP, SME turnover and SME GVA € billion. Population and number SMEs actual number.

numbers, the UK and Greece on turnover); (2) very small valleys (Scandinavia in numbers and turnover); and (3) data on SME turnover and GDP almost entirely overlapping.

On SMEs and employment in the EU

This study suggests that if Europe wishes to help its higher-risk capital markets, a focus on any particular firm organisational type (independent proprietor, small, medium, large) is unnecessary and perhaps counterproductive. But one reason governments (both the European Commission and national and local governments) focus on SMEs is that they view them as the primary agents of job creation and growth. While this is true, it should also be remembered that, if analysed separately (e.g. small vs. large, medium vs. large), large firms are actually the most important organisational type for employment (as well as turnover) within the EU.

Employment information can be divided first by employment statistics, which are less important from the perspective of capital markets, and then by turnover, which is more important.

First, from an employment perspective, the largest economies of the EU with the exception of southern European cases (Italy and Spain) are

Table 5.2 Size–class structure of non-primary private enterprise by country (1996)

Country	*Dominance*
Belgium	Very small
Greece	Very small
Italy	Very small
Spain	Very small
Austria	SME
Denmark	SME
Luxembourg	SME
Portugal	SME
Finland	LSE
France	LSE
Germany	LSE
Ireland	LSE
Netherlands	LSE
Sweden	LSE
UK	LSE
EU total	LSE

Source: European Network for SME Research, *The European Observatory for SMEs Fifth Annual Report, 1997*, The Netherlands: European Network for SME Research, October, 1999, p. 49.

Note
A country is said to be (1) very small, (2) SME, or (3) LSE dominated, depending on which enterprise type among these three contains the highest number of employees. Very small firms contain 1–9 employees, small contain 10–49 employees and medium 50–249 employees.

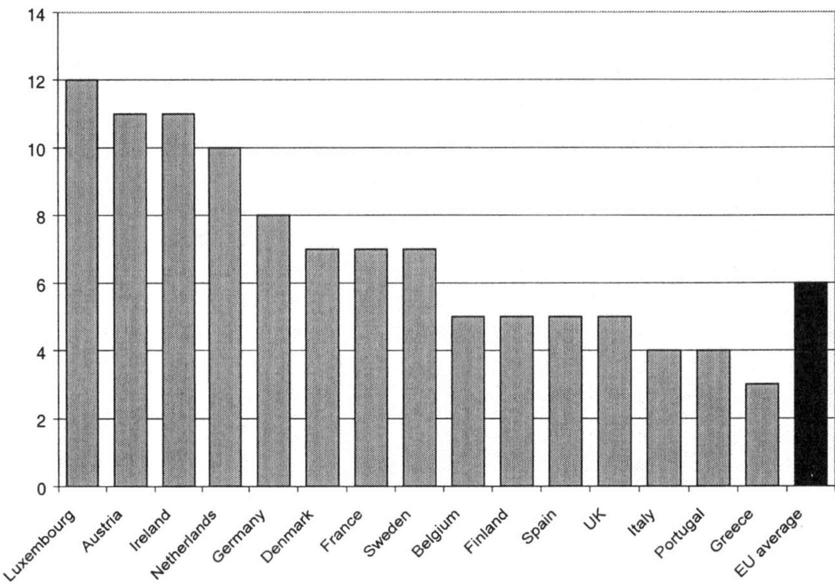

Figure 5.9 Average employment base of all sized non-primary private enterprises (1995).

Source: European Network for SME Research, *The European Observatory for SMEs Fifth Annual Report, 1997*, The Netherlands: European Network for SME Research, October, 1999, p. 49.

dominated by large enterprises, not small ones. In the chart below, a country is said to be 'dominated' by a firm of a particular size if it has a plurality of employees in that firm size.

It has already been stated that there is no clear correlation between wealth and SME numbers, and this chart helps to show the importance of large firms to most of the largest EU economies.

If we slice the information a different way in terms of the average employment base of all enterprises, we see particularly high figures for central Europe, followed by Scandinavian countries and France, with the UK and southern Europe towards the lower end of the scale.

Homing in on larger SMEs measured by employment and turnover

The European Observatory for SMEs provides statistics that are very useful for trying to filter out micro-enterprises (those with fewer than 10 employees) from more general statistics on SMEs. Filtering these very small firms out and focusing on the larger enterprises is important for better understanding the waters that angel investors, VC firms and espe-

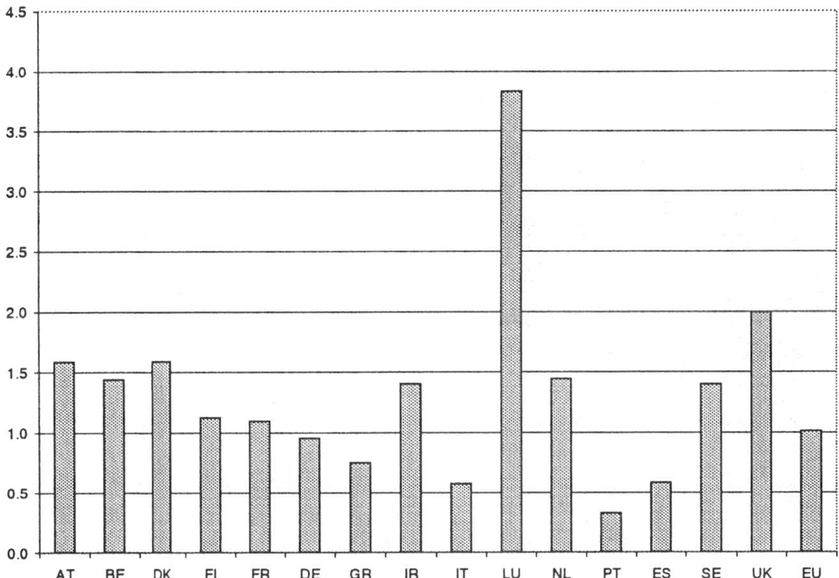

Figure 5.10 Average SME turnover by country (1995) (€ million).

Source: Eurostat.

cially small-cap exchanges might like to test. The smallest start-ups matter, and excluding them limits the analysis of targets for 'seed investment'. Still, the vast majority of these firms are not targets for any high-risk investors, and all of them combined do not matter as much as these larger SMEs to capital markets (at least not until they get bigger).

A graph focused on turnover of the average SME helps to show, perhaps not surprisingly, that countries with the largest numbers of SMEs have produced some of the smallest SMEs on average. By contrast, Luxembourg has many mid sized SMEs and its SMEs are by far the largest in terms of turnover. Of the EU's biggest economies, the UK's SMEs enjoyed the highest turnover of some €2 trillion.

How do European countries compare in their ability to develop these sizes of SME, that is, the larger small firms (10–49 employees) and the medium sized ones (50–249)? Figure 5.11 demonstrates that the EU's five largest economies tower over the rest in their ability to host the size of firms that is particularly attractive to high-risk venture capital. The most impressive foundations exist in Germany and the UK, so again, it is surprising that Germany trails significantly behind the UK in its ability to attract VC interest. Indeed, it is throughout German-speaking Europe (Germany, Austria, Switzerland and also in neighbouring Luxembourg) where small enterprises of 10–49 employees comprise the highest percentages of total enterprises – consistently at least 10 per cent of the total.

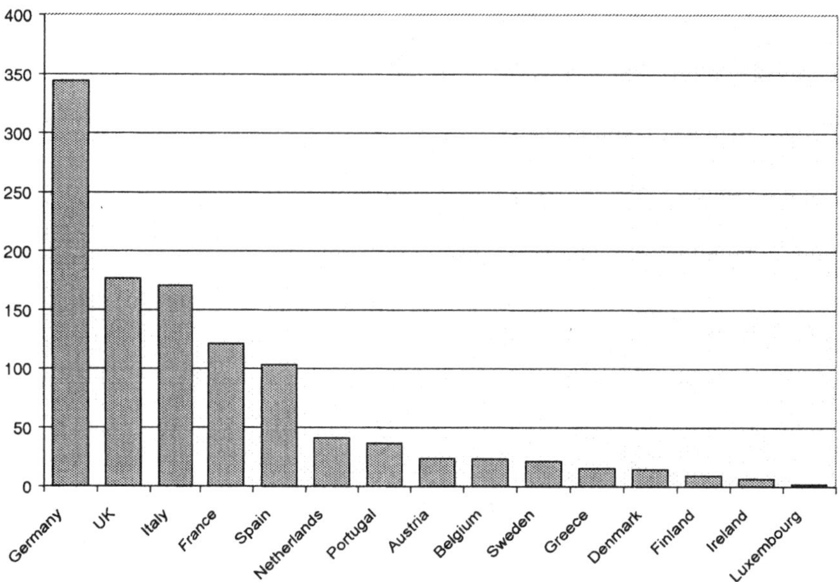

Figure 5.11 Number of small enterprises (10–49 employees) by country (1995) ('000s).

Source: European Commission, *Enterprises in Europe: Data 1994–1995*, Luxembourg: Eurostat, pp. 220–38.

There are far fewer medium sized enterprises (50–249 employees), yet these 170,000 firms are of a size quite likely to attract VC and institutional funding. The most successful among them in terms of revenue, profits and growth rates are the most likely to hit small-cap markets, if they did not already list as smaller firms. Here again, Germany is far and away the leading country in terms of numbers of mid sized firms, hosting more than one of every six in the EU-15. And the same four countries – Luxembourg, Austria, Switzerland and Germany – are again the countries most likely to emphasise firms of this size.

Germany can be described as more of a commercial banking country than a securities-based country like the UK. But recent changes in German tax law, capital gains and other deregulation efforts may push

Table 5.3 Medium enterprises proportion: EU four leading countries (1995) (percentage)

Luxembourg	12.4
Switzerland	12.1
Austria	10.8
Germany	10.0

Source: European Commission, *Enterprises in Europe: Data 1994–1995*, Luxembourg: Eurostat.

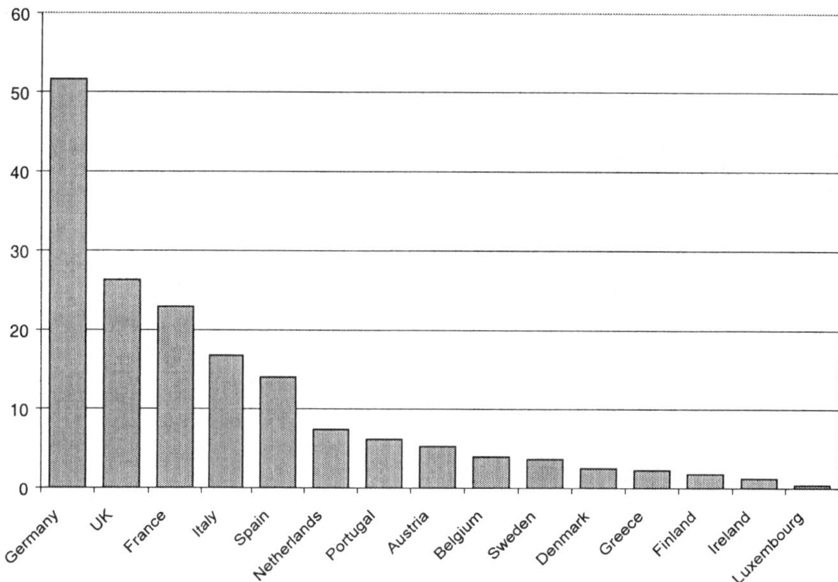

Figure 5.12 Total medium sized enterprises (1995) ('000s).

Source: European Commission, *Enterprises in Europe: Data 1994–1995*, Luxembourg: Eurostat, pp. 220–38.

Germany further in the direction of securities-based capitalism. The success of the Neuer Market and the incredible interest of the German people for at least some forms of high-risk securities (e.g. warrants) is also worthy of notice. Hence, while it is argued here that Germany has a great 'untapped potential' for more developed capital markets serving SMEs, it may be that this potential will soon be tapped. Germany and the rest of central Europe should be encouraged to continue to move in a direction which will allow these capital markets to flourish, and will allow Germany's vast SME base to blossom.

Opinions of SME representatives on capital and financing

SME representatives discussing constraints on short-term business developments focus extensively on governmental and non-governmental financial constraints: taxes, the cost of finance, and lack of working capital. The smallest companies are the ones that are most concerned with these issues.

Some of the largest differentials between the smallest and larger companies in opinions about the EU business environment emerge in opinions on taxes, where the largest percentage (almost 40 per cent) of smaller company representatives register concerns about this short-term constraint to their growth potential.

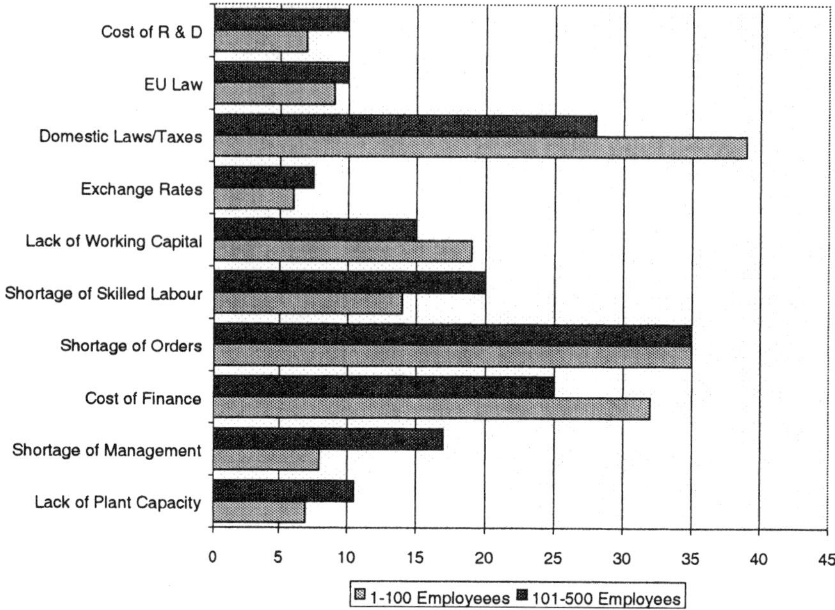

Figure 5.13 Short-term constraints on business expansion, percentage by class size (1996).

Source: European Network for SME Research, *The European Observatory for SMEs Fifth Annual Report, 1997*, The Netherlands: European Network for SME Research, October 1999, pp. 328–9; figures are approximate.

In the longer-term, smaller companies continue to worry far more than larger ones about taxes, the cost of capital, and lack of working capital.

Policy trends towards SMEs in the EU: specific cases

Governments, meanwhile, have responded to the concerns of SMEs with several policies designed to ease their credit-lines or in other ways alleviate their financial concerns. While most of this section focuses on the larger SMEs, some of these policies focus on the smaller start-ups, with the hope that they will thereby have a greater chance of becoming large.

Start-up credit-lines and loans

Many countries are offering new credit-lines, loan guarantees, and social security rebates for young enterprises.[3] *Austria* has implemented a new savings account that tops up founders' savings by 14 per cent (maximum €55,000) and a new credit line of (at most) €110,000 at 6 per cent interest. A new credit line is also available in *Finland*, with €60 million earmarked

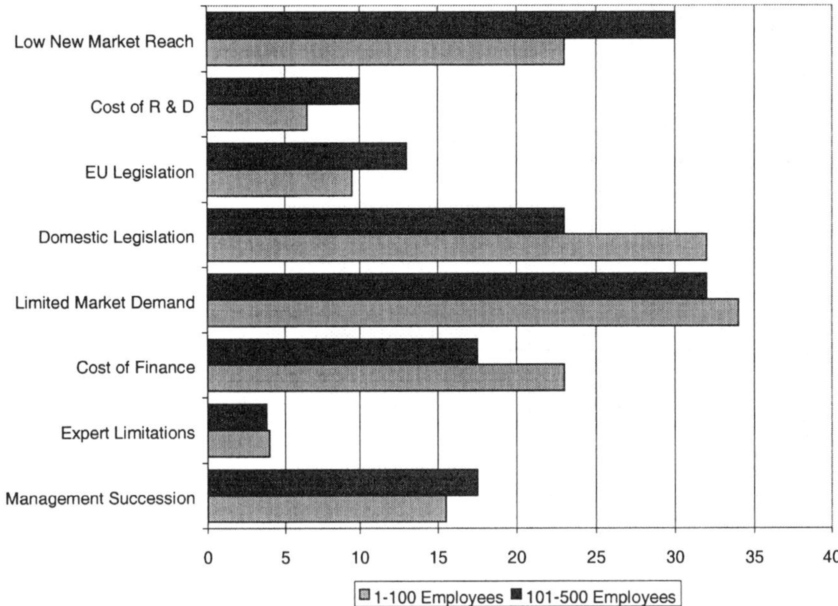

Figure 5.14 Long-term constraints on business expansion, percentage by size (1996).

Source: European Network for SME Research, *The European Observatory for SMEs Fifth Annual Report, 1997*, The Netherlands: European Network for SME Research, October 1999, pp. 332–3; figures are approximate.

for subsidised loans aimed at start-ups both in the manufacturing and the service sectors (a support policy that attracted a budget increase of some €25 million) only recently. *Greece* offers founders who cannot fully finance their business start-ups an allowance of up to €159,700. In *Belgium* a reduction of social security contributions and a new guarantee line reducing the risk on start-up loans are planned for business founders. Similarly, in *France*, BDPME, together with CDC, have set up a new start-up fund. For the same purposes, a new risk capital fund has been established for techno start-ups in the *Netherlands*.[4]

Other credit-lines and loans for SMEs

These include a traditional scheme that is operating in *Greece*. Commercial banks are obliged by the government to earmark 10 per cent of their loan portfolio as low interest loans to manufacturing SMEs. These loans are backed by state guarantees. The scheme is worth about €1 billion. If the banks do not lend as required, then their surplus is lodged with the Bank of Greece at zero interest until they comply. Hence, commercial banks either offer loans themselves or transfer their share to other banks for this purpose.

An even older scheme known as the Sabatini Act still operates in *Italy*. According to this scheme SMEs with less than 250 employees can receive a subsidised loan when purchasing or leasing production equipment or machinery. The credit line is managed by Mediocredito Centrale and therefore co-operates with other banks. Interestingly, the loan, with a duration of maximum 5 years, is only granted for a bill of exchange issued by the purchaser and then discounted by Mediocredito Centrale, thus enabling the purchaser to pay for the equipment immediately. 'According to surveys carried out on this scheme, some 44.7 per cent of enterprises questioned had actually been granted financial assistance under the Sabatini Act. Mediocredito Centrale reports that 36.6 per cent of capital went to specialised sectors, 34 per cent to traditional sectors, 32.5 to scale sectors and 13.3 to high-tech.'[5]

In the *Netherlands*, a scheme called the 'Borgstellingsregeling MKB. It offers SMEs with less than 100 employees (and start-ups) a loan guarantee for all kinds of measures related to business expansion. In 1997 a feature of the measure is that it is left to the banks to decide whether a guarantee under this scheme ought to be used or not, and if so, a second loan not guaranteed under this scheme has to be provided by the bank for the same amount. The loan conditions include normal commercial rates for low risk investments with duration of up to 12 years. The bank pays the state a one-off commission of 3 per cent. 'A total of 4,771 loans worth an average of €50,000 were secured in 1996. For that year the banks involved declared losses amounting to some €20 million, or about 1.6 per cent of the guarantees still open at the beginning of the year. Nonetheless, the net costs for the government were only €5.5 million in 1996.'[6]

For better access to venture capital, or to provide insurance for VCs funding SMEs:

'Apart from the recent establishment of secondary markets in small firm shares, new initiatives are generally geared to channelling private capital into the SME sector by means of guarantees.'[7] *Denmark* now offers loan guarantee facilities to development agencies that have equity in excess of €2.7 million and which invest in SMEs. According to the European Network for SME Research, this type of facility previously was restricted to agencies with equity of at least €6.7 million. Kera Ltd in *Finland* has widened the scope of its guarantees towards SMEs in the service sector. In *Italy*, SMEs facing a large share of short-term debt can convert it to medium-term debt via a new guarantee fund with a reserve of €52 million. Additionally, loans for capital investments can be secured via another €26 million fund. The Italian government has also allotted €182 million to banks and financial institutions for them to grant participative loans to SMEs. A guarantee fund geared towards SMEs lacking collateral for loans has been established in *Portugal.* It aims to secure 25–50 per cent of the loan risk not covered by collateral. In the *Netherlands* special facilities for innovative SMEs are provided under the existing loan guarantee scheme. Increasing the equity of SMEs with less than 250 employees is also the aim of a new guarantee scheme in *Austria*, according to which investments of up to €18,500 are granted a 100 per cent guarantee with 50 per cent guarantee for successive investments. The guarantee may be valid for up to 10 years.[8]

Belgium tries to channel private risk capital into SMEs with less than 100 employees by granting investors substantial guarantees. Furthermore, it is planned to reduce the tax rate on dividends from shares of SMEs to 15 per cent. The *Greek* government is currently formulating a new institutional framework for venture and seed capital that will add to existing interest rate subsidies for various kinds of investments and a subsidy on private investments in SMEs. In *Spain*, a new credit line aimed at innovative SMEs has been developed by ENISA, a public firm which specialises in enhancing innovation. It offers mainly participative loans to this type of enterprise. In the *United Kingdom*, a pre-finance service to help SMEs raise finance for innovative projects was established in 1996.'[9]

Germany offers a scheme called 'Eigenkapitalhilfeprogramm (EKH). The scheme is principally open to all business founders below 55 years of age and lacking the necessary financial means to start their business. It is also open to entrepreneurs who run enterprises no more than 2 years old. The programme consists of a loan of up to 10 years and €385,000 in a form that adds to existing equity rather than debt (participative loan). The loan does not require common collateral, and its rate is capped at 5 per cent from the fifth year onwards. The measure is run by the Deutsche Ausgleichsbank and considered to be successful because of its positive impact on strengthening the notoriously weak equity base of start-ups. Also geared towards start-ups is 'Naisyrittajalaina' run by Kera Ltd in *Finland*, and designed to promote female entrepreneurship by offering a subsidised loan to women starting up in business or becoming self employed. The average loan size initially from 1997 was some €12,155 with a fixed term of 5 years. The original budget of €8.6 million was exhausted by April and has been replenished with further €6.9 million only recently.

Generally, these programmes are making a positive contribution to the development of SMEs in all of the countries surveyed, yet it could be argued that, because they are geared towards isolated SMEs that qualify and receive the funds, they cannot have a very long-term effect on the economies of the EU. Instead, they may simply reward some firms that qualify or win awards, and punish others with non-market mechanisms. Because they are geared specifically towards SMEs rather than towards firms in general, they may also be shifting turnover from large to smaller firms in ways that create externalities, however small. It is likely that general policies to ease the supply of credit would have a more thorough impact. Policies could range from regulatory reforms on institutional investors (e.g. pension funds) and what they are allowed or encouraged to invest in (e.g. VC funds) to more expensive tax breaks on all firms, which might generate more financial resources in-house without creating market distortions.

Saving money and time by simplifying bureaucracy

The EU member states all sponsor initiatives to simplify bureaucracy among states, co-ordinate bureaucracy and eliminate some financial bureaucracy. The chart below suggests that these initiatives will be welcome throughout the EU, but particularly in southern Europe.

The *United Kingdom* has a deregulation unit charged with co-ordinating the UK government's deregulation policy between government departments, ensuring that business views are taken into account, and working to minimise bureaucratic and administrative costs. Similarly, *France* and

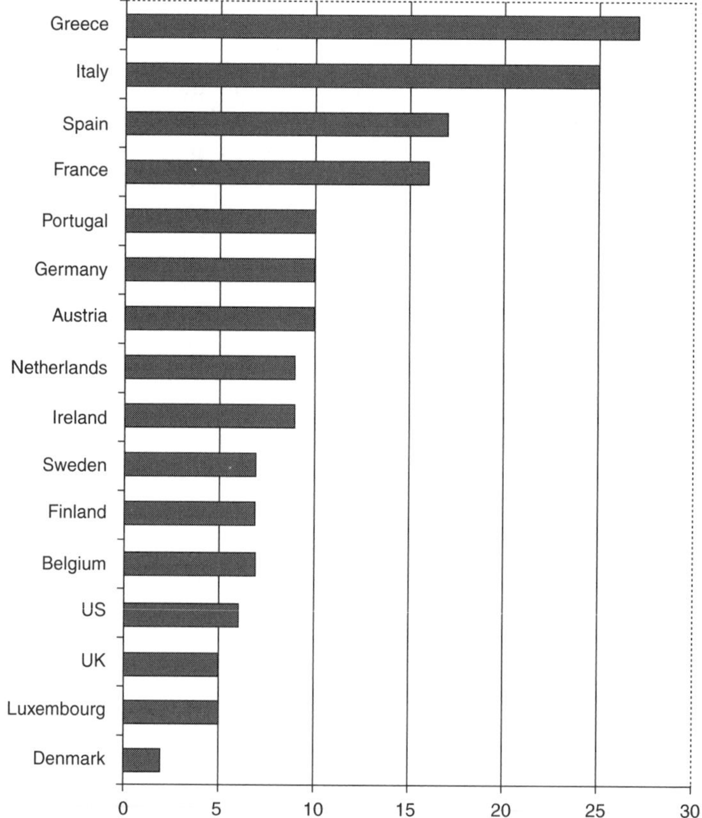

Figure 5.15 Number of procedures for company registration (1996).

Source: European SME Observatory.

Portugal have set up similar departments under the responsibility of their prime ministers. Most other member states have lower-level advisory committees working towards the same goals.[10] One of the initiatives of the *UK*'s deregulation unit was to provide flexibility in the upper threshold of the VAT accounting scheme at £300,000, so that firms can remain in the scheme until their turnover exceeds £375,000.

The *Flemish* Institute for Self-Employed Entrepreneurs (VIZO) in Belgium tries to encourage free and creative entrepreneurship while also providing services to better understand bureaucratic burdens for both SME leaders and civil servants. *Sweden* provides a single identification number to all enterprises making reorganisations of the enterprise and name changes easier. There is a business register in *Italy* with a similar function.

The same or similar bureaux have acted in co-ordination with other government units – in *Denmark, Belgium* and the *UK* – to create action plans complementary with others listed above for limiting the tax burden on SMEs.[11]

The EU now recommends 'seven basic principles for prompt organisation' that will hopefully limit administrative burdens for SMEs even further. The most important among them include the following:

- Centralising decisions for SMEs at one contact point
- Ensuring that an authority is appointed to take specific charge of many managerial systems, including licensing, target completion, SME advisory roles
- Ensuring proper feedback.[12]

Other

One unusual programme in the EU not discussed previously is the Joint European Venture (JEV) programme, which is a support mechanism for the creation of trans-national joint ventures for SMEs in the Community, approved 5 November 1997. The Commission's contribution would cover some of the expenses occurred in setting up a venture. In January 1998, the Commission proposed to allocate a larger sum for JEV, permitting some 1,500–2,000 projects to be financed.[13]

Notes

1 *European Commission, Enterprises in Europe: Data 1994–1995*, Luxembourg: Eurostat, p. 142.
2 European Network for SME Research, *The European Observatory for SMEs Fifth Annual Report*, 1997, The Netherlands: European Network for SME Research, October 1999, p. 143.
3 Ibid., p. 191.
4 Ibid., pp. 195–6.
5 Ibid., p. 205.

6 Ibid., p. 206.
7 Ibid., p. 191.
8 Ibid., pp. 196–7.
9 Ibid., pp. 196–7.
10 European Commission, *Improving and Simplifying the Business Environment for Business Start-ups*, European Communities, 1998, p. 7.
11 Ibid., pp. 8–12.
12 Ibid., p. 17.
13 European Commission, 'Access to Finance: Joint European Venture (JEV)', http://europa.eu.int/comm/dg23/financing/docs/jev2.htm

6 Private equity and venture capital in the European Union

This chapter provides a comparative analysis of the venture capital (VC) industries fuelling SMEs in different states of the EU. It first provides statistics that are broadly comparative, with a focus on the EU as a whole and the top markets. It then discusses VC activity within individual regions or states, to home in on strengths and problems that are important and comparable. This chapter is broadly comparative, focusing exclusively on VC markets, but with information about many EU countries. Indeed, some of the smaller countries are emphasised as much as the larger ones, to demonstrate the diversity of the markets, to introduce markets that may be less familiar to readers, and to avoid repetition.

Superficially, cultural explanations appear to matter in an understanding of strong vs. weak links between SMEs and VCs. Leaders rhetorically decrying 'cowboy capitalism' or 'Anglo-American capitalism' in Germany or France may be subtly degrading the very buy-outs and takeovers that are the primary source of liquidity for VCs. Yet France, paradoxically, was the largest VC and private equity market in continental Europe in the late 1990s, and its institutions will need to cope with the fact that France obviously profits from its increasingly aggressive banking industry.

Within European regions of similar (but not identical) culture and language, one also notes dramatic differences in VC activity towards all firms, including SMEs. For example, a previous section of this report questioned Sweden's traditional pattern of favouring large over small firms of all kinds, but this strategy may have some benefits in the financial industries, where recently large firms have had the easiest time attracting capital. There do appear to be natural clusterings of activities and economies of scale gained through size. Generally, Sweden invests more VC money, and attracts more private equity and buy-out activity than other countries in Scandinavia, even on a per capita basis. Assuming some similarities of culture within Scandinavia, something else could be at work beside culture.

Similarly, comparing the Netherlands with Belgium, Belgium is a far less developed private equity market despite a similar linguistic and cultural background at least in Flanders. (And Wallonia is less developed than much of France per capita.) Private consultants blame 'a high degree of state control and few large domestic investors.' In Belgium, the largest buy-outs are frequently funded by foreign investors, and the domestic corporate marketplace may be too heavily dominated by family-owned companies to attract more significant interest especially with respect to buy-out funds.[1] As the government relinquishes control of investment institutions, the situation is likely to change, but in the short term, 'cultural cousins' have produced very different outcomes.

We would again place an emphasis on tax and savings policies. In particular, the countries with the most dynamic pension and savings schemes appear to be those with the most dynamic capital markets and the most diverse institutional investors. By contrast, heavily regulated or government-owned savings methods and institutions tend to correlate with far more stagnant VC activity. This punishes all firms. And in countries where heavy regulations coincide with a reliance on small firms (e.g. Greece), it is likely that the smaller firms are the most punished.

Patterns in the VC industry also appear to reflect particularly large differences across nations based partly on the size of the country and also clustering within the country. Clearly, the larger the economy, the easier it is to generate VC momentum. Yet there is more to clustering than having a large national GDP. In the most recent years for which statistics are available, the correlation between the GDP of an economy and the new VC funds raised in that economy is not quite as high as the stronger correlation between the turnover of companies and new funds raised by VCs. It is interesting that, although much of the VC market focuses these days on the largest firms, later-stage funding, and MBOs, the countries where SME turnover is highest are also those that support the most dynamic VC industries. These correlations are shown below.

It also appears that countries that have managed to develop pockets of urban or regional momentum, in particular one or two dynamic financial centres, are those with the most successful SME industries. Countries within the EU that have one obvious financial centre appear to have particularly accelerated VC funding activities.

One can highlight the differences between, on the one hand, (1) the UK (London), France (Paris), and the Netherlands (Amsterdam), where there

Table 6.1 EU statistical correlations on new funds raised (1995)

Correlation of SME turnover and VC new funds raised	0.82
Correlation of GDP and VC new funds raised	0.60

Sources: European Venture Capital Association (for VC funds), World Bank (GDP), Eurostat (turnover).

Note
Both correlations measure the EU-15, excluding Luxembourg; all figures are for 1998 except SME turnover, which is for 1995.

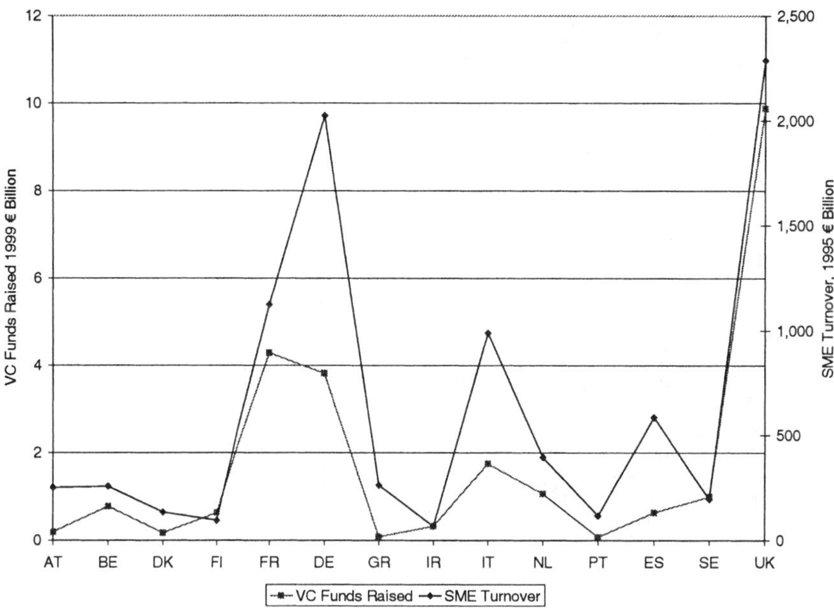

Figure 6.1 SME turnover (1995) and new VC funds in the EU (1999).

Sources: Eurostat for turnover; EVCA for new funds raised.

Note

Turnover (1995 data, the latest year where figures are comparable) focuses exclusively on SMEs, and units are € billion. New funds raised are figures for 1999 and units are € billion. Comparable data on new funds was not available for Luxembourg.

is an obvious financial/high-tech centre of urban or suburban activity; and on the other hand, (2) Germany and Italy, where activities are more dispersed throughout these two countries. Some of these issues are highlighted in Figure 6.1. Countries where the 'turnover' line runs far below the new funds raised by VCs are those with the most impressive VC industries adjusting for the size of enterprise production (the UK, France, the Netherlands, Sweden, Finland). Countries where the 'turnover' line touches the 'funds raised' one, or rises well above it (Germany, Austria, Greece, Portugal, Denmark), are those that can be considered comparatively shunned by the VC industry.

Yet one should remember that these statistics are measuring rapidly moving targets. Activity is picking up all over Europe, and activity is picking up in Germany in particular. Germany's markets are so large that it should be able to develop a dynamic VC industry even with somewhat dispersed financial and VC activity (currently centred around Frankfurt, Munich, Hamburg and Berlin, in that order). Italy also supports a very large economy and only a few regional centres of dynamism of significant interest to VCs. Still, it could be said that the industry is more dispersed across states than the US industry, and it is to some extent dispersed within states. While this is not a crippling handicap, it appears to be a hindrance at this particular stage of European VC development.

A comparative overview of VC industries

European venture capital investments were stagnant in the late 1980s and early 1990s due in large part to recession in Britain and slow growth elsewhere, but they grew steadily in the late 1990s. The European private equity portfolio was worth over €58 billion at the end of 1999, and 1997 to 1999 were banner years for fundraising.

These statistics demonstrate rates of increase comparable to those in the US, and generally help to support cyclical arguments about the nature of VC activity. European economies are picking up, and so is VC activity – dramatically.

Rates of activity within Europe

Which countries are raising this money? With over 48 per cent of European VC activity taking place in or through Britain, the UK stands out as

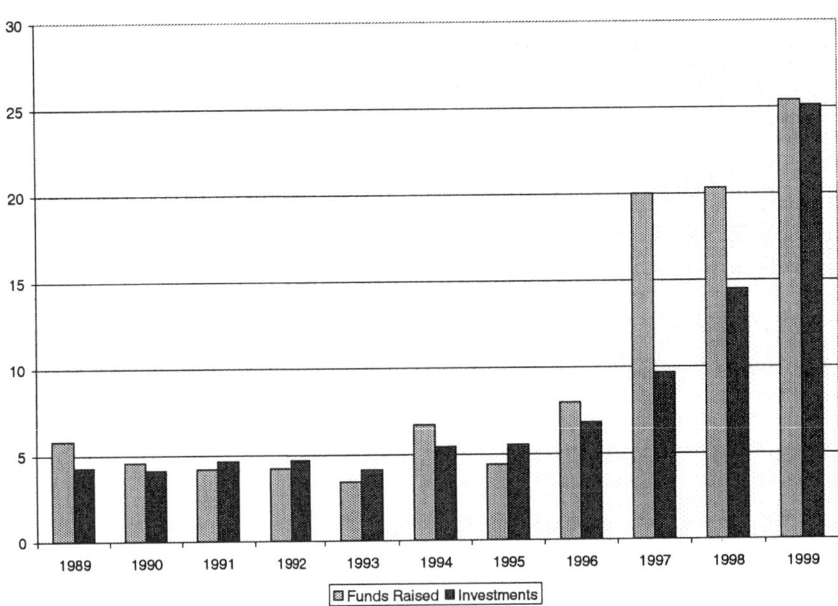

Figure 6.2 New funds raised and investments (1989–98) (€ billion).

Source: *EVCA Yearbook 2000*, European Private Equity Venture Capital Association, Luxembourg, p. 15.

Table 6.2 VC portfolios at cost (1999) (€ million)

Country	*€ million*	%
UK	28,044	48.1
Germany	7,896	13.5
France	5,279	9.0
Netherlands	4,571	7.8
Italy	3,618	6.2
Sweden	2,313	4.0
Belgium	1,796	3.1
Spain	1,493	2.6
Norway	759	1.3
Switzerland	741	1.3
Finland	530	0.9
Ireland	413	0.7
Denmark	344	0.6
Portugal	270	0.5
Austria	135	0.2
Greece	99	0.2
Iceland	51	0.1
Total	58,350	100.0

Source: *EVCA Yearbook 2000*, European Private Equity and Venture Capital Association, Luxembourg, p. 45.

the most impressive VC market by far. Its markets are roughly the size of those of the next five competitors combined.

Germany, by contrast, stands out as a market that, judging from the impressive size of its economy, could sport a much larger VC presence. The markets for smaller stocks and early-stage investments are picking up dramatically. But VC activity has been quite limited at the high-profit, high-value end of the market. In the short term, this appears good for SMEs, as they are more the centres of attention, but in the long term it is probably bad for everyone if bad for the industry as a whole.

France, meanwhile, is becoming more and more dynamic in its VC activity. France is also a bit like Britain with respect to the concentrated location of financial activity if not with respect to the much-ballyhooed 'Anglo-American capitalism'. Just as VC activities in Britain congregate around London, in France they congregate around Paris. Having anchor cities or suburban clusters (e.g. Silicon Valley, Boston, New York) appears to be useful for this business. But German activity is more dispersed even adjusting for the large size of its production base.

Among the smaller economies, Sweden and particularly the Netherlands are markets that stand out for surprising power, maturity, and diversity. Of the largest VC markets in Europe, the Netherlands ranks fourth, and its second place challenger, Germany, has an economy more than five times its size, with almost four times its population.

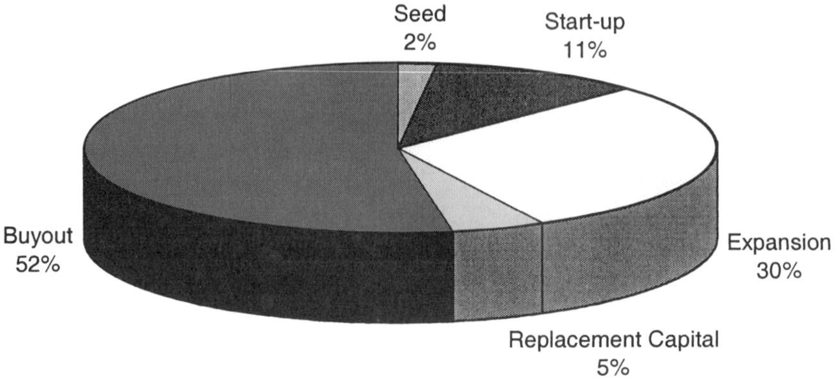

Figure 6.3 Stage distribution by percentage of private investment (1998).

Source: *EVCA Yearbook 2000*, European Private Equity and Venture Capital Association, Luxembourg, p. 33.

The investments can be broken down by stage as in Figure 6.3. The UK statistics, which are such a large portion of the pie, distort all of Europe towards buy-out and expansion.

Further, Figures 6.4 and 6.5 demonstrate that 'buy-out penetration' (buy-outs as a percentage of GDP), a primary factor in the dynamism and

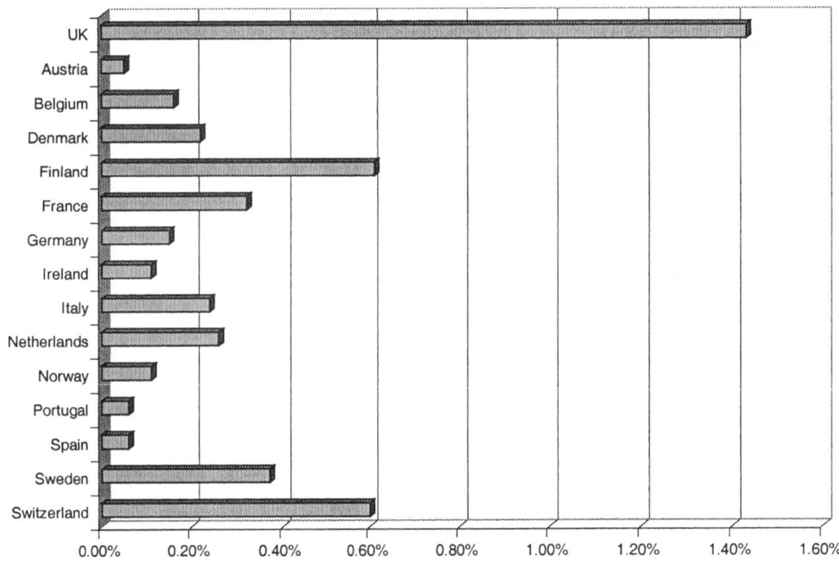

Figure 6.4 Penetration of buy-outs in Europe (1997) (buy-out activity as percentage GDP).

Source: Initiative Europe Ltd (various publication sources 1996–2000).

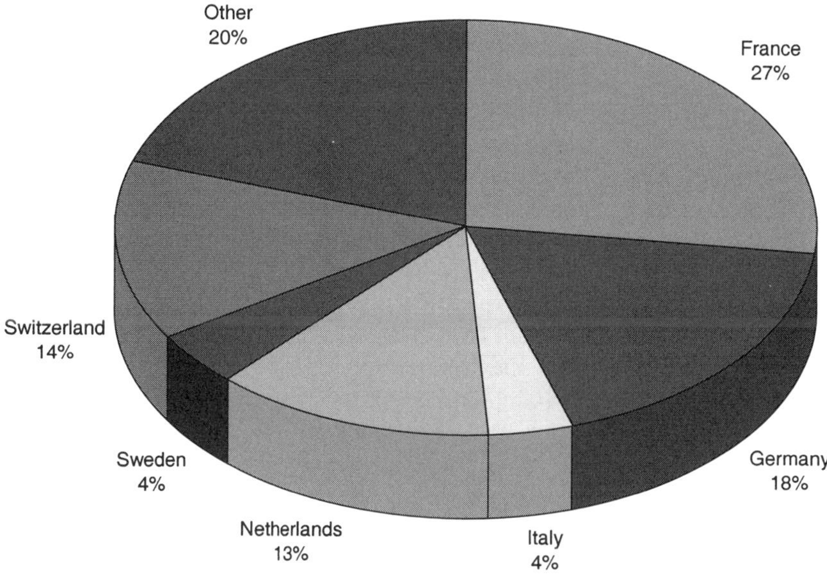

Figure 6.5 Number of buy-outs by country in Europe, excluding the UK (1997).

Source: Initiative Europe Ltd (various publication sources 1996–2000).

liquidity of the VC markets, is also far higher in Britain than elsewhere. But France, Germany, the Netherlands and Switzerland are the other large European markets for buy-out activity, and Finland, Switzerland and Sweden all stand out as markets where this financial activity is becoming a central economic feature.

The investors in all private equity in 1999 can be further broken down

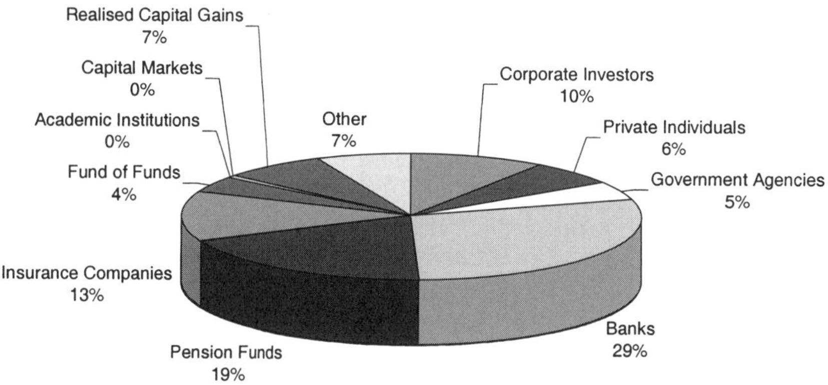

Figure 6.6 Private equity raised by investor type (1999).

Source: *European Venture Capital Association Yearbook 2000*, Luxembourg: European Private Equity Venture Capital Association, 2000, p. 30.

by type of investor, with banks and other financial institutions sponsoring the largest share of the investments as follows (see also Chapter 2).

Europe's largest markets: the UK, France and Germany compared

Analysing differences in the various countries of the EU is possible via other statistics from the European Venture Capital Institute, country venture capital associations, financial news and private consulting groups. A few key points stand out.

The VC markets outside of the UK are dominated by aid to the earlier-stage firms, and this aid for the British firms is indeed increasingly hard to come by. An illustration of the comparative investment styles of VCs filtering money through Britain, France and Germany is provided below. France devotes a larger proportion of VC money to start-ups than the UK and Germany emerges as the country most ready among these 'big three' to fund the highest-risk, earliest-stage projects.

If one filters these buy-out funds out of the equation, the UK's venture

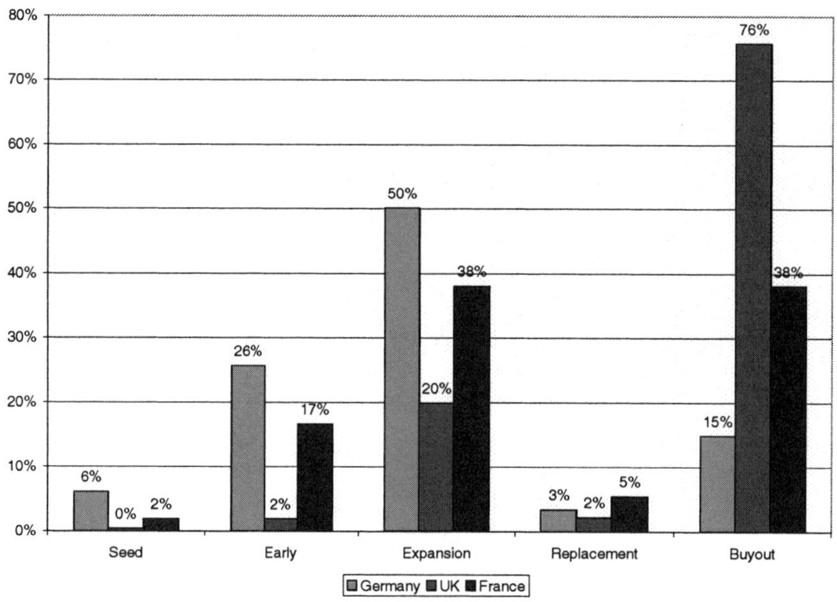

Figure 6.7 Percentage of VC money by investment type – Germany, the UK and France compared (1999).

Source: *European Venture Capital Association Yearbook 2000*, Luxembourg: European Private Equity Venture Capital Association, 2000.

Note

'0 per cent' implies less than 0.5 per cent of the total VC investment pie is geared towards seed money.

market is still bigger than that of larger economies like Germany, yet differentials narrow significantly. More important, it emerges that 'Cool Britannia' is actually rather nervous (or apathetic) when it comes to the more risky VC activities of providing seed and early-stage money for start-ups. Germany, by contrast, would be mischaracterised as a land of stolid banks and overly possessive Mittelstand owners. German start-ups have managed to attract more seed money than UK ones from their respective national investment communities, and the total pie of VC money in Germany is much more weighted towards the earliest stages of funding. These facts are again demonstrated by EVCA's information base.

Generalising across the biggest three markets for VC money, a few points stand out.

Germany

Despite problems noted above, the German markets demonstrate some significant strengths. There was a funding jump in the second half of the 1990s after unimpressive performance in the first half, and particularly healthy growth in seed and start-up funding – in 1999, 32 per cent of the total funds, 52 per cent of the number of investments – with over 1,000 companies receiving early funding.

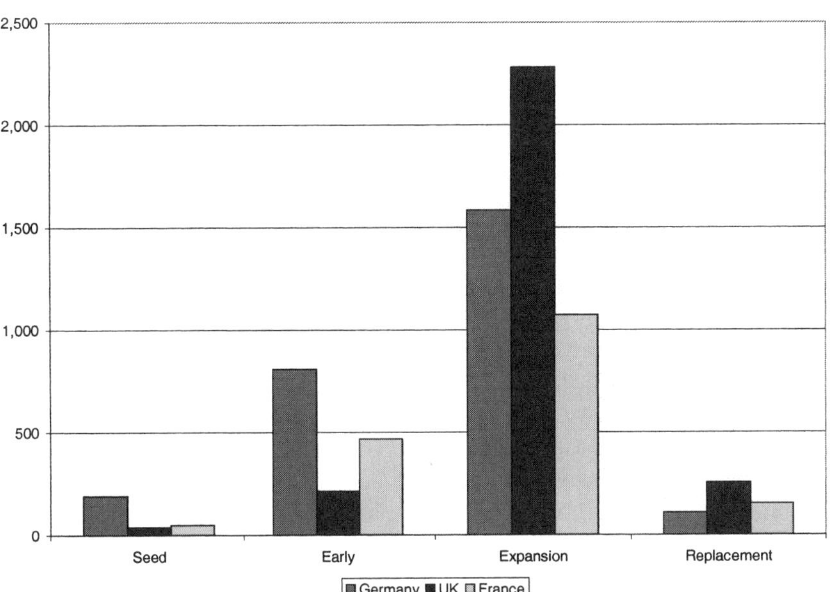

Figure 6.8 VC funding by stage (excluding buy-outs) (1999) (€ million – Germany, France and the UK).

Source: *European Venture Capital Association Yearbook 2000*, Luxembourg: European Private Equity Venture Capital Association, 2000.

Yet Germany's €3.2 billion investment in 1999 is such a small percentage of its capital pie that it is clear policy constraints, notably taxes and restrictions on the activities of public institutions and pension funds, are at work. Banks traditionally have been the big players, making over half the investments, but they have few incentives to play in high-risk markets and hence much of their potential lies stagnant. Recent changes have encouraged pension funds to put up more of the capital. Tax and pension schemes weaken interest. Further, the corporatism of boards may limit the power of VCs as board members so that the cost of knowledge and involvement for many investments exceeds the worth, and VCs are handicapped in the extent to which they can provide advice and control.

In 1997, the law for 'Unternehmensbeteiligungsgesellschaften' was modified – a problem that the German Venture Capital Association has focused on and lobbied for over the past years. With its liberalised regulations and tax incentives (tax rollover), the law was attractive to the majority of private equity houses. But with the tax reform of the new German government the tax rollover was cancelled. After that, individual investors could use tax incentives as long as they invest in venture capital.[2] In 1999 the laws were again being revised. The tax incentive contained in the 1997 law was cancelled. The end of 1999 saw tax reforms announced by the government. These proposed reductions in tax rates with set maximum rates of 25 per cent and 45 per cent for corporate and income taxes respectively. Most important was the proposal that capital gains would be tax free. These headline proposals have the potential to galvanise German private equity. However, the are some details still being ironed out.

It may be that some of the problem is also related to the dispersion of financing and talent across Germany. In that sense Germany is a microcosm of the European problem of economies of scale. A look at the location of VC firms in Germany helps to show that they are following dispersed industries with dispersed investment pools. The situation may profit from consolidation.

The German Venture Capital Association provides a useful interactive map permitting people to view the primary VC firms in their region of Germany. The number of firms listed for different German financial centres, with 165 firms total, can be seen.

The chart below demonstrates that the dispersion of VC activity is more pronounced than in all other primary markets for venture capital in this discussion (the US, the UK, France, Spain), with the possible exception of Italy. Although it cannot be the primary problem with the VC industry in Germany, this may be an industry where such equal distribution slows momentum.

In terms of buy-outs, their total value rose 42 per cent in Germany to £3.08 billion in 1998, meaning that it overtook its main continental rival, France, in terms of value for the second time. However, the volume of

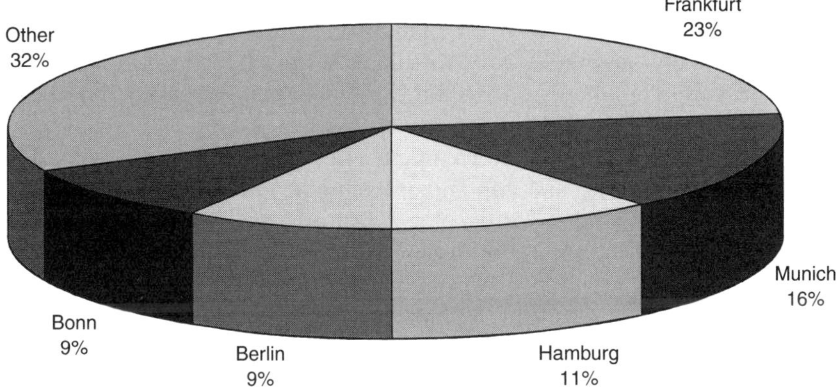

Figure 6.9 Location of VC firms in Germany (1998).

Source: The German Venture Capital Association, Bundesverband Deutscher KBGs: http://www.BVK-eV.de.

buy-outs only rose 15 per cent, leading to a marked rise in average deal value. Restructuring by large German conglomerates is finally taking hold, leading to a greater number of larger buy-outs.

Mittelstand companies are often blamed for a conservative and individualist management style that might suppress private and public capital markets, but according to at least one source, 'the gradual evolution of the Mittelstand group of companies is finally leading to more deals – the number of buy-outs from private shareholders now outweighs the number from corporates'.[3]

Partly due to the rise of the Neuer Markt, exit has also become somewhat easier. The level of German IPOs in 1998 has far outstripped all previous records. A large amount of equity funding is available from both international and domestic players. But as price levels rise, Germany's banks remain the players holding most of the cards.[4]

The United Kingdom

There are significant differences between British and continental styles of VC funding. The money pouring through the UK was far larger in absolute terms than the money invested elsewhere, but as previously stated much of the 'UK money' actually came from the US and funded buy-out activity rather than traditional venture work. Further, the UK emerges as the country with the most conservative VC investment structure in Europe. It is primarily geared towards buy-outs and replacement capital for later-stage firms rather than towards the earlier stages of funding. It should be stated that while this may seem on the surface to be a sign of weakness in the UK market for 'traditional' VC activity, it is instead in part a demonstration of the fact that UK VC institutions have found a more massive return on their investment through these larger investments. Buy-outs are now by far the most profitable hunting grounds in Europe for VC money, and Britain is taking a very large portion of the game.

The UK remains the most active market in the world behind the US for venture capital activity. The volume and value of UK private equity deals have consistently matched or exceeded the sum total of all continental European activity, and the last five years have seen a sharp rise in all types of private equity investments, with rising returns attracting the major US players. As a result, according to Labour Chancellor Gordon Brown, 'A strong venture capital industry supporting high-tech, high risk investments is critical to the future of Britain.'[5] Some 38 per cent of new issues on the London Stock Exchange were venture-backed companies from 1 June 1992 to 1 September 1998. The venture capital industry itself, with some 117 companies (or more when related financial institutions are considered), is believed to directly employ several thousand people (over 1,000 executives).[6]

Of course, it must be remembered that much of the most dynamic activity is for the biggest deals with companies that are not small and medium sized. The smaller companies are simply not as hot as the larger ones. Still, these deals provide a base of expertise for the smaller companies to profit from and a base of capital that rubs off on many of them; and smaller firms have also experienced record VC investments in the past few years. Indeed, even as the small-cap markets appear troubled, small-cap investments by private organisations remain buoyant. They don't receive the same sky-high valuations as FTSE (or especially NASDAQ) listed stocks, but they are growing quickly. The UK venture capital industry invested almost £5 billion in 1998.

VCs cluster tightly around London. Hemscott provides information on the distribution of major funds in the UK. If one includes the foreign firms, British-based VCs are quite concentrated, by the standards of

Table 6.3 Location of VCs in the UK (1999) (number)

London	64
Scotland	9
The North	7
Midlands	5
The South	5
Northern Ireland	4
East Anglia	3
Wales	1

Source: Data from Hemscott website, VC firm names and locations downloaded 8 February 2000.

Table 6.4 Major UK management buy-outs (1998)

Deal	*Value*	*Investor*
Willis Corroon	1,050	Kohlberg Kravis Roberts
IPC Magazines	860	Cinven
HMV Media Group	801	Advent International
Watmoughs	700	Investcorp
Dunlop Standard Aerospace	680	Doughty Hanson
Formica	650	CVC Capital Partners
The Tussauds Group	435	Charterhouse Development Capital
Total	5,176	

Source: Initiative Europe Ltd (various publication sources 1996–2000).

Europe, around London. This study suggests that this 'lopsided' concentration around a financial capital is actually very appropriate for the VC industry; it works for the US, and it appears to work in the UK.

Table 6.4 dates only from 1998, but it demonstrates that most UK buy-outs of private firms (as opposed to public mergers) do not exceed £1 billion in value. Some are nevertheless huge by the standards of the industry, and these large deals (having little to do with SMEs) greatly affect any statistics on UK VC activity.

The top UK private equity investors in the late 1990s are listed below by both volume and value of deals.

Table 6.5 Top UK private equity investors by deals (1996–8)

Investor	*No. of deals*
3i	688
NatWest Group	85
Murray Johnstone Private Equity	50
Barclays Group	38
Lloyds TSB Development Capital	36

Source: Initiative Europe Ltd (various publication sources 1996–2000).

Table 6.6 Top UK private equity investors by value (1996–8)

Investor	*£ Million*
3i	1,372
Cinven	657
NatWest Group	500
Charterhouse Development Capital	297
Electra Fleming	283

Source: Initiative Europe Ltd (various publication sources 1996–2000).

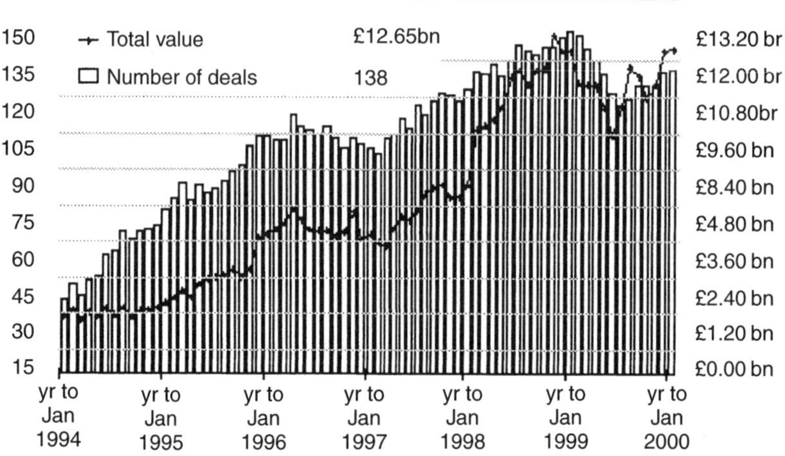

Figure 6.10 Number and total value of £10m+ buy-outs (1994–2000).

Source: private.equity.research.unit@initiative-europe

Note

Compound annual growth rate in volume of 106 per cent and value of 184 per cent.

Exit strategies

In 1998, 30 per cent of trading company floats on the Official List of the London Stock Exchange and 16 per cent of all floats on AIM were venture backed.

The BVCA, WM Company (WM), and Crossroads Management (UK) Ltd, in a 1998 Performance Measurement Survey of unquoted independent venture capital funds managed by UK firms studied the 'net' of all costs and fees to investors in VC funds. Included in the survey were funds that invested primarily in the UK and, for the first time, some funds with an overseas investment focus. The survey's results did not include quoted venture and development capital investment trusts, yet they are impressive. UK VC funds generated a net return to investors of 30.1 per cent even though a significant percentage of the assets were still being valued at cost, in line with BVCA valuation guidelines.

France

There is evidence that Germany has overtaken France in large segments of the private equity and VC investment market (e.g. buy-outs), despite France historically being the most significant private equity and VC player on the continent in the late 1990s, both for international investors and a growing number of domestic investors. In 1999, France was still the continental leader in commitments, raising €4.3 billion to Germany's €3.8

billion. Secondary buy-outs/trade sales are a prominent feature of the market, partly due to the lack of a good exit market, although the Second Marché and the Nouveau Marché are providing improved exit routes. The number of IPOs in 1999 was the highest since 1987.

Private equity and venture capital investment has been encouraged by the government: The 'DSK rule', whereby 5 per cent of insurance funds must be invested in venture capital or the Nouveau Marché, has provided a boost.[7] While this may be eliminated by the European Commission, it has helped to place French VC and public equity activity on higher ground. The European Venture Capital Association notes the following trends in French VC activity:

- Greater 'specialisation of investment vehicles' (by industry sector and type of investment);
- Increased 'business angel' and 'corporate angel' activities, with large industrial groups and banks rather than private equity, VC firms most important in fanning the flames;
- A tremendous increase in private equity. Funds raised during the year were €4.3 billion.

Banks remain the most important source of capital in 1999, although their share of the total funds raised fell to 25 per cent that year. Companies and pension funds, meanwhile, now comprise a larger percentage of the pie.[8]

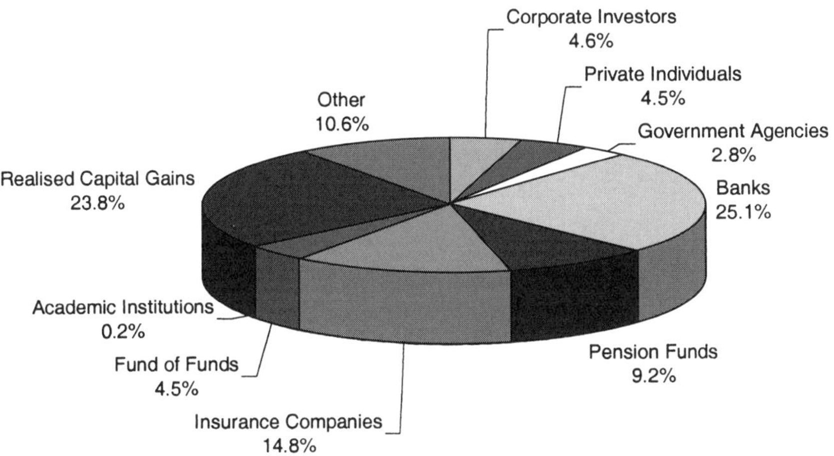

Figure 6.11 French private equity commitments by source (1999).

Source: *EVCA Yearbook 2000*, European Private Equity and Capital Markets Institute, Luxembourg, p. 30.

Southern Europe compared: Italy, Spain, Greece and Portugal

Although Italy had a highly successful year in 1999 in terms of fundraising, Spain was passed by the Netherlands and Sweden, far smaller economies, in the latest comparative statistics for venture capital activity, but these markets are still very dynamic, with rapid growth rates and strong prospects. By contrast, Greece and Portugal lag far behind major markets. Unfortunately, this may be in part due to their reliance on traditional 'old' economy small and medium sized enterprises as the foundations of production in their economies. But in large part it is due to heavily controlled regulation of the financial industry. In Greece, especially, one sees one of the most strictly controlled markets in Europe for capital and savings. These two markets are interesting despite their size, because they are the markets in Europe where SME concentrations are the highest, and yet in terms of VC activity they rank among the lowest.

Italy

The Italian Venture Capital Association (Ass. Italiana Inv. Istit. Cap. Ris.) provides pertinent information on the history and size of the venture capital industry in Italy. The AIFI Association was founded in May 1986 in order to promote, develop and represent, institutionally, private equity activity in Italy.[9]

Perhaps even more than the German VC industry, the Italian one seems small compared to the size of the Italian market. Its most up-to-date statistics date from 1999, when €1.8 billion was invested in 390 projects of one kind or another. Activity is lower than in smaller economies such as Sweden and the Netherlands. Yet it is more similar to the UK in its weighting towards later-stage projects. Although roughly 80 per cent of its investments are heading towards SMEs in terms of the number of investments, a far smaller percentage of the money invested goes to SMEs in terms of the value of investments. Almost exactly two-thirds of the money fuelled only 52 buy-outs. This leaves less than 40 per cent of the money for more traditional (early- and expansion-stage) VC activities. These issues are illustrated in Figure 6.12.

Figure 6.13 demonstrates cultural forces at work in Italian capitalism. Partly, VC markets may be suppressed by the fact that business leaders choose not to give up control for family projects to the general public. Even VC invested firms rarely exit through IPO. Despite 1999 being caught up in the furore of the Internet, only 13 divestments were through IPOs out of a total of 144

Over 40 per cent of funds come from banks. Pension funds and insurance companies invested only 12.3 per cent of new funds in 1999.

Finally, it is worth noting that Milan has developed the most momentum as a VC centre, with over 50 per cent of VC firms registered with the

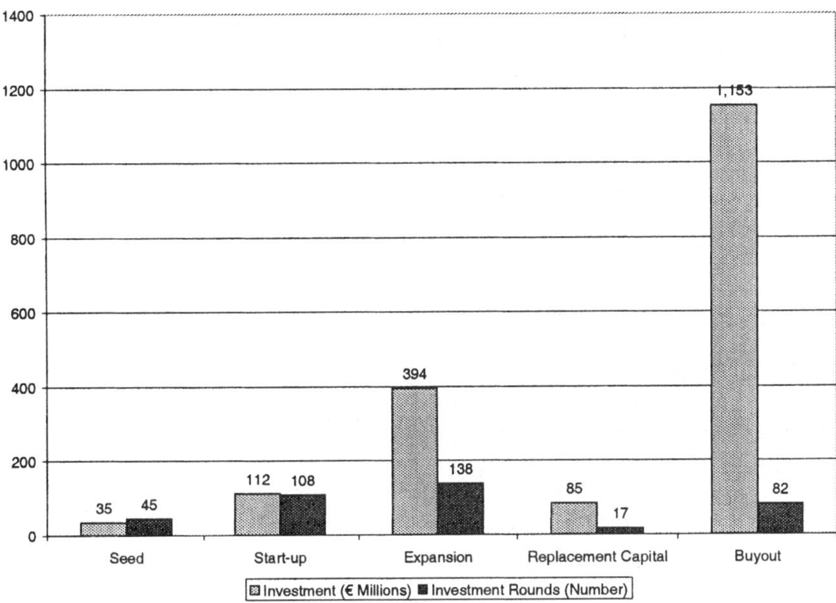

Figure 6.12 Stage distribution of Italian VC investments (1999).

Source: *EVCA Yearbook 2000*, European Private Equity and Venture Capital Association, Luxembourg, p. 38.

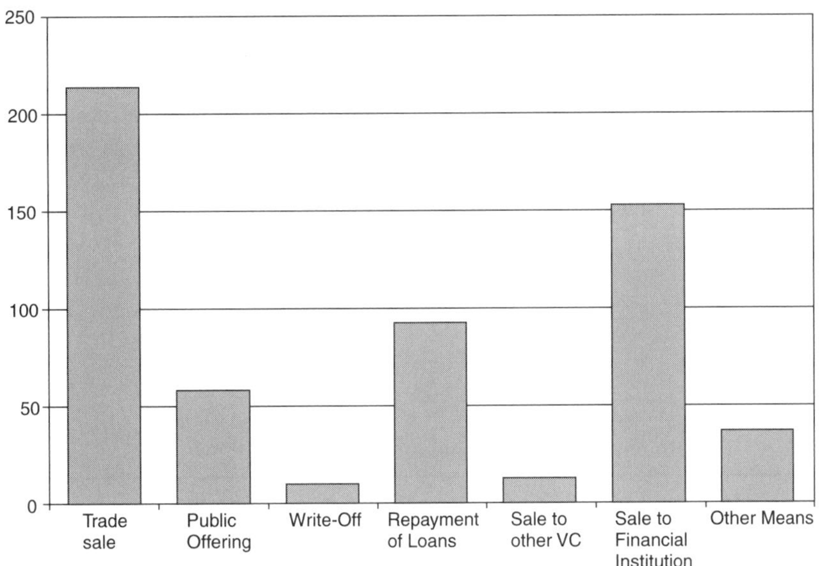

Figure 6.13 Divestment of Italian VC investments by type (1999).

Source: *EVCA Yearbook 2000*, European Private Equity and Venture Capital Association, Luxembourg, p. 44

Italian Venture Capital Association located there. Rome and Bologna are also dynamic centres of VC activity.

Spain

Most venture capitalists in Spain belong to ASCRI, the Spanish Venture Capital Association. This body, as well as being responsible for pursuing the interests of its members in terms of policy form and promotion, also produces an annual statistical abstract on the state of venture capital in the country. Further information about the society can be found through its website (http://www. ascri.org).

Venture capital in Spain is gradually coming of age. A total of 54 private equity companies operated in Spain during 1999. The majority (37) are independent with the balance being captive or semi-captive fund managers.

€630 million was raised by these funds during the year from a variety of sources. Both general economic well-being and the lure of Internet have fuelled appetite. Financial institutions have historically been and continue to be the major source of funds in Spain.

Unlike the UK, the majority of funds are destined to pure venture capital, with only 30 per cent earmarked for buy-outs. The year 1999 saw the majority of funds being raised domestically for the first time in recent years with the balance coming from Europe and the US (28 per cent and 15 per cent respectively).

Investments in 1999 doubled to €723 million but represented just 0.13 per cent of GDP – as compared with the European average of 0.3 per cent. There was also a shift in focus from later stage to earlier stage as investors sought to capitalise on the 'new' economy opportunities in telecommunications, Internet and media.

Fiscal incentives introduced by the authorities are seen as a significant inducement in private equity growth. Key measures recently introduced include:

Table 6.7 Divestment of Italian VC investments by type (1999)

Financial institutions	46%
Government agencies	15%
Pension funds	13%
Other	26%

Source: *EVCA Yearbook 2000*, European Private Equity and Venture Capital Association, Luxembourg, p. 136.

- Dividend receipts from portfolio companies are 100 per cent tax free.
- Taxation on capital gains from divestments made in the third to twelfth year are reduced by 99 per cent.

On top of this, the government is looking at technology start-up incentives.

As with other developing markets, Spain suffers from exit options. The most common method is buy-backs or repayment of loans/quasi equity followed by trade sales. Of the divestments made in 1999, only 4 out of a total of 220 companies were through public offerings.

Portugal

In Portugal, pension funds are a particularly suppressed element of the VC industry, as is demonstrated by Figure 6.14, diagramming the sources of Portugal's nascent VC industry which at the end of 1999 had a total of €270 million funds under management (at cost).

One would expect VC activity in a land of small firms to be concentrated in these firms, but they are barely served by the Portuguese VC industry. None of Portugal's 86 investments went towards seed capital in 1999, and only one-quarter towards early-stage capital combined. Yet the MBO/MBI industry in Portugal is also at quite a nascent stage. Hence, much of the money is not actually traditional venture capital activities. Two-thirds of the industry is focused on expansion, capital substitution, and restructuring of funded companies, all of which is similar to the activities of traditional relationship banks.

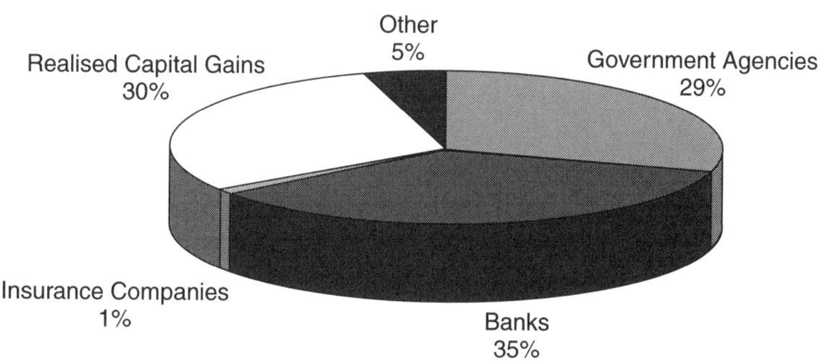

Figure 6.14 VC investments by type of investor (1999).

Source: *EVCA Yearbook 2000*, European Private Equity and Venture Capital Association, Luxembourg, p. 133.

Markets in northern Europe

Sweden's VC market is the largest by far in northern Europe, indeed like Finland's it stands out as one of the more impressive markets in the world on a per capita basis. The market is larger than Spain's, for example, although Italy's GDP is around five times larger than Sweden's, with a population base that is six times larger. Finland's market is also impressive. Yet again, it should be remembered that large markets are often the result of the domination of large firms going after large firms with buy-outs or the most advanced stages of expansion and replacement funds. Denmark, by contrast, is a country of smaller businesses; this has led to similarly high standards of living, but comparatively less capital market momentum. From the perspective of this study, some of the momentum in northern Europe will hopefully continue to trickle back to small firms, but for the moment a lot of it is interesting but not particularly important for these firms.

Sweden

Sweden provides one of the most developed private equity markets in Europe, a market that has been actively encouraged by the government since the 1980s. The number of buy-outs has fallen steadily since the early 1990s, but the total value and average value of buy-outs have both increased markedly with a rise in major buy-outs from large corporates. Expansion capital and technology deals are the most popular, with a rise in the level of funds allocated to such investments. Domestic players dominate the market and have all raised significant funds in the past two years, leading to a plentiful supply of financing. But international players also are taking a greater interest in Sweden, with Morgan Grenfell Private Equity, NatWest Equity Partners, and UBS Capital among others all responsible for big deals in recent years. The exit market, particularly IPOs, has been strong, but suffered during the market crash in mid-1998. There is still some degree of state intervention in the market, particularly in early-stage and development transactions.[10]

Finland

In Finland more than elsewhere in this survey, the venture capital industry is directly supported by government funds. Pension schemes, which receive extensive government support and regulation, are also far more prominent.

In 1999, venture capital investors made 364 investments. Of these, 60 per cent were initial investments.

In 1999 one-third of the money invested by the venture capitalists went into bridge financing. In monetary terms, the proportional share of venture capital investments made in early-stage companies (seed and start-up stage) has been decreasing recently. Partly as a result, the average size of the initial investments grew in 1999. The increase in the value of investment has mainly been directed to companies in the expansion, bridge and buy-out stages.

In terms of new capital, private venture capital funds account for 88 per cent and public funds 12 per cent. In 1999, almost half of total investments where high-tech. Investments were clustered around the province of southern Finland.

While the overall numbers are smaller than in many countries, those applying had a greater chance of success in Finland than elsewhere. Of all the investment requests by companies, 23 per cent were analysed in-depth by VC players and an initial investment was made into 6 per cent. Perhaps these percentages are so high because many of the VC 'investments' are actually closer to loans, as is evidenced by statistics on exits. Many of the VC investments were actually in debt instruments, and the most common exit was simply a company's repayment of debt. Management buy-backs were also common. Only 12 companies (with 19 VC investments between them) exited through IPOs; 41 exits resulted from bankruptcies.

Norway

Norway's private equity and VC investments surpassed those of Finland during some years of the late 1990s. However, markets are hampered due to a dearth of domestic investors; many of these focus on early-stage, development capital investment or technology investment. There is a high degree of government control of industry. Other deterrents for investors include a lack of attractive industries for investment and a relatively subdued M&A market, and a less developed exit market.[11]

Denmark

Historically, there has been little buy-out activity in Denmark, with expansion capital being by far the most common form of financing. The government is in the process of removing some barriers to private equity investment and, as a result, deal numbers are rising. Domestic investors used to comprise a small group of independent firms, but the level of investors and funds are rising with support from the government. 'A few international investors have woken up to Denmark's potential and are moving into the market':[12] the first non-domestic fund for investment in Denmark was not raised until 1998. Generally, dealflow is likely to come from both corporate restructuring and a mainstay of the Danish economy: small, family-controlled concerns. Exit prospects are good, with strong interest in technology companies from stock market investors and more activity from European and domestic trade buyers.

Other dynamic continental markets

Switzerland

The Zurich-based 'Swiss Private Equity and Corporate Finance Association (SECA) hosts a detailed website (http://www.innonet.ch/seca) that appears to exist primarily in English. The site lists 109 members, a large number for a relatively small country; but Zurich and Geneva are important financial centres. Many members are renowned international investment banks and well-known companies, both foreign and Swiss; SECA itself is based in Zurich.

In 1999 the number of larger buy-outs decreased, replaced by smaller deals, more expansion finance transactions and earlier-stage investment. The tax and regulatory environment makes buy-outs comparatively complex, discouraging some investors. Generally, there is an ample supply of both equity and debt financing, and the number of domestic investors has increased, mainly in the small to medium sized deal range. International investors are active participants in the Swiss market, completing many of the larger transactions (mostly buy-outs) over recent years. The exit market continued to perform well in 1999, with some high-profile flotations and successful trade sales.[13]

The Netherlands

The Netherlands is characterised by some private sources as 'continental Europe's most mature private equity market',[14] and this directly impacts on the quality and strength of the VC industry. The Dutch Venture Capital Association (Nederlandse Vereniging van Participatiemaatschappijen, NVP) services a small country that has nevertheless been an astute financial centre for centuries. Just as the Netherlands's capitalism dates from the beginning of the capitalist revolution, the NVP was founded somewhat earlier than many others in Europe (in 1984). It is also quite international, providing a significant portion of its news and information in English and also many statistical comparisons of use to international investors. The returns of 15 per cent for the latest year available (1998) are presented against foreign currencies.

The Netherlands occupied the fifth place on the ranking list of most investing countries in Europe in the years 1999 and its solid growth has created unusually high rankings in later years. In 1999, the total investment of the Dutch venture capital increased by 61 per cent and reached a new high of €1.7 billion. The total investment portfolio amounted to €4.6 billion in 1999. That same year, 40 per cent of the investments and 32 per cent of the portfolio value were invested abroad, and these numbers were increasing.

Again, as in other more mature markets, large deals dominate the industry and only a portion of this money is going to the smaller SMEs. Seed and start-up capital received almost 100 per cent more investments in 1999 than in 1998, but the total was still only 20 per cent total investments that year.

Generally, the VC industry was healthy, with rates of growth comparable to (or even better than) those in the world's most successful VC markets.

The Dutch VC world contains over fifty firms, but some dominant players. In 1997, 80 per cent of funds originated from eight venture capital companies.

Fifty per cent of the market was comprised of private companies, 44 per cent the 'captive' companies of banks and insurance groups, and 6 per cent government funds.

In terms of direct and indirect government support, like the authors of this report, the Dutch government primarily favours tax breaks to support the nexus between SMEs and the venture capital industry. Of the two government rules designed to support VC investments in SMEs, the first focused on tax breaks that would benefit the industry as a whole. The second focused on government matching funds, only affects a maximum of 6 per cent of the capital invested in the industry:

1. The first SME-friendly policy is the so-called 'Tante Agaathregeling' (rich uncle rule), which provides for a certain amount of interest to be received free of income tax by an individual who invests in a start-up company during an eight year period. If, during those eight years, the investment is lost, such loss may be taken as tax deductible up to an amount of 50,000 Dutch guilders (22,689). Venture capital funds are also allowed to take tax-deductible losses if large stakes in start-up investments go sour. Individuals investing in such funds also may claim a higher tax exemption for interest and dividends received than normally would have been applied.
2. The second involves certain incentives, particularly in the form of grants for so-called 'technostarters funds'. Subject to certain conditions (e.g. minimum size of the fund 10 million Dutch guilders (€4.5 million) the Ministry of Economic Affairs is prepared to participate, up to 25 per cent, in the total funding.[15]

The Netherlands has a favourable fiscal environment. Dividends received by a company in other company and capital gains on shares may be exempt from Dutch corporate income tax – the so-called participation exemption – if the shareholding meets certain criteria (at least 5 per cent). In other cases, withholding taxes of 25 per cent are levied on dividends and capital gains. Private shareholders also are not subjected to capital gains tax, provided that their share of total equity and their option on total equity is less than 5 per cent; yet generally, personal income taxes are extremely high in the Netherlands, which hosts one of the largest governments in the world measured by government spending as a percentage of GDP.

Belgium

Private equity investments by VCs are said to comprise just 0.12 per cent of Belgium's GDP, according to the Belgian Venture Capital Association ('Belgian Venturing Association' or BVA—http://www.BVAssociation.org). The association, which was formed in 1986, provides an impressive quantity of information to the public in Flemish, French and English, and most of this discussion on Belgium is derived from that site.

In terms of the size of the players investing the money, almost 50 per cent comes from independent sources and only 30 per cent from captive funds. This is in sharp contrast to markets in the German-speaking world.

On the other hand, as in Germany, funding for earlier-stage investments is much higher than average, with 25 per cent going to early-stage, high-tech ventures.

Table 6.8 Belgian private equity raised by source (1998)

	€ million	%
Independent funds raised in year	198	47.4
Amount invested by captives	126	30.1
Realised capital gains available for reinvestment	93	22.5
Total funds raised	417	100.0

Source: Belgian Venture Capital Association.

Table 6.9 Belgian expected allocation of funds raised (1998)

	€ million	%
High-tech early-stage	106.3	25.5
Other early-stage	0.3	0.1
High-tech expansion/development	109.0	26.1
Other expansion/development	138.3	33.1
Venture capital	354.0	84.8
Buy-out	24.8	5.9
Not available	38.7	9.3
Total	417.4	100.0

Source: Belgian Venture Capital Association.

Table 6.10 Geographical breakdown of Belgian VC commitments (1998)

	€ million	%
Domestic	336.8	80.7
Other European countries	79.5	19.0
Non European countries	1.1	0.3
Total funds raised	417.4	100.0

Source: Belgian Venture Capital Association.

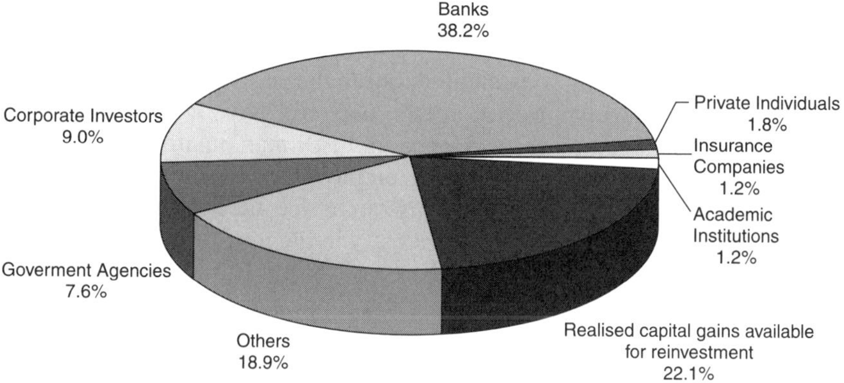

Figure 6.15 Private equity raised by investor type (1998).

Source: Belgian Venture Capital Association.

Figure 6.15 demonstrates the importance of banks, the largest investors; they are not as important as in the German case, but as in Germany, pension funds play a minor role (in this case, no apparent role).

Conclusion

One central problem addressed in this chapter is the lack of consolidation and internationalism of VC funding activities in Germany. National markets that are successful appear to have powerful financial capitals drawing resources towards the centre, but even these 'centres' are not particularly centralised from a Europe-wide perspective. The internationalism of investors and investment channels in countries like the UK, the Netherlands and Switzerland is contrasted with very limited cross-border trade elsewhere outside the market for large buy-outs (which are rarely SMEs). Greater international co-operation (joint-ventures or cross-border deals), and greater consolidation will take time, but trends in the banking industry towards internationalism and consolidation are likely to spill-over into the VC industry; the sooner the better.

Four of the top ten and five of the top fifteen cities for international equity management were located in the United States, and even within the US there is massive consolidation taking place in the fund management industry. US firms are also buying up European ones and occasionally vice versa, with the largest purchase in 2000 being Citicorp's acquisition of Schroders, one of Britain's most established and well-known financial houses. Price Waterhouse concurs that the institutional side of the industry will only continue to consolidate due to massive economies of scale in this field.

So Europe may need to be calm about the purchase of financial institutions and fund management organisations across borders within and outside the EU. Governments must worry about monopolistic practices in any industry that is truly consolidated, but in the short term the industry as a whole, and its most powerful actors, may still have a long way to go before they challenge markets. Hence, policies manipulating or blocking mergers for the purpose of protecting employment or (more likely in the financial industries) protecting prestigious domestic institutions may be particularly destructive to financial industry in the long term.

But while there are many differences in US and European VC funding sizes and styles, looking towards the future, one might conclude that part of the problem for funding of high-tech firms in Europe is being solved by market forces. As US investors become attracted to the potential to earn high returns on cheaper valuations present in European Internet firms, for example, European investors are influenced by US investment practices. In 1999, funds fuelling European Internet businesses multiplied more than ten times in the first three quarters alone. About one-third of the money went to the UK, and investments in firms in Germany and Scandinavia were also unprecedented. The number of non-US users of the Internet is said to have recently passed the number of US users, and this will only continue to demonstrate the importance of non-US markets in this field. So while tax structures and especially pension schemes could be more favourable (with more private funding complementing pay-as-you-go systems and more freedom to invest), a reasonable thesis would be that much of the differential in US and European markets is simply timing: as Europe recovers from slow growth and catches on to a trend for a new industry, it is more than pulling its weight in international markets.

Notes

1 Initiative Europe Ltd (various publication sources 1996–2000).
2 *European Venture Capital Association Yearbook 1999*, Luxembourg: European Private Equity Venture Capital Association 1999, p. 80.
3 Initiative Europe Ltd (various publication sources 1996–2000).
4 Ibid.

5 Quotation taken from a speech by Gordon Brown in 1998; British Venture Capital Association – www.bvca.com
6 The British Venture Capital Association; information from press releases of www.bvca.com downloaded on 8 February 2000.
7 Initiative Europe Ltd (various publication sources 1996–2000)
8 *EVCA Yearbook 1998*, Luxembourg: ECVA 1999, p. 73.
9 Further information can be obtained from the website of the organisation – http://www.betacom.it/aifi/
10 Initiative Europe Ltd (various publication sources 1996–2000).
11 Ibid.
12 Ibid.
13 Ibid.
14 Ibid.
15 See the Dutch Venture Capital Association (Nederlandse Vereniging van Participatiemaatschappijen) – http://www.nvp.nl

7 Capital markets in the European Union

The problems of small-caps generally were highlighted in Chapter 3, but Figure 7.1 demonstrates again that western small-caps performed relatively badly in recent years. North America's, at least, have picked up at the time of this writing, but the Morgan Stanley Indices demonstrate that the EU's, even now, are underperforming.

European small-caps only rose 35 per cent from March 1996 to March 2001, at a time when larger stock markets were booming in the US, in Scandinavia, in southern Europe, and by the last years of the 1990s in many European countries.

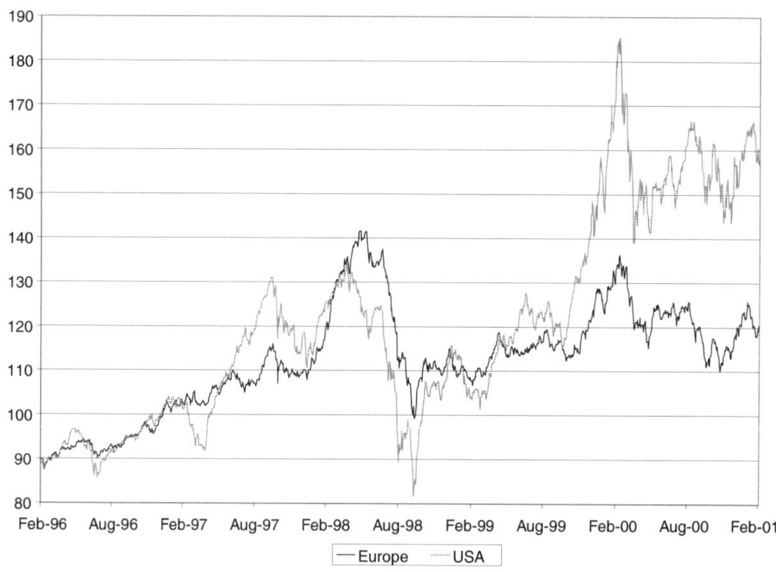

Figure 7.1 European and US small-cap stock performance compared (5 years to March 2001).

Source: Morgan Stanley Indices; www.msci.com.

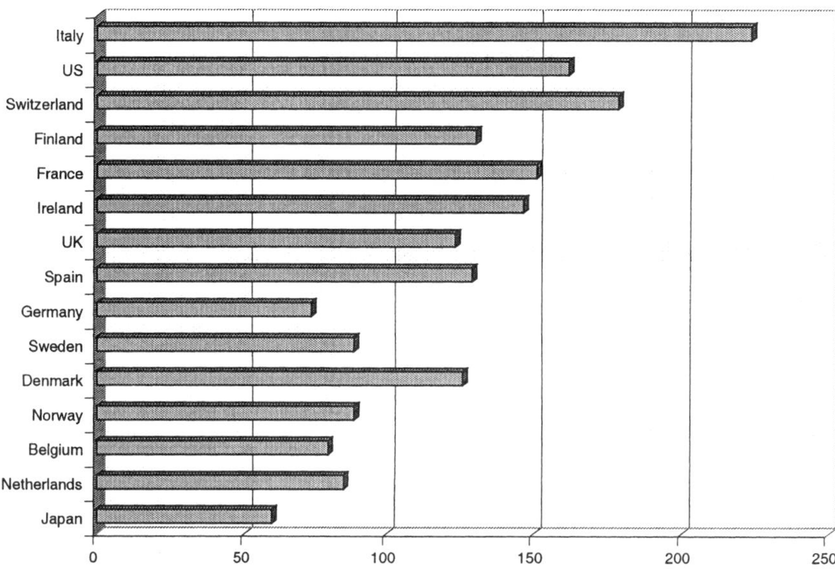

Figure 7.2 Market small-cap index performance in European countries, the US and Japan (December 1997–March 2001).

Source: Morgan Stanley Capital Index; www.msci.com.

Note
January, 1997 market cap = 100 in all countries.

Figure 7.2 provides comparisons across countries. The EU's small-cap markets outperformed laggard markets like those in Japan, but in the Netherlands and Belgium, markets actually decreased in value over three years of booming large-caps. Only the market of Italy outperformed the US small-cap markets, more than doubling in value over the three years studied.

While small-caps generally have a difficult time attracting attention in an age of mega-mergers and international conglomerates, this chapter demonstrates the extent to which markets in Europe, in particular, are hampered by dispersed regulations and trading platforms. An overriding theme relates to the complications that inevitably arise with 29 exchanges based in the EU-15, Norway, and Switzerland.

European exchanges: an overview of a dispersed market

The UK's stock exchange is the largest in Europe. For information on the 'big three' – UK, Germany and France – see Chapter 3. The relative market capitalisations are shown in Figure 7.3.

Yet Europe has far more than the bourses listed above. In 17 countries

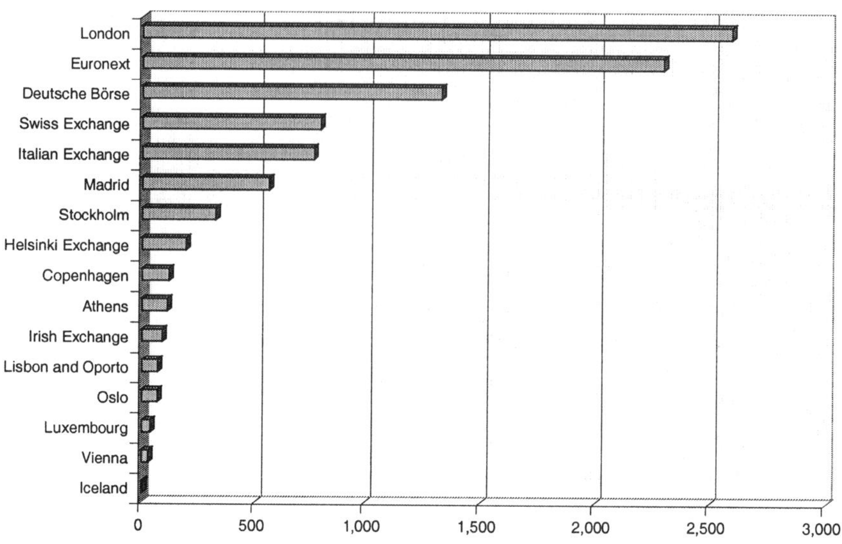

Figure 7.3 European market caps in January 2000 (€ billion).

Source: The Federation of European Exchanges; www.fese.be.

of Europe (the EU-15 plus Norway and Switzerland), there are no fewer than 29 national and electronic exchanges (not counting ECNs). In addition to these, there are independent pan-European exchanges, plus transnational trading alliances. There are several other alliances for cross-trading, settlement and cross-listing.

Within Europe, there are almost 70 markets for securities. We have analysed these markets in terms of their securities preferences as shown above. There are fifteen SME capital markets in Europe. Two of these exchanges are pan-European and the balance are located in individual countries. All of these exchanges have been established to offer high-growth companies with little or no track record an opportunity to seek equity capital from the stock market. In contrast, the US essentially has only one SME market, which is the NASDAQ small-cap market.

The Federation of European Stock Exchanges is an association of the stock exchanges from countries of the European Economic Area, and it claims great confidence in the continued expansion of the size and depth of European markets. New developments boosting FESE's confidence in EU exchanges include:

- An EU Investment Services Directive, which will confer the 'European passport' on properly authorised investment firms, and thereby bring about major changes in national securities regulation.
- Linkages between exchanges, bilaterally and regionally.

Table 7.1 European stock exchanges (2000)

Country	*Exchange*
Austria	Wiener Börse
Belgium	Euronext Brussels
Denmark	Copenhagen Stock Exchange
Finland	Helsinki Exchange
France	Euronext Paris
Germany	Baden-Württembergische Börse zu Stuttgart
Germany	Bayerische Börse
Germany	Berliner Wertpapierbörse
Germany	Bremer Wertpapierbörse
Germany	Deutsche Börse
Germany	Hanseatische Wertpapierbörse zu Hamburg
Germany	Niedersächsische Börse zu Hannover
Germany	Rheinisch-Westfälische Börse zu Düsseldorf
Greece	Athens Stock Exchange
Holland	Euronext Amsterdam
Ireland	Irish Stock Exchange
Italy	Italian Stock Exchange
Luxembourg	Luxembourg Stock Exchange
Norway	Oslo Stock Exchange
Portugal	Bolsa de Valores de Lisboa e Porto
Spain	Bolsa de Barcelona
Spain	Bolsa de Bilbao
Spain	Bolsa de Madrid
Spain	Bolsa de Valencia
Sweden	OM Stockholm Stock Exchange
Switzerland	SWX Swiss Exchange
UK	London Stock Exchange
UK	Ofex
UK	Tradepoint Stock Exchange

Source: Stock exchanges.

- Assistance to emerging markets in central and eastern Europe, increasing the draw and internationalism of European stock exchange platforms while further benefiting neighbouring countries to create a larger and more complete securities market throughout Europe.[1]

Still, the exchanges are said to face significant challenges, and all of them are magnified for the smallest-cap listings on the markets:

- Providing high-quality information.
- Settling trades speedily and safely.
- Growing competition as a result of the revolution in electronic and instantaneous access, providing more people with an opportunity to invest or list internationally rather than domestically.
- Ever-larger financial institutions straining the liquidity of some markets with the size of their investments.

Table 7.2 European capital markets by focus and exchange (2000)

		SME	*Small-cap*	*Mid-cap*	*Large-cap*	*Unlisted*	*Other*
Austria	Wiener Börse	1	1	1	1	1	1
Belgium	Euronext Brussels	1	1	1	1	1	
Denmark	Copenhagen Stock Exchange	1			1		
Eire	Irish Stock Exchange	1			1		1
Europe	EASDAQ	1					
Finland	Helsinki Stock Exchange	1	1	1	1		
France	Euronext Paris	1		1	1	1	1
Germany	Deutsche Börse	1	1	1	1	1	
Germany	Baden-Württembergische Börse zu Stuttgart		1				
Germany	Bayerische Börse		1				
Germany	Berliner Wertpapierbörse		1				
Germany	Bremer Wertpapierbörse		1				
Germany	Hanseatische Wertpapierbörse zu Hamburg		1				
Germany	Niedersächsische Börse zu Hannover		1				
Germany	Rheinisch-Westfälische Börse zu Düsseldorf		1				
Greece	Athens Stock Exchange			1			
Holland	Euronext Amsterdam	1			1		
Italy	Italian Stock Exchange	1			1	1	
Luxembourg	Luxembourg Stock Exchange			1	1		
Norway	Oslo Stock Exchange	1		1			
Portugal	Bolsa de Valores de Lisboa e Porto			1			
Spain	Bolsa de Barcelona		1				
Spain	Bolsa de Madrid		1				
Spain	Bolsa de Bilbao			1	1		1
Spain	Bolsa de Valencia		1				
Sweden	OM Stockholm Exchange	1		1	1		
Switzerland	SWX Swiss Exchange	1			1		
UK	London Stock Exchange	1	1	1	1		
UK	Tradepoint Stock Exchange					1	
UK	Ofex					1	
Total		14	15	12	14	7	4

Source: Stock exchanges.

States the FESE:

> Paradoxically, the institutionalisation of the market leads to a problem of financing small and medium sized enterprises. This happens because institutions tend to invest in the larger companies, leaving smaller companies dependent upon other sources of financing which often prove to be more costly.[2]

The exchanges are working to meet these challenges with longer hours of trading, the use of market-making and block-trading and the introduction of inter-dealer brokers to some markets, reducing settlement periods, and, of course, setting up special 'new markets' for high-growth, small-cap companies.

Listing requirements

Comparing within Europe, the London Stock Exchange's AIM is one of the most liberal locations for listing in Europe, with 'no minimum market capitalisation and no length of trading record' required. AIM allows the free market to determine minimum requirements, and only asks that companies have nominated advisors at all times and that the nominated advisor is satisfied that non-standardised 'minimum criteria' for a given company have been satisfied. Towards the other end of the spectrum, the Deutsche Börse has some of the most conservative minimum-listing requirements for SMEs, including, for example:

- Market capitalisation of €5 million (subsequently raised to €10 million)
- 20 per cent free floating
- 25 per cent 'are recommended not closely held'
- Three years of audited accounts
- €1.5 million in equity capital
- Only ordinary shares floated
- €250,000 total par value of shares
- 100,000 shares issued
- Must be a nomination of at least two 'designated sponsors'
- 50 per cent of an IPO should result in capital increase
- Must acknowledge Germany's 'takeover code'
- Companies must publish quarterly reports
- Companies must prepare their accounts according to IAS or the American GAAP standard.[3]

These requirements essentially match those of the Neuer Markt.

Trading methods

Continuous electronic trading (CET) is

> the single most popular trading and quotation mechanism among SMB markets worldwide. Most of the exchanges that use CET consider it such an economical and reliable price formation mechanism that they have adapted it directly from their main market. This has the further benefit of keeping procedures simple for an exchange's brokers and traders who are already familiar with the main market system.[4]

Most of Europe has adopted CET as a base for their quotation mechanism, and this is argued by many to be more efficient than, for example, NASDAQ's market makers. Yet unfortunately, Table 7.3 shows that Europe has adopted a wide array of trading methodologies, most of which use CET as a base but contain particularities. The lack of a standardised procedure may not only hinder market alliances but also the transfer of capital and skills across countries.

Mergers, takeovers and alliances

The number of European exchanges makes it difficult and very costly for market makers, specialists and brokers to have a truly pan-European representation. This is a vicious circle that leads to a lower average number

Table 7.3 Trading mechanisms for small-cap markets in the EU and the US (1999)

System	*Market*
Cont. elect. trading	Stockholm
Cont. elect. trading + market makers	Euronext Amsterdam Deutsche NM AIM
Cont. elect. trading + elect. price fixing	Swiss SWX NM
Cont. elect. trading + market makers + elect. price fixing	Euronext Paris
Cont. elect. trading + market makers for a period after IPO	Copenhagen
Cont. elect. trading + market makers + after market trading	Helsinki
Elect. price fixing + market specialist + cont. market maker	Euronext Brussels
Market maker	NASDAQ small-cap
Auction	Barcelona
Telephone based order driven system	Ireland

Source: Michael Ashley Schulman, *Medium Size Business Markets*, FIBV Working Committee Focus Group Study on SMB Markets, August 1999, p. 32.

Table 7.4 Pan-European exchanges (2001)

EASDAQ, based in Belgium – now NASDAQ Europe
Euronext. Merger of Paris, Amsterdam and Brussels stock exchanges

Source: Stock exchanges.

of market makers and specialists per listed security, less analysis and information published as the lower number of market makers cannot afford to produce the research, and therefore less confidence and less liquidity in the market. In contrast, the US has a large number of market makers per listed security, as exchange membership is much more cost effective. This enables analysis and research to be made available to investors at a more manageable cost to the market makers and specialists, and thus results in greater investor confidence and liquidity. This virtuous circle is one of the main contributory factors to the level of US market capitalisation.

In terms of trends, there have been several examples of outright mergers of markets within countries (e.g. NASDAQ and AMEX), but only one merger across borders within the EU – that of Paris, Brussels and Amsterdam exchanges to form Euronext. M&A activity is increasing, as alliances fail due to the inability to resolve critical aspects such as trading platforms, clearance and settlement.

The Euro NM formula was simple and hailed by its organisers as follows:

- Common admission criteria, geared specifically to the growing company

Table 7.5 Transnational European exchange alliances (2000)

Country exchange	
NOREX	Nordic Exchange. An alliance between the Stockholm and Copenhagen stock exchanges. It will soon also include the Oslo Stock Exchange and the Baltic exchanges of Latvia, Lithuania and Estonia.
Euro NM	European New Market Alliance. An alliance between the New Markets of Germany (Neuer Markt), France (Nouveau Marché), Netherlands (Nieuwe Markt) and Italy (Nuevo Mercato). The settlement and information centre was located in Belgium. The Alliance was formally ended in December 2000.

Source: Stock exchanges.

- Transparent market management based on established exchange practices
- Accessibility – a local gateway for European and international companies
- Tight integration of member markets
- Cross-market electronic trading
- High liquidity.[5]

In greater detail, the alliance contained the following members:

- Germany's Neuer Markt, which formed in March 1997 and quickly became the largest market in Europe for small-cap growth stocks
- Le Nouveau Marché, the first NM market in Europe dating from February 1996, managed by the Paris Bourse and listing over 100 companies
- The Nieuwe Markt Amsterdam, established the same month as Germany's Neuer Markt and containing over a dozen stocks with one of the highest index growth rates among the NM
- Euro NM Belgium, begun in April 1997, also containing just over one dozen listings
- The Nuovo Mercato of Italy, begun in 1999.

Another important alliance is the NOREX alliance between Stockholm, Copenhagen, and more recently Oslo. This is different from Euro NM in that it is between entire exchanges, and therefore has more chance of succeeding. The three Scandinavian bourses are hoping to further collaborate with a common electronic share trading system by 2001. At the time of this writing, Iceland is also considering membership in Norex. While they are not all for public companies, three Brussels exchanges (Belfox, Brussels Stock Exchange and CIK) have also united in 1999 to form BXS – Brussels Exchanges Ltd.

This trend is to be welcomed, but so far it has progressed only to a limited extent. Markets remain quite fragmented. Further, the incomplete nature of some of the alliances weakens their importance. For example, the Euro NM alliance is currently most pronounced as a single-entry gateway to multiple exchanges, yet there is still a very strong need for harmonisation of all of the following:

- Accounting rules for firms that list
- Taxation rules
- Market platforms, for example, for execution of trades (see also above).[6]

Highlights within two countries: the UK and Germany

We provide some details on what are now the two largest capital markets in Europe, the UK's and Germany's.

The United Kingdom

The London Stock Exchange saw record volumes traded on its international and domestic markets during 1999 – with international business up 10.1 per cent by value and domestic business up 36 per cent. Yet the year, and indeed a number of recent years, have not been as impressive for small- as for large-caps. The UK small-caps picked up gained value rapidly in 1995/8, and as a result they competed almost at par with large-caps. Morgan Stanley's all-cap index for the UK rose 93 per cent from 1995–2000, whereas the small-cap index rose 70 per cent. But much of the gain in the small-cap index was already achieved by the middle of 1998, and it has only recently begun to rise again. More importantly, much of the gains were actually in companies that were much larger than the average SME.

At the end of 1998, 79 per cent of the value of the whole London stock market was represented by the FTSE 100 and a further 14.5 per cent by the FTSE 250. This left the other 2,049 companies (including AIM) comprising only 6.4 per cent by value. These very small companies as a percentage of the total market cap of the country were declining in the UK (and the US) rather rapidly as large-caps grew far faster than small-caps. For example, the same residual category (neither FTSE 100 nor 250) were worth around 15 per cent of the market, or 2.5 times as much as in 1998, in 1996.

The primary disadvantage of investing in small-caps is lack of liquidity, and some 81 per cent of fund managers in a poll saw liquidity problems as the most serious. However, the same survey more recently has shown an improving situation, with only 25 per cent feeling that liquidity is worsening in 2000/1 compared with 41 per cent in 1997/8. Pressure on fund managers to invest larger sums than they might otherwise do continues – 57 per cent investing more on average compared with 41 per cent in 1997/8. Fund managers are hoping for a free float of around half the shares or a minimum of around £50 million, but just under half (48 per cent) of London's listed companies had the implied market cap of around 100 million criteria together (implying a market cap of 100 million).[7] A very significant number of existing quoted countries are outside any of the FTSE indices, and these extra-index companies are often shunned by fund managers.

What is a smaller-cap company in the eyes of professionals? Interviews conducted by KPMG Corporate Finance with fund managers demonstrate some changes in the way fund managers are beginning to (more critically)

Table 7.6 Comparisons of large- and small-cap indices (1999)

	Companies in Index (number)	*Value of companies in Index (£ million)*	*% of total quoted market (%)*	*Average market cap of companies in index (£ million)*
FTSE 100	100	1,072,940	79.2	10,729
FTSE all share	840	1,334,275	98.5	1,588
FTSE 250	250	197,380	14.6	789
FTSE small-cap	490	63,955	4.7	130
FTSE fledgling	828	16,806	1.2	20
AIM	312	4,438	0.3	14

Source: 'Investment in Smaller Capitalisation Companies', *KPMG Corporate Finance*, Spring 1999, p. 4.

view small-caps. Aside from prospective profitability and quality of management, market position is increasingly important, with managers looking towards niche players. Other top concerns from the latest survey are listed in Table 7.7.

Most of these concerns have only risen in importance for the fund managers, and generally, the survey appears to demonstrate a conservative 'flight to quality' and traditional valuation methodologies at a time when the US appeared to be less and less tied to traditional valuation methodologies, especially in high-tech sectors.

Fund managers would lobby to UK exchanges to promote all of the following:

- Reduce/simplify/establish different taxes for smaller companies (27 per cent)
- Abolish/reduce capital gains tax (20 per cent)
- Abolish stamp duty (10 per cent)
- Create better tax breakers (10 per cent)[8]

Table 7.7 Fund manager criteria for judging small-caps in the UK (2001)

Issue	*% of managers viewing an issue as important*
Prospective profitability	98
Quality of management	98
Cash flow analysis	96
Market position	92
Level of gearing	70
Past profitability	65
Attractiveness of the sector	63

Source: 'Attitudes Towards Smaller Quoted Companies: A Study Amongst UK Fund Managers', *KPMG Corporate Finance*, March 2001.

Table 7.8 New issues: the LSE (1994–8)

	Privatisations		*Other*	
	No.	*£ million*	*No.*	*£ million*
1994			256	11,519
1995	1		189	2,962
1996	2	3,321	228	7,287
1997			135	7,100
1998			124	4,196

Source: London Stock Exchange.

Around half of those polled hope that companies on the small-cap exchanges would:

- See shareholders more often
- Disclose information more frequently.[9]

All UK stocks demonstrate in the late 1990s a clear correlation between size and performance, with smaller cap indices demonstrating far inferior performance to the FTSE 100, and performances decreasing as the size of the cap decreases. Further, among the small-caps, issues and the values gained from issues are both decreasing, as is shown in Table 7.8.

Germany

German stock markets are likely to pick up speed in the next few years with changes in German tax laws, but the German markets were laggard performers in the second half of the 1990s.

The MSCI Small Cap German–US Dollar Index has fallen 32 per cent whilst the equivalent indices in Europe and the USA have risen 35 per cent and 81 per cent respectively. Commonly quoted indices of decreasing size for the German capital markets are as follows: (1) The German share price index (DAX) consists of the 30 largest German equity leaders listed for the market segments. (2) The MDAX (Midcap Index) consists of 70 German medium sized companies in terms of volume and capitalisation, and the (3) DAX 100 combines both DAX and MDAX. One can use the smaller cap indices or the Neuer Markt as proxies for SME activities in public markets, yet, as stated before, these are very rough proxies.

Generally, Germany's small-cap markets are growing, and the participation of true SMEs – as opposed to firms that are large but not international conglomerates – is also growing, although from a much lower base and with more limited results.

> An increasing number of SMEs are finding their way to the exchanges, where new shareholders are boosting their equity levels. Since 1985,

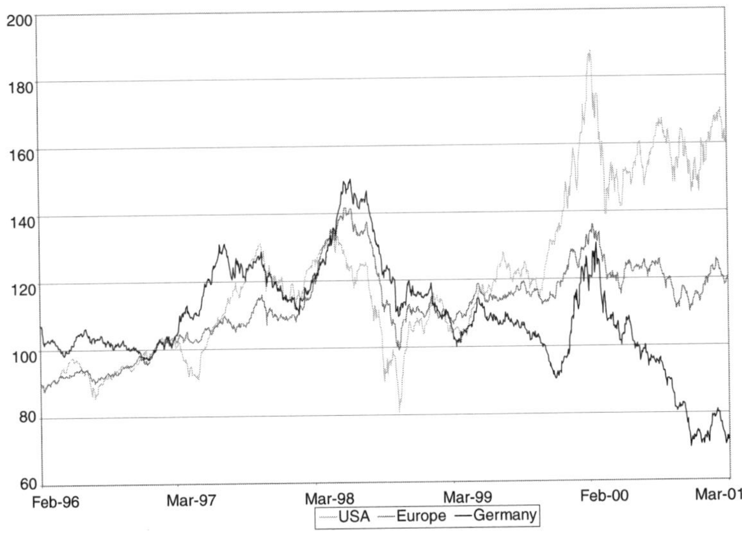

Figure 7.4 German small-cap performance vs. Europe and the US (1996–2001).
Source: Morgan Stanley Capital Index.

> the volume of placements has averaged DM 67 million (€34 million). There has been a correspondingly strong rise in the equity ratios of newcomers to the stock market, with equity on average rising from 26.8 to 41.8 per cent as a proportion of assets in the wake of the IPO.[10]

Nearly all the IPOs take place in Frankfurt, home of the world's fourth-largest exchange, where 80 per cent of the volume of trading in German shares occurs. Frankfurt also boasts by far the largest numbers of market players.

Before the Neuer Markt was created in March, 1997, companies first went public an average of 50 years after being founded, and only 10 or at most 20 companies dared to opt for an initial public offering each year. Further, there were hardly any smaller high-tech enterprises among them. The Neuer Markt shows that there is a rising trend among young, fast-growth companies to take their place on the exchanges. Defenders of the exchange are pleased that more and more companies of less than DM 100 million (€51 million) and less than 10 years old are going public.

Further, stock ownership in the Neuer Markt appears to be less from conservative institutions such as banks and more from corporates and private individuals than on the main exchange, as is demonstrated in Figure 7.5.

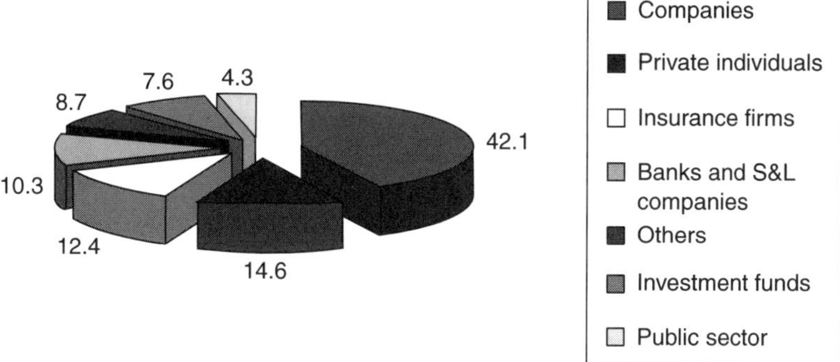

Figure 7.5 Spread of share ownership in Germany (1999) (percentage).

Source: 'Going Public: Guide', *Business and Financial Markets Magazine*, Deutsche Bourse, January, Vision and Money Special, 1999, p. 8.

While the Neuer Markt has attracted many companies, because its listing standards are comparatively rigorous, some corporate leaders have chosen the easier OTC route, which provides access to much less capital but also imposes fewer regulations:

- No obligation to immediately disclose new information that has a bearing on share price
- Much less informative perspectives.[11]

Generally, despite successes, there are still several problems with the German capital markets, and they tend to affect SMEs more seriously than larger firms. A disadvantage of going public in Germany is inheritance tax; the companies' share values are taken as the basis for the assessment. And since the market price is usually higher than for comparable companies not listed, heirs must pay considerably more tax.

Another disadvantage is that habits of disclosure, and rules governing disclosure, are less well-developed than elsewhere in the eyes of exchange organisers themselves. 'Even if investor relations in Germany is no longer in its absolute infancy, it has still not yet achieved the status it enjoys in the United States.'[12] An example: ad hoc disclosures of insider discoveries, news, or information that could significantly influence market price in Germany were not required until 1995. Hence, 'Despite the opportunities, only a little over 10 per cent of German joint stock corporations[13] are quoted on the stock exchange.'[14]

One segment of the German market that is expanding is the growth segment for high-tech companies. The exchange's statistics demonstrate that software and service providers form two-thirds of these companies, with the remainder occupied by automobile components, biotechnology, and telecommunications.

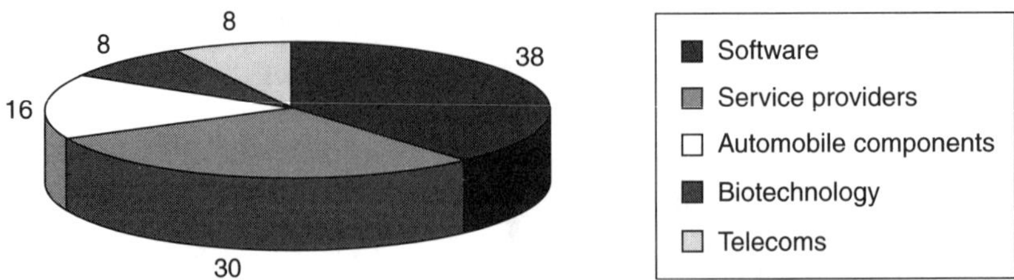

Figure 7.6 Growth segment for high-tech companies in the Neuer Markt (1998).

Source: 'Going Public: Guide', *Vision and Money Special, Business and Financial Markets Magazine*, Deutsche Bourse, January, 1999, p. 13.

Securities trading at stock exchanges and by market participants by banks largely involved 'self-regulation' in the 1980s:

> stock exchange reforms of the 1980s led to increased activity on the exchanges but also to a wave of insider dealing and fraud allegations involving some of Germany's largest banks. The self-regulatory system manifestly failed to stop insider dealing, especially since violations of trading practices hardly ever led to sanctions.

The rules became more stringent in the 1990s, and the stock exchange activities of banks in the securities markets have been supervised by the Federal Securities Supervisory Office (FSSO) established on 1 January 1995.[15]

Summing up the German case, Mittelstand traditions may be a reason that the stock market began from a low base of public equity and limited traditions of aggressive investment banking; but new rules on disclosure, newly aggressive investment banks, and the success of the Neuer Markt ensure that the volume of new issues now will be high, and the stock markets of Germany vibrant compared to many major competitors. Changes in tax rules, already planned or underway, are likely to push the markets forward that much faster.

Highlights of other large markets

France

In 1999, the Paris Bourse had its busiest year ever in terms of the number of trades, the amounts traded and the amounts raised by issuers. The Paris Bourse system recorded 58.59 million trades, the first time the total has topped the 50 million mark. At the end of December 2000, there were 1,144 companies listed on Paris Bourse markets, a signficant number of which are small- and mid-cap stocks. Of this total, 486 are large-caps listed on the Premier Marché – the Bourse's main board. The Paris Bourse has a thriving secondary market which combines both small- and mid-cap companies. Of the 372 companies listed on the Second Marché, no fewer than 60 are SME quoted stocks. There are a further 111 growth stocks listed on the Nouveau Marché and finally a further 175 listed on Marché Libre. French companies represented a market capitalisation of €1,472 billion (FRF 9,655 billion).

Yet, as France experienced healthy capital market growth, small-caps outperformed the European average, growing by 65 per cent since March 1996 but still behind the USA.

Italy

Italy's small-caps were the best performers in Europe in the second half of the 1990s: Morgan Stanley's index for Italian small-cap stocks rose 143 per cent, outperforming both Europe and the USA.

Spain

In response to the interest in high-tech stocks, Spain launched the Nuevo Mercado (10 April 2000), which is a segment of the Madrid Exchange. However, unlike the most recent entrants to the Neuer Markt, the companies that have sought listings are those that already do so on other

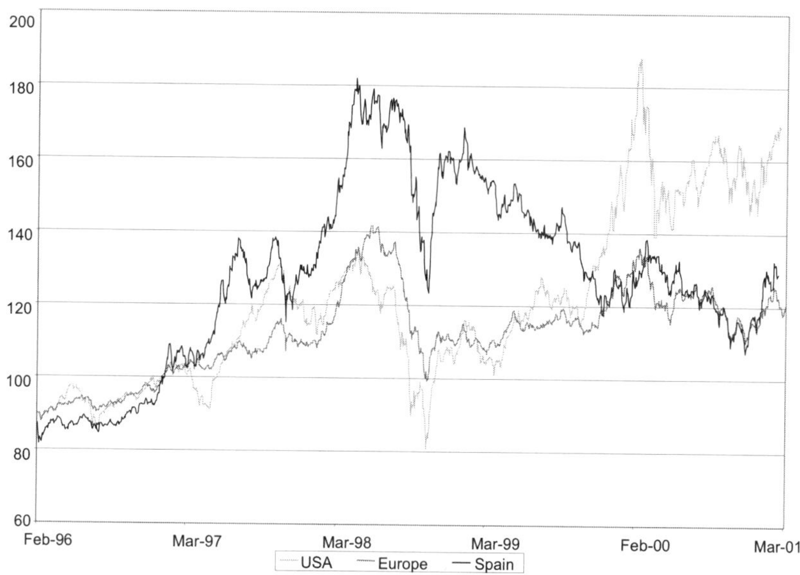

Figure 7.7 Spanish small-cap performance (1996–2001).

Source: Morgan Stanley Capital Index.

markets (including the Spanish National Market in Madrid) and who are some of the largest technology players in Europe. Thus, the Nuevo Mercado will in the short term be rather like London's TechMARK index – rather than Neuer Markt.

In the meantime, Spanish small-caps have performed moderately well, growing by 48 per cent since the mid-1990s.

The Netherlands

The Amsterdam Nieuwe Markt, now part of Euronext Amsterdam following the merger last year with Paris and Brussels, has been judged relatively successful in terms of attracting new listings and issues. However, the overall performance of small-cap stocks in the Netherlands is poor. The MSCI small-cap index for the Netherlands shows stocks virtually returning to the 1996 valuation levels and registering a growth of only 4 per cent.

Stocks have been at this level since the end of 1999 with little change between then and March 2001. In a country that attracts significant international business and is dominated by large enterprises, this seems hardly surprising – but is something of a dichotomy given the maturity of Dutch venture capital.

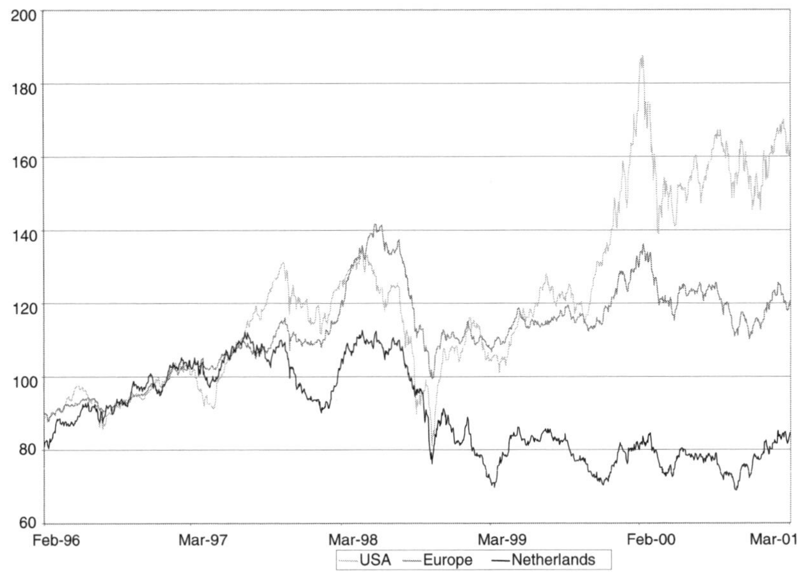

Figure 7.8 Dutch small-cap performance (1996–2001).

Source: Morgan Stanley Capital Index.

Sweden

Sweden's small-caps rose a below average 20 per cent in the second half of the 1990s. Sweden took a decisive step towards joining the European single currency when the leadership of the ruling Social Democratic party formally backed membership for the first time during January 2000. Hopefully, this will contribute at least slightly to the harmonisation of Swedish small-cap markets, and market rules, with those of other continental markets.

NASDAQ Europe (formerly EASDAQ)

It seems worthwhile to say a few words about the goals of the exchange and the extent to which they are realised on it or any other European exchange. It is the only 'pan-European stock market', not intended for any particular national market. Indeed, it is designed to encompass not only Europe but also any state interested in listing in Europe and following a rule set on accounting and disclosure largely taken from the US. Yet it claims to be 'Designed expressly for a unified Europe': 'Its unique structure and independence from any national market make it a perfect fit for innovative companies and forward-looking investors from across Europe and beyond'.[16] Yet is this an accurate description?

The country most represented on NASDAQ Europe is actually the US, followed by the UK. Some of the most important continental markets (e.g. Germany) are barely represented. The rigorous accounting and disclosure standards of NASDAQ Europe are expensive for European small-caps, which must hire expert accountants who are competent not only in the many rules and regulatory requirements of their home countries but also in those of NASDAQ Europe, which largely mirror US laws. It is not surprising, then, that the countries most likely to list on NASDAQ are actually those most likely to list on NASDAQ Europe, and it has not yet quite lived up to its pan-European promise.

While NASDAQ Europe clearly has problems, it has at least had significantly improved market performance during 2000, as is demonstrated in the chart below. One would hope that this performance will only continue in the coming years.

Yet it is unlikely that NASDAQ Europe will be able to lead the European charge towards harmonisation, and its future is still in question at the time of this writing. Other exchanges, meanwhile, have not even adopted the goals of NASDAQ Europe. They arise from national exchanges as secondary markets for a particular state. Only afterwards have they started to expand outward. The pattern is thus much the same as the pattern for many of the European Union's other harmonisation work, first on the trade of heavy industrial goods and recently with the birth of the EURO. This may be the most realistic pattern to follow for small-caps as with other things, but it is a pattern that yields somewhat slow results.

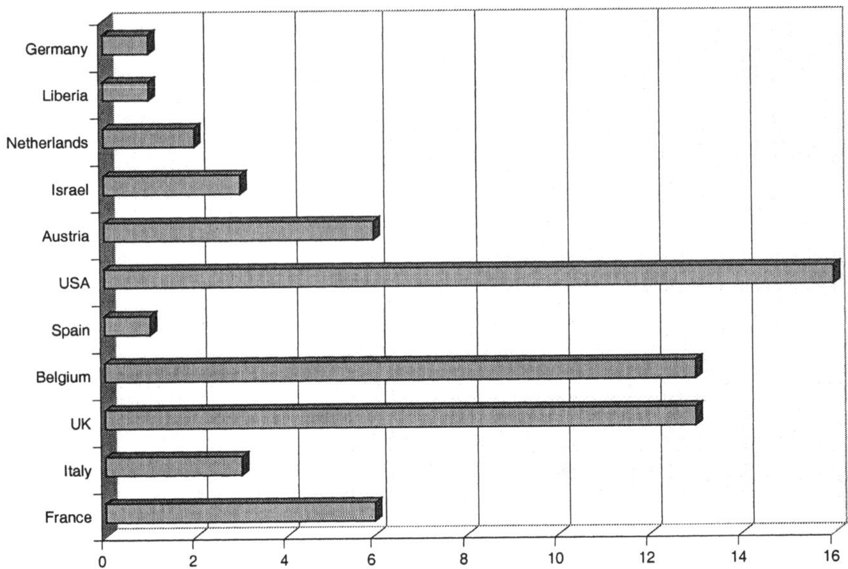

Figure 7.9 EASDAQ composition by country (IPOs to March 2001).

Source: www.nasdaqeurope.com.

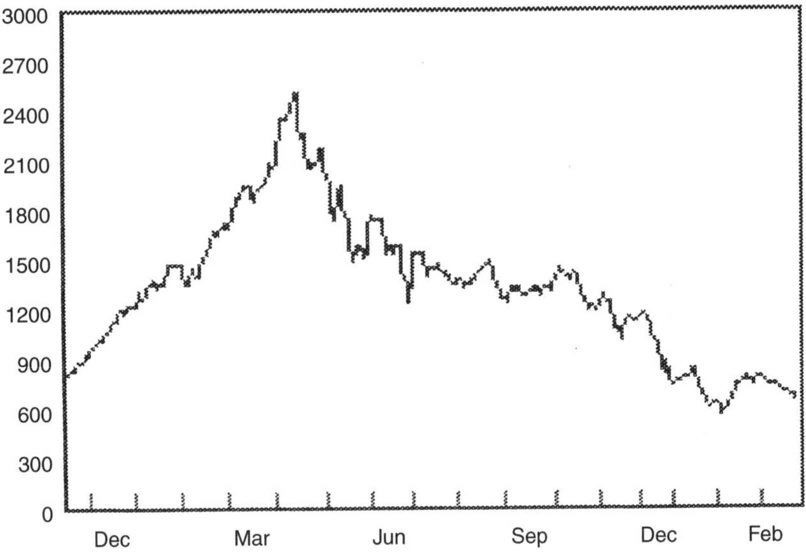

Figure 7.10 NASDAQ Europe market performance (March 2000–March 2001).

Source: www.nasdaqeurope.com.

Conclusion

The European Commission has identified the main barriers to the development of a pan-European market as follows:[17]

- Fragmentation, both institutional and regulatory
- Taxation
- Paucity of high-tech SMEs
- Human resources
- Cultural.[18]

The European Union currently has 33 regulated stock markets and 18 regulatory organisations. Each national market has lower capitalisation and liquidity, and consequently less exit routes, than a combined market. The diversity of regulations and taxation systems across the member countries makes the integration of national exchanges complicated.[19] Our conclusions revolve primarily around the need to consolidate markets, although other regulatory themes on taxes and savings also receive some attention.

Fiscal

The first set of policy recommendations relates to the reduction or removal of taxes on investments. Specifically:

1 Provision of tax relief for investments made at a seed or early stage. This would significantly increase capital supply-side interest in the smallest ventures.
2 Granting of capital gains relief to VCs who list on a parallel market.
3 Reduction or removal of capital gains tax
   - Only on share trades
   - Only for retail investors
   - Only for parallel markets
   - Only for shares made over x years (to discourage short termism)
   - For everyone.
4 Introduction of ‘prudent-man’ regulations for institutional investors removing the raft of specific regulations that govern their areas of investment both at home and internationally.

Standardisation and harmonisation

The second set of recommendations relates to standardisation of trading systems through alliances such as NOREX, mergers such as Euronext or takeovers such as NASDAQ’s acquisition of EASDAQ.

1 Single-entry multiple-exchange trading platform. Membership in one exchange would give membership to all alliance partners. This would increase the number of market makers per stock, broaden the capital

base, and make the market more attractive to new companies seeking funding from a broader range of sources, and increase the number of analysts per stock, thereby increasing transparency and information provision to investors.

2 Harmonisation of listing and compliance related issues
   - Harmonisation of listing requirements as was proposed with the Euro NM alliance.
   - Harmonisation of disclosure and reporting requirements.
   - Harmonisation of oversight. For example: the introduction of the Federal Securities Supervisory Office (FSSO) in Germany.

Geographic focus

A third set of recommendations relates to the geography of EU activities.

It may be that the number of SMEs over all fields correlates closely with population, and improving the business environment for start-ups is no more useful than improving the business environment for any other firm. Indeed, we believe that while centres of SME activity are worthy of study, lessons from their successes will not necessarily help to generate increased wealth elsewhere.

On the other hand, a more well-honed sector analysis reveals that high-tech and VC activities naturally cluster around certain centres of high-population density, high-convenience, high-education, and high-finance. Further, in the US, both entrepreneurs and investors in high-tech ideas are far more clustered in certain geographic locations, and this seems to contribute to the rapid growth of their ventures. One might think that this is surprising given the comparative uniformity of cultures and economic systems of the states that comprise the US: if they are somewhat uniform, why would some states (especially California and Massachusetts) emerge so prominently as leaders in these industries? Yet it appears the nationally unified market allows for much greater mobility of labour, capital and market inputs so that any natural clustering in high-tech fields can indeed take place.

In Europe, despite some clustering around Cambridge in the UK and other centres of wealth and education in many EU states, greater diversity generally has led to greater geographic dispersion of high-tech growth. Europe might profit from the encouragement of greater concentration of investments nationally within countries or (if possible) in only a few areas of the EU that already seem to be developing at a comparatively impressive pace.

Since much of the EU's work on SMEs is geared towards boosting employment, many programmes instead fund areas of greater poverty and unemployment. Some of the potential benefits of such investments are out of the scope of this study, but it is suggested here that capital markets might be better served with the opposite approach.

Legal and regulatory environment

A fourth set of recommendations relates to the improvement of legal and regulatory environments for SMEs developing intellectual property. The European Commission describes the overall European patent system as

> profoundly unsatisfactory ... Alongside national patents, which continue to exist, there is a European patent, which, once granted by the European Patent Office in Munich, operates to all intents and purposes like a national patent. However, the system is complex and expensive and does not provide a unitary patent for all the Member States, in the form of a Community patent.[20]

As a result, while more than 640,000 inventions are patented each year in the world, compared with 220,000 in the 1960s, most of this growth comes from Japan and the US. In seven recent years in Europe, the percentage of applications for European patents from Europe has decreased by 11 per cent, while during the same period the US applications have increased by 32 per cent. Further, European industry files less than 43 per cent of all European patent applications. Among the 170,000 European SMEs that do produce inventions every year, an estimated two-thirds of them do not apply for patents. Hence, according to the EU, 'urgent reform is necessary'.[21]

Capital market ownership

Privatisation of exchanges themselves. Stock exchanges should become public to

- increase efficiency and reduce costs to members
- improve transparency
- pave the way for stronger and more formal alliances
- share price of exchange reflects performance
- give shareholders more power to influence the policy and strategy of the exchange.

However, some have concerns about disclosure and proper regulation of market information – this might encourage short-term gain from authorities whose job in the past involved a great deal of self-regulation.

Availability of information

A final set relates to the provision of more standardised, more up-to-date, more comprehensive, and more accessible (e.g. web-based) information provision related to smaller-cap publicly traded firms.

One scholar[22] warns: 'Care must be taken to explain the composition of indices, and avoid frequent modification (inclusion and exclusion of stocks) because of the possible negative effect on issuers, investors, the credibility of the exchange as the market operator, and on the exchange's relation with issuers and investors.' A further recommendation related to the Internet: 'SMB markets should create and maintain a dedicated, easy to navigate website, fill the website with knowledge and information for investors and issuers, use the Internet to economically distribute information and build a relationship with investors.' All of this is done to some extent at the European bourses, but not at all in a standardised fashion. Also, the vast majority of the information is unavailable in a format that people can quickly download for the purpose of research on market trends, covariance, etc.[23]

Notes

1 'Federation of European Stock Exchanges' – www.fese.be
2 Ibid.
3 Michael Ashley Schulman, *Medium Size Business Markets*, FIBV Working Committee Focus Group Study on SMB Markets, August 1999, pp. 23–4; see also 'Going Public: Guide', Vision and Money Special, *Business and Financial Markets Magazine*, Deutsche Börse, January 1999, p. 10.
4 Michael Ashley Schulman, *Medium Size Business Markets*, FIBV Working Committee Focus Group Study on SMB Markets, August 1999, p. 32.
5 'The Successful Alliance of Growth Markets in Europe'. Copyright Euro NM (www.euronm.com, 1999), p. 2.
6 European Commission: 'Risk and Capital Markets, A Key to Job Creation in Europe: From Fragmentation to Integration', *Euro Papers* (No. 32), January 1999, p. 10.
7 'Attitudes Towards Smaller Quoted Companies: A Study Amongst UK Fund Managers', March 2001, KPMG Corporate Finance.
8 Ibid.
9 Ibid.
10 'Going Public: Guide', Vision and Money Special, *Business and Financial Markets Magazine,* Deutsche Bourse, January 1999, p. 7.
11 Ibid., p. 10.
12 Ibid., p. 17.
13 Joint Stock Corporation – generic name for a public company limited by shares that has the legal structure required to list on the stock exchange – equivalent to AG in Germany or SA in Spain or PLC in the UK.
14 'Going Public: Guide', Vision and Money Special, *Business and Financial Markets Magazine*, Deutsche Bourse, January 1999.
15 Oonagh McDonald, 'Financial Regulation in Germany and the UK: A Comparison', Financial Markets Group, the London School of Economics Special Paper No. 82: March 1996, p. 7.
16 Text taken from the web site – www.nasdaqeurope.com
17 'Risk Capital: A Key to Job Creation in the European Union', Communication of the European Commission, SEC 1998, 552 final, April 1998.
18 Bank of England, *Finance for Small Firms* (6th Report: Bank of England, January 1999), p. 59.

19 Ibid., p. 59.
20 'Risk Capital: A Key to Job Creation in the European Union', Communication of the European Commission, SEC 1998, 552 final, April 1998, p. 18.
21 Ibid., p. 18.
22 Michael Ashley Schulman, *Medium Size Business Markets*, FIBV Working Committee Focus Group Study on SMB Markets, August 1999.
23 Ibid., p. 44.

Conclusions

We would reiterate that industrial policy, if it should exist at all, should not concentrate solely on small and medium sized enterprises. An emphasis of support on these firms is neither the key to greater wealth, nor an obvious route to higher long-term employment. It is certainly not the central pillar on which private sector capital operates. One could argue that if it works for the private sector – why should not governments also follow suit. On the other hand, successful SMEs do bring economic benefits to regions that are also served by angel capitalists, venture capital funds, investment banks, specialist advisors, and public equity markets. This type of clustering has been wildly successful in northern California. The US government has been a player, but it is difficult to argue that they had a decisive, rather than just an important, role and that it would not have happened anyway.

Our recommendations concentrate on strengthening and diversifying the bridges between SMEs and the financial communities that serve them. While a concentration on SMEs and their funding sources need not be the first priority of governments, it would usefully fuel high-growth sectors, financial industry diversity, and investor sophistication through broadening investment opportunities. Furthermore, our recommendations might be beneficial and complementary to other aspects of economic development, as they focus on the enabling environment rather than sector-specific policies. Other improvements to the enabling environment, beyond those covered above, are relatively easy to ponder but beyond the scope of this study.

SME policy

With respect to policy on SMEs, we would recommend a stronger focus on the enabling environment and less focus on structural fund donations and government support. Neo-liberal policies emphasising tax burdens provide part of the answer. Burdens on corporations and individuals generally should be lowered in those states that view the financial industry and its institutions as both likely to expand and an important priority. Here,

Germany and France stand out as countries with somewhat high taxes compared to many competitors. France in particular has a tax regime that is higher than the EU average, despite a large internal market (and hence lower international trade risk than, for example, in Belgium, the Netherlands, or Denmark).

Yet taxes are only part of the answer. Europe demands the world's highest employer social security contributions. Although these contributions are vast, the organisation of contributions is frequently undiversified, unsophisticated, and expensive. Social security contributions should be balanced or supplemented by 401K-style individual accounts that are managed both individually and through privately managed funds profiting from prudent-man rules. A move that is underway with the Individual Savings Account (ISA) in the UK. Non-state funded pensions generally should be expanded and diversified. The EU is now considering a 20 per cent minimum tax on savings to limit tax breaks and level differences in tax rates between states. This is a bad idea because it 'standardises' in a way that limits competition on experiments in lowering the tax burden. At the time of this writing, Germany is formulating plans to lower capital gains tax burdens. These should be encouraged. France has permitted publicly managed savings to be invested in (domestic only) NM markets, smaller-caps and private equity. Similar policies (though not limited nationally to domestic investments) should be encouraged elsewhere.

The result of more liberal tax and savings policies will mean far more resources available for both large and small financial players to invest in both large- and small-cap firms. To take again the examples of France and Germany, these two countries are fortunate to have a comparatively high potential to expand both their large- and small-cap markets for equity, with large, pre-existing financial centres, some of Europe's largest banks, and (especially in Germany) a vast pool of successful mid sized firms. Hostile and friendly merger activities in the financial industries of both these countries recently suggest that the high street banks of Germany and France are readying themselves to develop more aggressive and successful investment banking divisions to complement more diversified financial markets. Witness the jockeying amongst leading European banks and financial institutions including Dresdner and Allianz and Royal Bank of Scotland and National Westminster. Increasingly aggressive financial institutions of all kinds may benefit larger firms first, but the benefits are likely to trickle down to the smaller deals, the smaller-cap equities, and the unlisted private firms with rapid expansion plans.

The European Union sponsors structural programmes that are rarely geared towards the link between SMEs and equity markets. While the European Commission concentrates particularly on SMEs and has good intentions for these firms, some of its measures lack focus. There are too many programmes providing different levels of financial support for different reasons. These conflicting programmes also often compete, as some forbid SMEs signing up for more than one programme simultaneously. SMEs are perhaps the least prepared of the companies to spend time and money on the bureaucracy that is frequently required to gain funding approval. Funds are most likely to go towards depressed regions: those that are least likely to create the momentum required to build 'the next Silicon Valley' – or to reinforce the development of those already being built, in the southeast of England, around Munich, in Catalonia, etc. The policies on SMEs are frequently reinforced by a desire to increase employment, since SMEs are seen as vehicles for job growth. But the high-growth firms most likely to require an expanding employee base are not usually those most likely to receive funds, or other breaks and incentives.

We recommend a rationalisation of EU programmes and increased focus on the financial industries of member states. A small step might be to shift more of the structural investments into equity rather than debt packages. A bigger and perhaps more useful step would be to provide money to privately managed funds who choose the winners rather than the government bureaux that presently choose them. They would employ the money under specific policy guidelines outlined by the European Commission. But goals and incentives would be more tied to profits and less to the minimal goal of quick, successful allocation (dispensing) of resources. Even bigger steps would focus on the enabling environment – especially tax and savings schemes – and the supply of money rather than on the end users of services and their demand for money.

On the bureaucratic front, we also recommend that the EU consider establishing a more visible and effective point of contact for SMEs and VCs. Although access to Brussels is not particularly difficult, the sector could do with a more permanent 'one-stop shop'. The United States has achieved this through the SBA facility. The latter is 'plugged in' both at the federal and states level. The information it provides to the public is vast, and its policies are more focused. A further study might focus on a better way of co-ordinating and disseminating EU programmes for the SME sector.

Country-by-country, requirements for the registration of new firms should be simplified, and the times of payment for services rendered should be shortened. Here, southern Europe has the most punitive policies and response rates, to the detriment of southern Europe's millions of small firms.

Investor policy and VCs

US consumers are aggressive spenders and even more avid gamblers. They are not afraid to invest surplus capital, even their primary retirement accounts, into high-risk investments. Because of greater inequalities of wealth, despite similarities in GDP per capita, there are more people in the US who are very wealthy. These rich people have a greater ability to diversify their assets (and therefore their risks) by allowing a portion of their savings to form a large pool of high-risk investment in new firms or new industries with less-tested risk-assessment methodologies. The US also has immense non-profit institutions with large endowments and an interest in high-growth industries tied to technological research and health care. So the US may begin with some comparative advantages that build bridges between SMEs and financiers while fuelling angel and venture capital firms and industries with vast capital and resources.

Yet European markets for private equity are becoming more impressive every year. They are already more than double the size of the markets of the rest of the world (excluding North America) combined. The expansion of activity in Germany, from a low base, has recently been striking. Many of the countries in southern Europe, with the deregulation of financial industries and other liberalisation measures, saw the most rapid expansion of private equity activity in the 1990s.

Again, with respect to VCs, we would focus on savings policies. In the US, 50 per cent of investments in VC/private equity come from public and private pension funds.

One central problem addressed in this book is the lack of consolidation and internationalism of VC funding activities in Europe. National markets that are successful appear to have powerful financial capitals (London, Frankfurt) drawing resources towards the centre, but even these 'centres' are not particularly centralised from a Europe-wide perspective. The internationalism of investors and investment channels in countries like the UK, the Netherlands, and Switzerland is contrasted with very limited cross-border trade elsewhere outside the market for large buy-outs (which are rarely SMEs). Greater international co-operation (joint-ventures or cross-border deals), and greater consolidation will take time, but trends in the banking industry towards internationalism and consolidation are likely to spill over into the VC industry; the sooner the better.

Even within the US there is massive consolidation taking place in the fund management industry. US banks and funds are also buying up European ones and occasionally vice versa (e.g. Deutsche Bank's purchase of Standard Chartered, Dresdner purchase of Wasserstein). Europe may need to be calm about the purchase of financial institutions and fund management organisations across borders within the EU and outside the EU. Governments must worry about monopolistic practices in any industry that is truly consolidated, but in the short term the industry as a whole, and its most powerful actors, may still have a long way to go before they challenge markets through monopolies. Hence, policies manipulation or blocking mergers for the purpose of protecting employment or (more likely in the financial industries) protecting prestigious domestic institutions may be particularly destructive to the region's financial industry in the long term.

As shown in the other sections of the report, only 6 per cent of all funding raised by European VCs comes from other EU member countries. This is less than half that raised from non-EU sources. Greater freedom of international fundraising and creation of international funds will lead to greater financial resources moving towards the SME sector.

Policy on capital markets

France helps to illustrate what happens when tax and savings policies are diversified. The government introduced a new type of life insurance policy that is tax exempt if half of the amount is invested in shares and at least 5 per cent is invested in SME capital markets. Billions of francs have since flowed into the Nouveau Marché. This alone has increased liquidity, which in turn has led to an upsurge in IPOs in that market.

The German government also offers investors in the Neuer Markt tax breaks on their investments. The effect of this measure has been similar to that in France. It is not surprising that these two countries have a significant percentage of Europe's SME market capitalisation. Clearly, there is a lesson here for all other markets, policy-makers and SME market supporters.

Yet French policies were limited to national investments within France, and as a result were roundly attacked by other countries and non-French securities exchanges, including especially NASDAQ Europe. Diversifying French savings methodologies was a good idea, but the French law aggravated another problem: SME capital markets in Europe are fragmented. In particular, there is a need for improved harmonisation in operating rules and increasingly standard, open information – a basic ingredient to increase investor confidence and greater liquidity. The objective is to create the 'virtuous circle' that exists in the USA today.

Harmonisation has already started to take place in the SME capital markets of Europe. The process needs to be given the freedom to be accelerated and consolidated through market forces. The announcement of NASDAQ Europe, coupled with the harsh realities of globalisation of financial markets – along with the encroachment of ECNs upon what was a traditional market preserve – has acted as a wake-up call to the managements of European exchanges. The Neuer Markt in particular has taken heed of these developments, placing itself as the pre-eminent SME capital market in Europe in a relatively short space of time. Increased harmonisation of trading, settlement, listing and regulation are the key factors behind its success. The ability to trade stocks across all markets from a single point of entry has also widened the capital base. The cost savings this confers on the members, coupled with electronic trading, has meant that there are multiple analysts, market makers and specialists for each stock. The shake-up has already started. The Brussels exchange has merged with its counterparts in Paris and Amsterdam to form Euronext – which is the second-largest exchange in Europe by capitalisation. The exchanges in Vienna, Dublin and Helsinki have formed alliances with Frankfurt. Within the myriad of clearing houses and systems in Europe, there are also similar moves towards consolidation. Euroclear and Sicovam have announced a further consolidation of their strategic alliance with the opening of direct accounts. Cedel International and Deutsche Börse Clearing are merging to create Clearstream. Euroclear and Brussels Exchanges have announced the formation of a strategic alliance with the opening of direct accounts.

Some of the problems of European markets are cyclical. Indeed, one of the reasons for success has been the liquidity of certain home markets – particularly those in Germany and France. One of the key drivers of this success has been the positive economic environment as a result of the introduction of the Euro. Interest rates in many countries have plummeted, causing retail investors to re-examine their savings strategies. Expanding economies have also fuelled IPOs and small-cap public and private firms. Yet many problems of harmonisation, even after the launch of the Euro, remain unresolved.

Information access

We close this study with a discussion of information access and disclosure. Despite some structural problems, the European market's comparative inability at generating high-risk capital and low-volume liquidity can be alleviated through more transparency in the quantity, quality and timeliness of information.

A key conclusion is that timely, accurate and consistent data and analysis focused on SMEs and their capital demands is far less successfully organised, analysed, and distributed in Europe. In this study, we have relied extensively on SME data from 1995, because, although far more recent data was available for the US, the best, comparable data Europe-wide was last collated for the middle of the 1990s. Some Eurostat data is not even compatible with other data – as Eurostat readily admits. To take an important example, Eurostat relies on two different sources for information: first, on numbers of firms and their employment base, and second, on the gross value added and turnover of these firms. So any conclusions on the cost of labour or the efficiency of firms based on this data are rather compromised. Eurostat also relies extensively on nationally organised statistical bureaux that provide different definitions and calculations for some issues that are relatively basic. For example, 'Mittelstand' enterprises in Germany are sometimes 'large' by the EC's definitions.

Public and private resources should be utilised more effectively, and more resources should be made available over the Internet. Some governments stand out as providing relatively unimpressive information over the web (e.g. France's national administration, although various ministries are greatly improving their websites). Europe needs a one-stop statistical facility and website providing information on SMEs, or all corporate activity, providing the following kinds of information.

More up-to-date statistical information on corporate activities

- More analysis relevant to venture capitalists, investors, policy-makers and industrialists providing a clear macro-picture of the state of SMEs in Europe, on an annual if not a quarterly or monthly basis.
- Better benchmarks and indices for SMEs using existing private indices or producing new ones if necessary. (It appears that private indices for small-cap public equity are as sophisticated as in the US, but more information on private equity is difficult to find.)
- Standardised information and news on IPOs in member states of the EU.
- Analysis of systemic risk and economic indicators and their effect on public small-caps and private SMEs.
- Standardised information about European exchanges and markets, including listing requirements, contact details for markets, changing average firm sizes and overall market caps, sponsors, etc.
- A general knowledge base for investors, containing information about SME stocks and statistics centred in one site.

Some of the services above could be provided better by a private corporation than by a public one, but others resemble 'public goods' that might best be expensive and thankless to produce in the short term, but yielding significant benefits for policy-makers and corporate decision-makers in the long term.

Postscript

As we write this conclusion, the longest bull run in the history of the US equity markets, and a revival of high growth rates in many European countries, inevitably influences our conclusion on the likely future directions of markets. Is the US's 'formula for success' merely what US Federal Reserve Chairman Allen Greenspan referred to long before the (still unseen) end of the current boom as 'irrational exuberance'?, with his deputy describing most Internet companies as 'a thousand times nothing'. Alternatively, is the high valuations achieved in the markets under the 'new economy' merely a shift in the way shareholder returns are generated. Rather than receiving most income from dividends under the old model, they come from trading instead. Similarly, the Euro has helped to boost European confidence in the possibilities of integration, but is its recent dip in international markets evidence that many of our recommendations above are overly 'exuberant' about possibilities?

We have considered the cyclical effects of markets as important intervening variables. But one can't help but consider that markets on *both* sides of the Atlantic are on a more secure footing than ever before, and this will continue to positively impact upon SMEs, private equity and the financial markets that serve them. The post-cold war world has created violent turmoil and tragic problems on the borders of western Europe, but throughout Europe, as in north America, it has helped to firmly establish an agenda that, if not 'neo-liberal', is at least unabashedly liberal. Liberal goals throughout almost all Europe have fuelled democratisation. Greater freedom to choose, greater freedom of access to information, valuing competition, organisations designed to promote wealth-maximising outcomes. These are clearly beneficial and complementary not only to democratisation and political liberalism but also to small, private players in the markets and the financial firms that they employ. Firms have rushed to NASDAQ as its index has risen. However, while *valuations* are growing more slowly in Europe, the pace of IPOs is high, and the number of firms listing on the European SME markets has also doubled in the last year. The former index began its life in the early 1970s and the latter (e.g. Neuer Markt) only in the second half of the 1990s. One wonders if this is the most profound difference that separates the two markets, with one providing a window towards understanding the future of the other.

The 'culture of entrepreneurship' and risk in Silicon Valley is impressive and now known the world over; but in Europe as in America, cultures are growing more accepting of financial risks and the tools that help to diversify them. This may first benefit world-famous 'large-caps' in northern and central Europe with consolidations, buy-outs, and mergers; but small-caps throughout the European Union are beginning to see positive results from diverse financial instruments that are, in the end, simply impersonal tools no more 'foreign' to European than any public or private securities – which, of course, were instruments first invented in Europe.

Glossary

401K Plan Government-backed scheme that encourages additional voluntary contributions through providing matching funds. Created to counterbalance underfunding fears resulting from most pension schemes being defined contribution rather than defined benefit schemes.

ADR American Depository Receipts. Negotiable certificates that represent a non-US company's publicly traded equity or debt. Depository receipts are legal, US securities that trade freely on major exchanges or in the over the counter (OTC) markets. Denominated in US dollars, they pay dividends or interest in US dollars and settle, clear and transfer according to standard US practices. Commonly used in global equity offerings by non-US companies. They facilitate cross-border trading and settlement, minimise transaction costs and may broaden the investor base of that company through attracting US institutional investors. Sometimes called Global Depository Receipts (for marketing purposes).

An American Depository Receipt (ADR) is a physical certificate evidencing ownership in one or several ADSs. The terms ADR and ADS are often used interchangeably. ADRs provide US investors with a convenient way to invest in non-US securities without having to worry about the complex details of cross-border transactions; they offer the same economic benefits enjoyed by the domestic shareholders of the non-US company. ADRs are issued by a US bank, that functions as a depository. Each ADR is backed by a specific number or fraction of shares in the non-US company. The relationship between the number of ADRs and the number for foreign shares is typically referred to as the ADR ratio.

ADS An American Depository Share (ADS) is a US dollar denominated form of equity ownership in a non-US company. It represents the foreign shares of the company held on deposit by a custodian bank in the company's home country and carries the corporate and economic rights of the foreign shares, subject to the terms specified on the ADR certificate.

Balanced Fund Venture capital firm strategy of investing in companies across a range of investment stages – seed, start-up, expansion and buy-out.

Business Density Calculated as the number of businesses divided by the total mid-year population expressed per 1,000 capita.

Business Start-up Activity Calculated as the number of business start-ups divided by the number of businesses at the start of the year, expressed as a percentage.

Captive Fund More than 50 per cent of the fund is owned by a parent organisation.

Direct Participation Programme (DPP) A business venture usually organised as a limited partnership that is structured to pass through income and 'tax losses' of the underlying investments to investors. However, its use as a tax shelter has been severely reduced by recent tax legislation.

EADSDAQ European Association of Stock Dealers Automated Quotation. Refers to the Belgium-based stock market, now known as NASDAQ Europe following the takeover of the company in 2001.

Europe Within this text, taken to mean the fifteen countries of the European Union, unless specified.

Eurostat Eurostat, part of the European Commission, is the body charged with the collation and dissemination of EU statistics.

EVCA European Venture Capital Association. Trade organisation representing European venture capitalists.

FTSE Stock exchange index calculation specialist. Autonomous organisation owned by the London Stock Exchange and Financial Times Group.

GDP Defined simply as the total value of goods and services produced by a nation within that nation.

Gross Value Added Total turnover of individual enterprises within a region net of intra-regional trade.

Independent Fund Less than 20 per cent of the equity of the fund is owned by a parent organisation.

Innovation Can mean different things to different people. The neatest definition is that provided by Ed Roberts of MIT who said that innovation was invention plus exploitation. See discussion page of *The Innovation Journal* website address for further definitions: http://www.innovation.cc/articles/definition.htm

IRA Individual Retirement Account. State scheme that encourages individuals to save through pension plans by offering tax concessions.

ISP Internet Service Provider. Provides individuals and businesses with access to the Internet. Examples include AOL, T-Online, Terra Lycos, Wanadoo and Tiscali.

Management Buy-in Financing provided to enable a manager or group of managers from outside the company to buy-in to the company with the support of private equity investors.

Management Buy-out Financing provided to enable current operating management and investors to acquire an existing product line or business.

Market Maker Positions Sum total of issues in which markets are made. This number, divided by active market makers gives the average number of market makers per issue.

NACE NACE or *Nomenclature statistique des Activités économiques de la Communauté Européenne* is a system of classification of economic activity uniformly adopted by EU members and others submitting statistics to Eurostat.

NASDAQ National Association of Stock Dealers Automated Quotation. World's first electronic stock market. Major market for technology companies such as Microsoft and CISCO.

NASE Non-Agricultural Self-Employed.

New Business Formations Measured by new firms with employees collected from state employment security agency quarterly reports filed with the US Department of Labour's Employment and Training Administration. This may result in an overcount, when an employer has employees in more than one state.

New Business Incorporations Compiled by SBA and incorporates data from Dun & Bradstreet.

NVCA National Venture Capital Association. Trade organisation representing US venture capitalists.

OECD The Organisation for Economic Co-operation and Development has a 30-nation membership, which traditionally included the world's richest nations, but recently has expanded to encompass all those interested, recent joiners include Slovakia, Czech Republic, Hungary and Poland amongst others. Its purpose is to promote market economy principles, democracy and human rights.

R&D Research and Development. Spending on the development of new products (or even new knowledge), or on improving products already being made. R&D costs vary widely by industry; semiconductor firms, biotechnology companies and other businesses whose products are rapidly evolving tend to have high R&D expenses. Some other industries, such as retailing, traditionally spend little on R&D. And some industries, such as newspaper publishers, probably need to spend more.

SBIC SBICs are Small Business Investment Companies. These are private companies that borrow money from the US Small Business Administration (SBA) and then provide equity capital, long-term loans and management assistance to qualifying small businesses. For the purpose of this programme, small businesses are defined as companies with net total assets of less than US$18 million and profits after tax of less than US$6 million in the preceding two years. Should these criteria not be met, then the standard definitions apply.

Semi-captive Fund Parent organisation owns between 20 per cent and 50 per cent of the fund.

SME Small and medium sized enterprise.

S&P Standard & Poor. Stock exchange index calculation specialist. Responsible for producing a range of indices including the S&P 500 (consisting of 500 stocks chosen for market size, liquidity and market representation. It is a market-value weighted index with each stock's weight in the index proportionate to its market value).

True SMEs Those that meet the definition adapted by this study. In considering capital markets, we differentiate between the latter and small-cap companies – which may not meet this strict definition.

VC Venture Capital Fund or Venture Capitalist or Venture Capital *per se*.

Warrant A certificate that gives a shareholder the rights to purchase a security at a specified price within a predetermined time period or perpetually. Corporations issue warrants directly and they are sometimes offered along with a security as incentive to buy. The abbreviation 'WT' is used in newspaper stock listings.

Index